Y0-BVN-896

American Democracy

American Democracy

Aspects of Practical Liberalism

Gottfried Dietze

The Johns Hopkins University Press
Baltimore and London

This book has been brought to publication
with the generous assistance of the
Karl and Edith Pribram Endowment.

Printed in the United States of America on acid-free paper

The Johns Hopkins University Press
2715 North Charles Street
Baltimore, Maryland 21211–4319
The Johns Hopkins Press Ltd., London

Library of Congress Cataloging-in-Publication Data
Dietze, Gottfried.
[Amerikanische Demokratie. English]
American democracy : aspects of practical liberalism / Gottfried Dietze.
p. cm.
Includes bibliographical references and index.
ISBN 0-8018-4507-6 (acid-free paper)
1. Liberalism—United States. 2. Liberty. 3. United States—Politics and government. 4. United States—Social conditions. 5. Democracy. I. Title.
JC599.U5D5313 1993
320.5'1'0973—dc20 92-44137

A catalog record of this book is available from the British Library.

In Memoriam

William S. Carpenter

Thomas I. Cook

Hardy C. Dillard

Ernst Fraenkel

Carl J. Friedrich

Louis Hartz

Alpheus T. Mason

Carl McFarland

Frederick D. G. Ribble

Carl B. Swisher

Eric Voegelin

You and I, as individuals, can, by borrowing, live beyond our means, but for only a limited period of time. Why, then, should we think that collectively, as a nation, we're not bound by the same limitation?

Ronald Reagan, *First Inaugural Speech*

Contents

Preface to the American Edition

The year 1992 is an important anniversary. Five hundred years ago, in 1492, Columbus arrived in the New World. And 1792—two hundred years ago—was the first full year in which Americans enjoyed their Bill of Rights.

The Spanish military conquest for absolute monarchs in the name of an absolute church, sooner or later aided by Indian chiefs used to absolute rule over their people, laid the ground for what became known as a Spanish-American dictatorship. The English crossing the Atlantic were civilians who had come to settle, fleeing from what they felt was oppressive in the old country with its absolute monarchy. They established the basis for what has been called American liberalism.

In Spanish America, dictatorship was seconded by Roman law and subsequent legislation. In English America, liberalism was supported by common and customary law.

Thus the two major parts of the New World have a different heritage. To a large extent, they have remained the captives of their traditions, which in a way they could not help and for which they ought not to be blamed.

This does not mean that they ought not to be helped. Observations of, and comments on, countries, their people, and their governments can do some good. Having been to, and studied, all the nations in the Western Hemisphere, I might, at some future date, write a book on Spanish America. For the time being, I am content with again trying my hand at one on the United States.

The present study is my translation of my *Amerikanische Demokratie: Wesen des praktischen Liberalismus*, published in 1988, a hundred years after the publication of James Bryce's *The American Commonwealth*. As these titles suggest, there have been many changes in the land of unlimited opportunities and the pursuit of happiness.

Whether they were for better or worse is for the reader to decide.

Preface to the German Edition

American democracy is characterized by liberal variants and variations, their never-ending new creations, and changes in all directions for better or worse. Whether Americans created the kind of democracy best suited to them or whether democracy formed the American people, there can be little doubt that both acted upon one another, revealing liberalism in all its simplicity, multiplicity, multifariousness, and duplicity.

The long years of my residence in the United States have been full of changing impressions of that ever changing country. Above all, two things have filled me with ever new and increased wonder—but also with fear, the more I thought about them: the blending of what is American with the democratic and with liberal law. In the land of the automobile, believed by many to be God's own country, people more and more live for their own advantage according to their desires, worrying less and less over the death of God. They challenge the starred heaven above and increasingly respect only those laws that, in the mood and play of the moment, they give to themselves in order to be happy.

In 1787 there was drafted in Philadelphia—the city known as one of brotherly love and sisterly affection and that gave birth to the Declaration of Independence—the U.S. Constitution, which put government into the hands of the people. In 1788, that Constitution became law in the nine states that had ratified it. The following year witnessed the establishment of the first federal government.

The bicentenaries prompt the question as to what has come about under the Constitution and an examination of the present constitution of American ways of life. The findings could, among other things, reveal what is questionable in democracy and in liberalism, both of which probably have developed the furthest in the United States.

Introduction: America's Liberal Democracy

The United States of North America is a liberal democracy driven by the quest for freedom. The integration of the American and the democratic is well known. It is so obvious that frequently America is identified with democracy and vice versa. One can speak of American democracy as a specific way of life. It manifests itself in a far-reaching blending of the American with the democratic. And behind everything lurks the great agitator in the human breast, the insatiable drive for greater freedom. Freedom beckons powerfully, tempts incessantly. Its throne has not been shaken to this day.

As did his predecessors, President Ronald Reagan paraded this truth again and again. For instance, he was quoted in *Parade Magazine* of the *Washington Post* of September 15, 1985, that America's founders "believed first and foremost in freedom, which they approached abstractly and practically. They created with a sureness and originality so great and pure that I can't help but perceive the guiding hand of God, the first political system that insisted that power flows from the people to the state, not the other way around." He added that it was the great task of Americans to further extend freedom. In my opinion, Americans today enjoy more freedom than other people. I ask myself whether their always asking for more shows that their freedom is losing its measuredness. The drive for freedom has been so strong that it seems to be the destiny of American democracy.

Over a hundred and fifty years ago, the great French observer Alexis de Tocqueville published his famous book, *Democracy in America*. In the introduction he wrote that the American development toward equality of condition would be followed in France and Europe. He was right.

Tocqueville lived at a time when the United States was a rather insignificant nation on the periphery of world politics. Today, it is a super power, as Tocqueville envisioned. Therefore, whatever happens there is of great importance for the rest of the world. This thought prompted me to write this book.

It cannot be denied that in America equality and democracy have advanced greatly. Still, to me America primarily appears to be a land of freedom and of an incessant drive for more freedom. Tocqueville wrote that "a great democratic revolution is going on among us, but all do not look at it in the same light. To some it appears to be novel but accidental, and, as such, they hope it may still be checked; to others it seems irresistible, because it is the most uniform, the most ancient, and the most permanent tendency that is to be found in history." These words apply today to the quest for freedom. People want equality of condition and self-government in order to enjoy greater freedom. It must not be forgotten that equality and democracy were emphasized within the liberal movement and thus are parts of that movement; they are subordinated to the drive for freedom and are its servants, for the word *liberalism* points to liberty only and to nothing else.

Our time is characterized by insatiable strivings for freedom. Liberation movements abound. They have increased ever since the beginning of the movement known as liberalism, especially after World War II. They are appraised, condemned, and praised in different ways. Some people see in them fashions of limited duration that are controllable. Others consider them aspects of the irresistible evolution of the most basic, most constant, and most powerful drive of the human race, the quest for freedom.

If, in conformity with the innate meaning of the term, *liberalism* means the drive for more liberty, then the history of humankind appears to be that of liberalism, even though the word *liberalism* came about only around the turn of the nineteenth century, when, after the American and French revolutions, the modern liberal movement came to enjoy recognition, and the so-called liberal century began. Concepts follow their conceptualization. There was a greater awareness of the importance of liberty at that time than there had been previously. People spoke of the liberal movement, of liberalism, and of the liberal age. All these terms, however, only show the generalization, illustration, and crystallization of liberal striving, a striving that existed from the beginning of the human race, long before the modern historical movement known as liberalism, which began at about the time of the Reformation.

The first relationships between man and woman, creditor and debtor, ruler and ruled probably brought about the desire to gain more freedom from the other, for basically everybody wants to be free from others. The striving for freedom from political potentates became well known. Oppressed people revolted against foreign domination, slaves against their owners, subjects against governments. The struggle for liberty from oppression often was celebrated, as in the *Funeral Oration* of Pericles and the Rütli oath. Although the quest for more liberties under less tyrannical conditions was less known, it existed nevertheless. Even a bearable foreign domination is still foreign domination. Even under good slave owners slaves felt they were slaves and desired to be free. We know this from not too distant American history. The quest for more freedom existed not only under the Theistic kingships in France and other continental nations, it also could be found under the feudal English monarchy, which delineated the rights and duties of the monarch and his vassals. The Magna Carta Libertatum is ample proof of this. We know from Kant that the desire for freedom existed under enlightened despotism as well as under its harsher predecessor. It has existed even under constitutionalism, under American free government, under the German Rechtsstaat and similar governments.

The demand for more freedom increased considerably with the historical movement known as liberalism. That movement was substantially aided by discoveries that destroyed the firm foundations and limitations of the Middle Ages and became harbingers of emancipation. Cosmological advances were liberated from traditional opinions on the cosmos, geographic explorations from those on the nature, culture, and population of the earth. They demonstrated that things were different from what governments wanted people to believe. Emphasis upon biblical texts led to freedom from papal dogma. New nations brought about liberation from feudalism. To these were added the results of search and research in the natural sciences and in technology, the invention of the invention, the emphasis upon the advantages of free trade and of a science of politics that favored, for the sake of the freedom of the individual citizen, limitations upon governmental power.

When the American Revolution began and brought forth the first bills of rights, liberalism had arrived in many respects and was ready to spread out in further directions. Perhaps it is symbolic that the very year Americans declared their independence from England, Adam Smith in his book on the wealth of nations advocated free trade and independence of the economy from governmental control. This meant additional emancipation from regulations by the state, because once freedom has achieved one victory, other victories follow. The fact that the bills of rights of the American states elevated aspects of freedom to the status of subjective rights that citizens could claim left its imprint upon the development of American liberalism, making the drive for liberty egocentric and diverse. Subjective rights result in subjective behavior.

Liberalism did not appear the same way everywhere. In his *Spirit of the Laws,* Montesquieu wrote that different factors such as environment, ethnic composition, religion, and tradition led to different governments and degrees of freedom. Wherever there was a drive toward greater liberty, it took specific forms depending on local and temporary conditions. Thus one could speak, for instance, of the liberalism of the eighteenth and nineteenth centuries, of English, German, or French liberalism, and all of them were interpreted in different ways. They were split into groups, subsections, and still smaller units. They could deal with freedom from the state (protection of private property, religious freedom, etc.), with the right to participate in politics (active and passive suffrage, etc.), or with other liberties. In due time, ever new aspects of liberalism were revealed. They grew from generation to generation, decade to decade, year to year, month to month, often in veritable geometrical proportions. We are living at a time of liberalistic explosions and inundations never experienced before but characteristic of modern liberalism.

Although modern liberalism appears to be derived from eighteenth-century liberalism, it has changed both qualitatively and quantitatively. Montesquieu, Adam Smith, Kant, and perhaps Jefferson probably would not recognize it as their kind of liberalism. They saw the liberal movement as something measured, opposing the absolutist police state but not the public order as such. They favored a good balance between the freedom of the individual and the authority of the government. The individual liberated from governmental oppression was not just supposed to obey the laws. He also was to be guided by ethical and moral considerations. This is obvious in the work of Montesquieu. Adam Smith published *The Theory of Moral Sentiments* before he emphasized morality in his *Wealth of Nations.* Kant followed his liberating *Critique of Pure Reason* with *Critique of Practical Reason,* with its categorical imperatives. In his treatise on the nature of human freedom, published in 1809, Schelling warned that freedom was an ability to do good and evil. Hegel, who considered that treatise the most important contribution of his former roommate at Tübingen, favored the free individual in the state, that "reality of the moral idea" and "concrete freedom," the institutions of which are "a guarantee of the public weal and of reasonable liberty" (*Philosophy of Law,* sec. 257, 301). Similarly, a measured liberalism was favored in the United States. The Constitution is a work of measure vis-à-vis the designs of the masses. The *Federalist,* its first and best-known commentary, frequently warns lest freedom be used and abused in an evil way. Jefferson, who was called an apostle of freedom, emphasized the need for legal and moral restraint.

At the end of the eighteenth and the beginning of the nineteenth centuries, liberals thus favored more liberty for the individual from the state—but within the state's order. They strove for a diminuition, not an abolition, of government. As indicated by the word *liberal,* the idea of *libertas* was foremost. Equality and democracy were considered means for the promotion of the individual's freedom. On the whole, the liberal argument was simple and self-evident: since the exclusion of the people from absolute monarchical government had been tantamount to their oppression, popular self-government would result in their freedom from the state, for it could not well be assumed that people would oppress themselves. All of this was to take place under liberal laws. Irrespective of the liberality of these laws, the authorities were to be strictly obeyed. Thus liberalism was a movement for the emancipation of the individual according to the laws in a liberal order. Its motto was ordo et libertas.

However, the fact that the word *liberalism* points only to liberty and not to order raises the question as to whether sooner or later the drive for more and more liberties would be at the cost of order. That possibility grew when Manchester liberalism led to liberalistic practices that Adam Smith would have resented and Karl Marx found revolting. It was likely to further increase after John Stuart Mill's *Essay on Liberty* (1859), probably the most widely read liberal tract, stated in its last chapter that "liberty consists in doing what one desires." That sentence could lead people to believe that freedom was without limitations. Applied to the drive for more liberty, it means that every behavior and misbehavior is justified by liberalism and that the free individual no longer is bound by legal, ethical, moral, or other limitations. On account of its marked brevity, Mill's sentence was likely to be quoted out of context and to have a great impact. Now everything could qualify as liberalism, as long as it served the extension of liberty, irrespective of whether it was good, evil, beautiful, ugly, or what not, for liberalism no longer was required to distinguish between values. The will alone mattered. Freedom appears to be pure because it is purified of all attributes and restrictions.

It is similar with liberalism or the quest for freedom—it can do good and evil. Just as pure freedom is not restrained by law, ethics, or morals, pure liberalism is devoid of any limitation. The modern liberal movement is nothing but a crystallization of earlier drives for more freedom. These drives appeared in different types and subtypes, partially realizing the general idea of liberalism, from which all particular forms of liberalism are derived. And that idea is that of pure liberalism, free from all restrictions, always out for more specific liberties, irrespective of whether or not these are used in praiseworthy or reproachable ways. Nourished by that idea—and ideas are powerful sources and reservoirs—more and more liberalisms came about beyond the measured ones favored by men like Montesquieu, Smith, and Kant. They may be compared to Goethe's sorcerer's apprentice, calling as they do for liberal spirits and devils, which in the end lose all measure. For even measured movements toward liberalism might fall prey to the insatiability of pure liberalism. After all, they all are interested in liberalization.

For Hegel, history demonstrated an ever-growing emancipation of people within the order of the state protecting them. Tocqueville emphasized the drive for equal conditions and the march of democracy connected with it. As his compatriot Montesquieu a hundred years earlier had seen England as the land of liberty, he saw the United States primarily as one of equality and democracy. In this country, an important part of which prior to independence was considered New England, emphasis upon freedom was followed by that upon equality, a republicanism oriented toward freedom followed by egalitarian democracy. Nevertheless, even Tocqueville, much as he may have trembled for the survival of freedom, showed how the fight for equality and democracy often was motivated by a quest for more liberty. Since today people enjoy not only a great degree of equality and democracy but also a high degree of freedom, it can be assumed that all these features derive from pure liberalism.

Despite its emphasis upon the freedom of the individual, the movement known as liberalism was loyal to the public order. This cannot be said of some modern liberalisms. Of course, there are still liberals today who have a high regard for the laws and who believe that the minimum of legal restriction characteristic of the liberal state requires a maximum of obedience to the laws, even though it is in the nature of laws to curtail freedom. After all, the growing liberalization during the nineteenth century brought about a growing recognition of the rule of law. That rule was advocated by Americans admiring their Constitution, by Germans favoring the Rechtsstaat, by Albert V. Dicey's *Introduction to the Law of the Constitution* (1885) which, running through ten editions, saw its twenty-fourth printing in 1960. The rule of law was recognized by others who saw in obedience to the laws the characteristic feature of a free society. On the other hand, liberalistic drives have increasingly shown a disregard for authority.

In Rome and in the writings of Thomas Aquinas a distinction was drawn between power (*potestas*) and authority (*auctoritas*). The latter was legitimate, whereas the former—sheer might—was not. From the seventeenth to the nineteenth centuries, the liberal movement was primarily directed against monarchical omnipotence and its oppressions. The latter were criticized by John Adams in *A Defence of the Constitutions of Government of the United States of America,* by James Madison in letters of December 18, 1825, to Thomas Ritchie and of August 2, 1828, to Thomas Lehre. Lord Acton wrote Bishop Creighton that power tends to corrupt and absolute power corrupts absolutely. Jakob Burckhardt, at the end of his discussion of culture determined by the state, in his reflections on world history, called might "evil." However, these authors did not attack legitimate authority, which was considered conducive to freedom under the constitutionalism created by the liberal movement.

Nevertheless, the legitimate order of constitutionalist nations came under attack. Culprits hoped to get away with their behavior. If brought to justice at all in liberal societies, they often would not be found guilty, let alone severely punished. Still, they constituted a minority, and only a few among them felt their behavior was justified because it was conducive to liberty. Generally speaking, their attacks upon the liberal legal order were not motivated by the idea of pure liberalism. By contrast, today legitimate institutions are challenged illegally with liberal arguments. Since these institutions are part of the Establishment (a term coined in America) of the existing liberal order, attacks are directed against that order. Under the aegis of pure liberalism, the drive for more liberties has gained new dimensions. While originally directed against the police state, it now frequently came to fight the basically free order of liberal democracy, an order based upon the protection of the individual's freedom and equality and generally considered the very opposite of the police state. In the name of liberalism, the very principle of government that for centuries had been desired by liberals has come under attack.

There have always been attacks upon liberalism: one need only think of conservatives, of communists, of fascists. However, those belonging to these groups did not claim to be liberals. Irrespective of how they would propagate liberty and liberations—conservatives with the argument that Jacobinism means serfdom, socialists by pointing to the exploitation of the workers—they still recognized the authority of the state. By contrast, today liberal establishments are attacked by those giving loud lip service to liberalism. It will be argued that liberals have always attacked other liberals; that new liberals attack old liberals, New Whigs, Old Whigs, and so on; that such attacks are in the nature of liberalism as a drive for more freedom; that there cannot be a static liberalism nor, in the last analysis, can liberals be loyal to the state; and that progress always requires innovation. This is correct, although what is new, while it constitutes progress from the point of view of innovation, is not necessarily progress in the sense of improvement. At any rate, the struggle among liberals for the most part took place within the framework of liberal constitutions. People moved in the forms prescribed by the laws. By contrast, many of those posing as liberals today attempt to attain their goals illegally. They do not even refrain from violence and terror. They justify their actions with confessions to freedom and enjoy the sympathies of large parts of the population, notably of intellectuals. The latter, after all, always have been the torchbearers of liberalism.

Given violations of the ethical minimum of the law under the theory of pure liberalism, it is not surprising that recognized principles of ethics and morals would be challenged. Even after the Victorian age, people for some time turned up their noses at unmarried older couples living together. Today it is quite common for unmarried youngsters to live together. After the abolition of penalties for homosexuals, the latter for a time were content to follow their inclinations inconspicuously. Today they organize street festivals in which they happily dance together. Candidates for elections play up to them. I read that in San Francisco, at the Golden Gate in the Golden West, a mayor needs their support to get elected. Liberalism increasingly has lost its bounds. Carl L. Becker, who wrote the first and still the best study on the Declaration of Independence, published *Everyone His Own Historian* in 1935. One chapter bears the title "Liberalism—A Way Station": liberalism is a mere stop on the way to further liberations and emancipations under ever new liberalisms, all of them new stations on the many ways to greater freedom. And the driving force behind them is the idea of pure liberalism.

Nowhere has pure liberalism been realized. So far America probably comes the closest to its realization. It is true that England generally has been seen as the cradle of liberalism. However, the nation that developed out of New England, in which Englishmen sought refuge because their mother country was not liberal enough for them, where during the fight for independence the first bills of rights were framed guaranteeing subjective rights to individuals, became the land of liberalisms and neoliberalisms, of variants and variations of innumerable liberation movements.

It probably is significant that it was a high-ranking American who furthered the challenge of traditional liberal establishments by modern liberalisms. In his "Quarantine Speech" in Chicago in 1936, President Franklin Roosevelt denounced authoritarian regimes. He thus no longer distinguished the respectable concept of authority from the dubious one of power. Therefore, it is not surprising that in the following years doubts would be cast upon the legitimacy of authority. People increasingly felt entitled to disregard or even attack it, especially in view of the fact that a few years later the United States was at war with "authoritarian" regimes in Germany, Italy, and Japan. Following their defeat, the principle *vae victis* came to be applied to authority as such, helped by American anti-authoritarian education. The negation of the family was followed by that of the public order. Only the individual was to possess authority.

This new look upon authority under the auspices of pure liberalism can mean the decline of traditional authority and can undermine long accepted concepts of law and morals, for pure liberalism does not care about law and morals. It is only interested in extending freedom, which can be used for good or evil. Whereas specific liberal movements may be restrained by laws and morals and thus be limited in their extensions of liberties, pure freedom, resulting from pure liberalism, permits doing whatever one desires.

Although pure liberalism seems to have been realized in the United States more broadly than anywhere else, it has not yet been completely achieved. America still is restrained by limited liberalisms. In principle, the law still rules, and moral and similar considerations hinder drives for freedom. However, such considerations are decreasing due to the thrust of pure liberalism. To me for one, the growing replacement of legal, moral, and similar evaluations appears to be the essential feature of American democracy. I plan to demonstrate this fact in the present book.

It is not my purpose to just satisfy curiosity but to learn and draw lessons from it. The replacement of limited freedom by an unlimited one in the leading—and strongest—Western democracy could serve as a lesson to other nations as well as to democracy and liberalism in general. Tocqueville thought that democracy and equality in America would be important for other countries. I should like to claim a similar importance for liberalism as practiced in America, a liberalism of which democracy and equality are mere aspects and which, for better or worse, has tended toward an ever greater purity and its concomitant value-freeness.

I plan to be guided by observations. They have demonstrated to me that things American and democratic have blended, that American democracy is characterized and branded by an ever growing variety of liberal variants and variations derived from pure liberalism. An examination motivated by the desire for objectivity cannot adjust to preconceived opinions. On the other hand, my experiences have led me to believe that American democracy increasingly reflects pure liberalism. Without claiming that my observations are important or right, I plan to marshall facts in support of that opinion. I will be content to see my study stimulate discussion: at any rate, I have attempted to follow Fichte's advice in the foreword to his lectures on the calling of the scholar and not to care whether something will be popular and pleasing but only whether it conforms to the truth.

Understanding American democracy is important because widespread Americanizations have raised the question whether John Locke's words in his *Second Treatise,* "in the beginning all the World was *America*" (sec. 49), can be complemented by saying that in the end all the world will be America. This could mean the return to a situation in which money is not known or, as a result of liberal developments, the coming of a civilization in which everything turns around money. I consider the latter alternative the more probable one. Locke had in mind some Golden Age prior to the coming of the whites—as it was described by Rousseau or, in Germany, by Winnetou, the hero of Karl May. However, when the immigrants pushed the Indians back, they pushed back the idea of a previous Golden Age with the idea of a future characterized by material rather than ideal values. Perhaps the time will come when Americans will change their minds, for many a thing is possible in the land of unlimited opportunities. On the other hand, American history so far has demonstrated, above all, a materialistic turn of mind. It has shown that the morals of the masses in a large measure are determined, if not pushed aside, by their sensualism.

As the title of the book indicates, I shall deal with America, the American people, and American democracy. However, it must be kept in mind that these concepts cannot be kept strictly apart. One flows into the other. A nation is in large measure what its inhabitants make it. I have often thought of the words I heard a Swiss orator tell his countrymen: "Your country is small. It is up to you to make it great!" America hardly can be imagined without her people, their doings and omissions, their use and abuse of liberty. Also, American space with its vastness and its riches has put its stamp on the population. In short, American democracy is not conceivable without the land and its people. The American melting pot is not just one of ethnic groups—it also is one of concepts. But perhaps American popular government can be appreciated better if the three concepts mentioned are dealt with consecutively.

I

America

1 The New, Freedom, Faithfulness

America is known as the New World. This attribute is essential to understanding it. It points to its colossal extension, to immense proportions. Everything in this attribute is to be noted: the definite article, the concept of the new, the world idea.

America is not considered a new world, but *the* New World. There is not merely some new world added to older worlds. Rather, the one and only New World is juxtaposed to the Old World. Now the new was distinguished from the old previously—the New Testament comes to mind, and the new science of politics. The ancien régime has been clearly contrasted to what came into existence with the French Revolution. However, all these cases were concerned with particular things in this world, such as faith and politics. One did not speak of them as new worlds as such, irrespective of how much they might influence the whole world.

On the other hand, calling America the New World indicates enormous dimensions. It will be argued that the term *New World* has only a geographical connotation: before 1492 the earths and waters then known were considered *the* world; after the discovery of America, they became known as the Old World. However, in this Old World there were whole continents—Asia, Africa, Europe. One could easily have added the newly discovered continent and spoken of it simply as the new continent America, especially after further discoveries left no doubt that America was indeed just such a continent. No, one spoke of the New World. The clear—and emphasized—distinction shows a contrast between the Old and the New Worlds of a magnitude that seldom comes to mind when a distinction is drawn between the Old and New Testaments or the old and new science of politics. This prompts an examination of the nature of the New World and of what really is new in it.

Something can be new because it never was heard of, because it is unknown and for that reason unusual, eerie, producing fear or hope. Thus Moses in his song on the Lord's justice and faithfulness rebuked those who were not faithful to God and brought sacrifices "to Gods whom they knew not, to new *gods* that came newly up" (5; 32, 17). According to Acts of the Apostles (17; 18), Epicureans and Stoics suspected Paul of seeming "to be a setter forth of strange gods." Luther, on the other hand, in a well-known song, has the angel announce: "I bring you good new tidings." Klopstock's *Messias* spoke of the new, godlike man. Götz von Berlichingen looked for new distant worlds. Faust's early groan, indicating that, in spite of his studies, he could not *know*, showed his striving for the new unknown. The diastolic is evident throughout Goethe's drama, at the end of which there could well come the words, "the eternal new pulls us on." Perhaps God's grace points to the new.

The drive for the new is strong indeed. People are interested in all new things: new books, new rulers, new ideas, new directions in art, new fashion, new sensations—news. From time immemorial, a fascination with the new can be found within all strata of society, among young and old alike. We think of the great explorers of the globe and the cosmos. A Columbus put up with the risks of the sea, a Sven Hedin with those of the desert, an Auguste Piccard with those of the atmosphere and the depths of the ocean. The desire to know new things often exists just for the sake of knowing, free of egoistic motives. A mountaineer will put up with the hardships of climbing a new peak simply "because it is there." An American admiral, obviously impressed by the polar expeditions of Peary and Byrd and the conquest of Everest, asked me why Germany lacked explorers like those. My answer came quickly: Germans were primarily interested in finding out new things in the sciences, as is testified by their great share of Nobel Prizes. One can imagine the triumphant feeling of the unknown country doctor Robert Koch when he discovered the tuberculosis bacillus, of Otto Hahn when he succeeded in splitting the uranium atom on his small workbench. Max Weber described such feelings in *Wissenschaft als Beruf* (1919). There were new things in other fields, like politics. We think of modern *isms* such as liberalism, communism, fascism. They appeared to some as whole new worlds of angels, like the star that according to Herder's *Turteltaube* came with Christ.

People are not just interested in what is totally unknown. They also want to know what is different from what has been known so far. "To new shores beckons a new day," Faust said after Wagner left him alone. Every day brings new joys, but in Schiller's *Maria Stuart* one reads that "every day brings new suffering" (1, 2), and in *Macbeth* (4, 3),

Each new morn
New widows howl, new orphans cry, new sorrows
Strike Heaven on the face

Whenever a new ruler assumes office, people look forward to his rule with both skepticism and hope. One wonders how a new employee will turn out and what new things will prove to be. Hopes are accompanied by doubts. One of Picasso's most touching pictures is that of Pierrot at the beginning of the twentieth century. In a disturbing way it mixes the cheerful celebration of the fin de siècle with the fear of the new century and is remindful of Edvard Munch's *The Cry.* Tennyson's "In Memoriam" greeted the new year:

Ring out the old, ring in the new
Ring, happy bells, across the snow:
The year is going, let him go
Ring out the false, ring in the true.

A year later, there is cast aside as false what twelve months earlier was hailed as true. The new year again is praised as true, and so it goes year after year. We congratulate others on their birthday, at the beginning of another year of their life; on the occasion of their wedding as the beginning of a new life together. There always is joy at leaving the old behind, joy that it is possible to leave it and all its troubles. But there also is fear of the new, as in Matthew Arnold's "Dover Beach":

Ah, love, let us be true
To one another! for the world, which seems
To lie before us like a land of dreams
So various, so beautiful, so new,
Hath really neither joy, nor love, nor light
Nor certitude, nor peace, nor help for pain.

Hope and doubt can also be encountered with the new in the sense of a restoration of the old, for it also can result in good and evil. In contrast to the quest for the unknown, there prevails a nostalgic desire for what has been lost, the longing for the good old, the renaissance and restoration of which appears as something new. A French proverb goes, Ce qui est nouveau est vrai. One has spoken of the new Jerusalem, of the Renaissance. Ecolompad is a new Abiram. Luther is considered a new Hus, having written in *Wider Hans Worst* that he did not invent anything new but merely kept God's word. Rückert spoke of the new Rebekka, Wieland of the new Adamis, Rousseau of the new Heloise. In *Torquato Tasso* (I, I) we read that "this new green and this sun bring back to me the feeling of that time." In all these cases, the skepticism characterizing the expectation of the absolutely new and unknown, of the new in contrast to what is now, is less evident. One hopes that the new, reborn, will be better than what exists now.

Whatever may be the doubts about the new, it fascinates. The quest for it is insatiable. In his remarks on *Neuigkeit,* Kant wrote in *Anthropology:* "The *new,* including the rare and what is kept hidden, enlivens *attention.* For it is an acquisition; the sensual imagination gains greater strength thereby. The *common* or *usual* eliminates it." In Gellert's *Fabeln und Erzählungen* (1763, p. 161) we read: "A thing may be as foolish as possible. As long as it is new, the mob will like it." In time, this statement applied less and less to just the mob. Today there exists, generally speaking, a veritable craving for what is new, a veritable oversupply of new things and of news. Curiosity is prominent on a world scale. Again and again it is satisfied by the press, the radio, and television and again and again stimulated and provoked by them. The new is the glittering promise. Is it the gold that everyone clings to, everyone is after? It will be argued that one can cling only to what is old, it being essential to the new to get rid of the old. However, clinging to the new is quite possible if one sees in it the eternal desire to question what is old and to renew things. Even when the old was still being honored, people were after new things: "Old faith ranks highly with you. Still, you abandon it for a new one," wrote Friedrich von Logau in *Sinngedichte* 2 (Zugabe 180). "News is news," they say in America. The content counts less.

"The new as such is especially liked," we read in Goethe's remarks on Marivaux. This is true, for men are by nature curious, and the new as the younger, fresher, stronger replaces the older, withered, weaker. "The old falls, times change, and new life blossoms out of ruins," we see in Schiller's *William Tell* (4, 2). On the Gettysburg battlefield Lincoln expressed his hope for "a new nation, conceived in Liberty." Faust asked Wagner to lead him away "to a new, colorful life!" In their calls for the new, they are all repeating old ideas. St. Paul advised the Ephesians to "put on the new man, which after God is created in righteousness and true holiness" (4, 24), and the Colossians, to "put off the old man with his deeds; And have put on the new *man,* which is renewed in knowledge after the image of him that created him" (3, 9–10).

Young and fresh, the new is not used up, not violated. A new coin, a new piece of jewelry, new porcelain give pleasure on account of the beauty of their perfection. Untouched and unsoiled, not worn off, not derided, the new appears to be not just beautiful but also good. A beautiful person is considered good and unspoiled, combining beauty and goodness.

However, what is not touched and not soiled is pure not only in the sense of aesthetics and ethics but also in the sense of purity. The significance of the new as something purely new, something merely new, ought not to be overlooked, for it has increasingly come to the fore. Although the drive for the new often derives from the desire to improve things, it also can be motivated by that of merely bringing about something purely new, just because it is new, irrespective of its quality. Such a desire could instigate and stir up many a thing. The new as something more beautiful, better, more moral, and so forth, is replaced by the new simply because it is new. No longer is the question asked whether the new is better or not. The new is preferred merely because it is new. This attitude has become obvious in our time in which the Establishment is criticized without a thought to the nature of the new that is to replace it.

This development is not surprising. It follows from the quest for the new. While desires for something new are likely to invoke praiseworthy grounds for such desires, the praiseworthiness of such grounds will become more and more dubious, until in the end it no longer exists at all. The drive for the new will thus become bare of ethical, moral, and similar motives and be motivated merely by a desire for change for the sake of change. Let us assume people request, as did Paul, something new because it was desired by God. Then, the godlike of the new probably underwent change when Theism was replaced by Deism. Later on, the probability of the dedivinization of the new had to grow with the increasing divinization of humans, until with the emphasis upon the death of God something godlike could hardly be seen in the new. Or let us consider beauty. Often, schools of painting desired innovation. In due time, there came about so many aesthetic motivations among painters that, for instance, less and less consideration was given to perfect drawing, until it no longer mattered at all. It was asked of Edgar Degas why he was always concerned with the same subject. He answered that the same thing could never be drawn often enough to achieve perfection. But since then, the new for the sake of the new has emerged. Those who were good at their craft were pushed aside by those favoring innovation, few of whom have ever proven that they master the artistic rules of their craft. They don't even sell their products any longer under the motto *l'art pour l'art,* preferring the principle *le nouveau pour le nouveau.* The situation is similar in other fields. Hence the call for a new Shakespeare, a new Mozart.

In view of the liberty taken to request the new merely for the sake of the new, it seems appropriate to examine its relationship to liberty. There can be no doubt: the new liberates. Abstract painters found their innovations as liberating from the expressionists as the latter considered their works as emancipations from the rules of the salon. Those who said God was dead believed that their new ideas were as liberating as the reactions of Deists to Theists, of Protestants to Catholics. English revolutionaries propagated their new program in the name of the Magna Carta Libertatum as liberation from the despotism of the Stuarts and their theory of the divine right of kings. The word *liberty* stands at the beginning of the slogan of the French Revolution, which put an end to the ancien régime. The new discovered by men like Hahn, Koch, Kant, Galilei, and Copernicus liberated. So did Wagner's music, which with its new chromatic in *Tristan* paved the way for Schönberg and modern music. The discoveries of new parts of the earth and the cosmos also were liberating. All these innovations bring emancipation. They emancipate even if only by temporarily freeing individuals from the urge to innovate—which in the last analysis is that of individuals. In that respect it is similar to the drive for freedom and, like freedom, is essentially egoistic.

Just as the new liberates, liberty creates the new. In his long address of February 27, 1860, at the Cooper Institute, Lincoln called conservatism "adherence to the old and tried, against the new and untried." On the other hand, F. A. Hayek, long considered the spokesman of those who in the United States call themselves conservative, stated at the end of his book on the constitution of liberty, published a hundred years later in Chicago (in the home state of Lincoln and Reagan) why he was not a conservative. He emphasized his liberal inclinations because only the quest for more freedom could bring innovation and thus promote progress. This thought also was expressed by Reagan when he announced a new beginning in 1980, a new freedom in 1984 at the beginning of his second administration, and prophesying that Americans "haven't seen nothing yet" as to the prospects of more freedom and more free enterprise.

The new exists on account of freedom. Even under the worst despots, thoughts are free and create new things. Kant's belief that freedom of thought could not really exist as long as its expression was limited (*Was heißt: Sich im Denken orientieren?*) is not quite correct, for an opinion that cannot be expressed and is not expressed also presupposes liberty. Those who do not fall prey to a dictator's propaganda actually retain their inner freedom. It goes without saying that there is more liberty if one need not hold back one's thoughts. Prohibitions on freedom of expression denied to many the fulfillment of Luther's favorite words in Psalm 118, "I shall not die, but live, and declare the works of the Lord." They could not avoid the cup of sorrow. The same applies to the voicing of nonreligious opinions, which often are also considered works of the Lord.

Basically, every thought is new, even if just repeating what is already known, for it always is arrived at anew. Yet freedom of thought also produces what has not existed so far. Every innovation can be traced to the liberty to create it. Generally speaking, restrictions on liberty are less likely to lead to innovation than guaranteed liberty. The latter has grown since the Enlightenment. In his *Beantwortung der Frage: Was ist Aufklärung?* Kant wrote that further enlightenment would result in more freedom to bring about further enlightenment. In that long process, more and more liberties could create more and more innovations, with people taking ever greater liberties to replace existing accomplishments by something new.

Much as one may see in an ethically motivated drive for innovation an ethically motivated drive for freedom, in an aesthetically motivated desire for innovation, an aesthetical desire for freedom, and so on, a quest for innovation not motivated by ethical, aesthetical, or other considerations, but merely interested in the new as such, in pure innovation, can be seen as a drive for mere or pure liberty. Just as qualified innovation can result in qualified freedom, pure innovation can bring about pure freedom, which in turn can produce new things. All this is not without risk.

Freedom does not, as Spinoza believed, produce just good. Following the Lisbon earthquake of 1755, an event that considerably muted the optimism of the time, the dangers of liberty were pointed out by the authors of the *Federalist Papers* and by Kant, who followed thoughts expressed earlier by Hobbes, Locke, and Blackstone. Schelling was not the first author who considered freedom as the ability to do good and evil. Similarly, innovation can result in good and evil. The fear and courage, and the hope and the skepticism accompanying it, are proof of this. Furthermore, it must not be overlooked that, while progress is not possible without innovation, the latter can retard civilization. The drive for the new is an essential feature of civilization, which has been characterized by both progress and regress. It has been debated which one of the two has been predominant.

The drive for the new is the opposite of faithfulness. It will be argued that this is true only of the desire for the absolutely unknown, whereas striving for the restoration of something shows faithfulness. However, even in that case one is not faithful to the currently existing. Thus there is an element of faithlessness in every drive for innovation. Since what is new sooner or later will be old, the quest for it is bound to bring about never-ending drives for innovation. Its boundlessness thus demonstrates faithlessness upon faithlessness, without limit. It must not be overlooked that freedom as such (unrestrained, absolute, pure freedom) implies the absence of all limitations. It means that one may without scruple disrespect everyone and everything, that one is absolutely free of ethical, moral, and other inhibitions vis-à-vis everybody and everything, including feelings of fidelity. As the negation of every kind of limitation, freedom invites infidelity.

The enormous possibilities inherent in America as something new, to bring about innovations for the sake of all kinds of liberations and liberties, now become obvious. These possibilities are even larger on account of America being not just a new country but the New World. Certainly, the potential of innovation is greater in the big world than it is in a mere nation. The drive for the new, for liberation from the old, for the freedom to innovate is likely to grow with the variety and the differences of things and persons, with the bigness of society and the territory inhabited.

Within a family, the individual's desires for new things will be modest. It is not becoming for a child to make big claims. Youngsters usually will desire more and adults still more. Basically, however, every member of a family will remain within family custom. Quests for innovation and the drive for more freedom to bring it about will be on a modest scale. The situation is different in a village community. Here children and youngsters will get together to press their demands for innovation and the freedom to achieve something new. Even if within a specific community order fathers alone speak for the whole family, the different opinions they advance in the interest of their families will enlarge the number of attitudes on desirable innovations and the liberty to innovate. That number will be further enlarged in a town, a county, a province, a state, a nation. The drive for different kinds of innovations and liberties to bring them about potentially grows with society and its members, groups, and parties.

It also grows with the territory where people live, be it measured vertically or horizontally. Those crowded into high-rise apartments are likely to have different opinions on the desirability of innovation and freedom from those living in one-family homes surrounded by gardens. Those inhabiting wide stretches of land will think differently from those living in small territories—and not just because of climatic differences. This has been emphasized by Jean Bodin and Montesquieu. Similarly, the *Federalist* mentions that the probability of an increase of different drives for innovation and freedom grows with territory. One need think only of Hamilton's and Madison's remarks on factions in essays 9 and 10. In a large nation like the United States the drive for innovation will be extraordinarily great, especially in view of the fact that the New World presumes innovation. And all this implies infidelity.

The different ways of life in the original thirteen states, reaching from temperate to subtropical zones, were conducive to a great many different conceptions of desirable innovations, of a greater freedom of getting somewhere, of producing something. These conceptions would increase with the growth of that territory. New stretches of land in the wilderness farther west brought about ever new ideas on innovation and freedom, even after these regions had become more civilized and been admitted into the Union. Today the United States stretches over enormous distances of land and sea, from the arctic of Alaska to the tropics of Hawaii, from proper Boston to the city of the angels, Los Angeles, not known for its morality, from Harvard University, with its learned luster, to Hollywood, with its empty glitter. More and more the United States became, with the extension of its territory, a new world.

The liberal drive for innovation—older than its recommendation by William Carlos Williams's *In the American Grain* during the Golden Twenties—often approaches a veritable obsession with the new, assuming the strangest forms. Libraries and reading rooms are built without the blessings of daylight and natural air, which are replaced by electric light and air conditioning. It is similar in museums, such as the Hirshhorn in Washington, D.C., and the Guggenheim in New York. Even in art galleries there is a tendency toward banning natural light and beaming strong doses of artificial light upon pictures, thus falsifying them, making them monotonous and lifeless. Impressionist paintings, which due to their lightness and easygoing nature are favorites of Americans, are especially victimized, since for them change of light is especially important for a correct appreciation. These examples make it obvious that the new is not the true. However, Americans do not particularly resent this. They mind such artificialities as little as sound amplifications in chamber and symphonic concerts. They seldom ask whether this new world is a sane world. Rather, they consider these things proof that they are right in seeking innovation and, thus, an always progressing, "progressive" civilization, in which people may move according to the principle "As you like it."

2 Heterogeneity and the Melting Pot

America's diverse character grew further with the growth of its population. The *Federalist* could well emphasize that the large geographic extension of the thirteen states happily was balanced by the fact that they all were colonized by Great Britain and that their inhabitants shared a common culture. John Jay stated, in essay 2: "Providence has been pleased to give this one connected country to one united people—a people descended from the same ancestors, speaking the same language, professing the same religion, attached to the same principles of government, very similar in their manners and customs. . . . This country and this people seem to have been made for each other, and it appears as if it was the design of Providence, that an inheritance so proper and convenient for a band of brethren, united to each other by the strongest ties, should never be split into a number of unsocial, jealous, and alien sovereignties."

Jay was basically correct, even if it was the point of view of the white rulers. But already by that time there lived French people in the upper Midwest, Dutch people in New York, Finns in Delaware, Germans in Pennsylvania, and Spaniards in the Southwest. There were also Indians and blacks. Later on, the ethnic factors making for disintegration grew still further. The Civil War between the North and the South was not due just to slavery. A hundred years later, there was unrest between blacks and whites bordering on civil war. Furthermore, the ethnic groups arriving after the eighteenth century (about 60 million, 90 percent of whom were white) intensified the original division between whites, blacks, and Indians by new divisions within the white population. America increasingly became a microcosm of the world, something it had been from the time of its independence, as was emphasized by Harold Laski at the very beginning his 1948 book on American democracy.

To André Siegfried, the ethnic division was so evident that in *Les Etats-Unis d'aujourd'hui* (1927) he dealt with it in the first two chapters, speaking of an assimilation crisis. He emphasized the "really fantastic ethnic diversity" and enumerated the various ethnic groups: Africans, Armenians, Bohemians, Moravians, Bulgarians, Serbs, Montenegrins, Chinese, Croats, Slovenes, Cubans, Dalmatians, Bosnians, Herzegovians, Dutch and Flemish, Indians, English, Finns, French, Germans, Greeks, Hebrews, Irish, Italians from the north and south of Italy, Japanese, Koreans, Lithuanians, Magyars, Mexicans, Pacific Islanders, Poles, Portuguese, Rumanians, Russians, Ruthenians, Scandinavians, Scots, Slovaks, Spaniards, Syrians, Turks, Gauls, West Indians, and those referred to by statistics simply as "other people" because it was impossible to know their origin. Siegfried divided whites into two major groups, the Nordic from Great Britain, Germany, France, Belgium, Holland, Switzerland, Denmark, Sweden, and Norway, and the Slavic-Latin from Austria-Hungary, Russia, Finland, Poland, the Balkans, the Mediterranean, and Portugal. He emphasized that immigration by the first group was increasingly replaced by that of the second one and that there were severe rivalries between these groups and within them.

American authors arrived at similar conclusions. In the first chapter of *Send These to Me* (1975), John Higham wrote that in 1972 Americans reported their national and racial origin as follows: 14.4 percent British (including Anglo-Canadian), 12.5 percent German, 8 percent Irish, 2.5 percent Polish, 4.3 percent Italian, 2.6 percent French, 1.1 percent Russian, 4.5 percent Spanish and Spanish-American, 37.6 percent other white (Swedish, Dutch, and Norwegian among them), Negro 11.1 percent, Indian 0.4 percent, and Asian 1.0 percent. That author's *Strangers in the Land* (1955) demonstrates how immigrants more and more transformed the new world into a New World. Not only were they different from each other, they were considered strangers by those who had come earlier. At the beginning of the third chapter of Max Lerner's *America as a Civilization* (1957), we read that a roughly chronological chart of the waves of immigration—English, Dutch, German, Scotch-Irish, French, Scandinavian, Irish, Mediterranean, Jewish, Balkan, Slavic, Mexican and Latin American, Filipino, Middle Eastern, Oriental—corresponded roughly to the descending scale of prestige in the ethnic hierarchy. He mentioned more or less derisive names given to them: Wop, Dago, Sheeny, Kike, Nigger, Norske, Mick, Spick, Polack, Hunkie, Bohunk, Chink, Jap. Limey, the name given to those of English descent, and Kraut, given to those of German origin, he omitted, but his message is clear.

In the American movie *Summertime,* made in the midfifties and set in Venice, a telling statement by an American tourist was that it was nice to meet Italians in Italy. This could be applied to other nationalities. It showed a mentality that, since the immigration law of 1924, had official sanction and that indicated that the mainstream was increasingly fed up with America being a microcosm of the world. For a long time, immigration into the United States had been unlimited. Without any restriction on immigration, America became a New World because its immigration policy corresponded to J. R. Lowell's *Commemoration Ode,* which says of America:

> She of the open soul and open door,
> With room about her hearth for all mankind!

This changed after World War I. In February 1921, Calvin Coolidge published a popular article under the title "Whose Country Is This?" in *Good Housekeeping* magazine. Its message was a far cry from Lincoln's famous "house divided" speech, in which the emancipator of the slaves stated that a nation divided into free and slave states could not exist. Coolidge believed in the superiority of Nordic immigrants and maintained that biological laws show that Nordics deteriorate when mixed with other races. In tune with this article, his first annual message to Congress called for some action in order that America might be kept American. Secretary of Labor James J. Davis, Welsh by birth, compared old and new immigrants with beaver-men who built America and rat-men who try to tear it down. He said that obviously rats could never become beavers. More and more voices were heard requesting that immigrants from eastern and southern Europe be prevented from endangering the dominant position of the "great race" that had built up America, so that old American stock would not be "hopelessly bogged down in the mire of mongrelization" (*Saturday Evening Post,* February 11, 1922).

Representative Albert Johnson, chairman of the House Committee on Immigration, wanted to put European immigration on 2 percent quotas computed from the 1890 census, thereby lowering the Italian quota from 42,000 to about 4,000, the Polish from 31,000 to 6,000, the Greek from 3,000 to 100. Also, if possible, he wanted to completely exclude the Japanese. Following debates influenced by the considerations of not letting immigration restrictions appear un-Christian, undemocratic, and discriminatory and yet maintaining the principle of Nordic superiority, the Johnson-Reed Act was finally agreed upon. President Coolidge, after refusing to give a hearing to immigrant leaders hoping for his veto, signed the act into law in 1924. It had passed Congress by a great majority of votes. The vigorous letter-writing campaign by the Ku Klux Klan in support of the Johnson bill probably made no material difference. Congress was expressing the spirit of the nation. Even the American Federation of Labor, which at first was mildly critical of limitations on immigration, ended by endorsing it as a way of maintaining America's predominantly Nordic character.

Until 1927 the new law limited immigration to 2 percent of the number of foreign-born residents of each nationality counted in 1890. After 1927 a total quota of 150,000 would be parceled out in the same ratio as the distribution by national origin of the 1920 white population. The share of people from eastern and southern Europe was relatively small because, given their more recent immigration, they had not yet produced second and third generations. Thus immigration quotas especially restricted eastern and southern Europe. In order to prevent immigration from the Far East altogether, the Japanese were no longer permitted to come at all.

There also were campaigns emphasizing the necessity of Americanizing the immigrants. Michel Guillaume Jean de Crèvecoeur wrote in his third *Letter of an American Farmer* (1782) that in America individuals of all nations were melted into a new race of men. In 1856 the program of the Democratic party called America the asylum of the oppressed of all nations. Abraham Coles' poem "My Native Land" spoke of the

> Great Empire of the West
> The dearest and the best,
> Made up of all the rest.

According to Walt Whitman's "In Thou Mother with Thy Equal Brood," America was the résumé of the earth, containing the other continents. Israel Zangwill's *The Melting Pot* saw America as God's crucible, the great melting pot where all the races of Europe melt and reform. Woodrow Wilson mentioned that thought in a speech on April 19, 1915, as did his predecessor, Theodore Roosevelt, in a speech on September 9, 1917. Earlier, both had denounced immigrants who did not break with the country of their origin fast enough as hyphenated Americans. At the convention of the Republican party in Saratoga, Roosevelt stated that there "can be no fifty-fifty Americanism in this country." In Bridgeport he remarked: "America is not to be made a polyglot boarding house for money hunters of twenty different nationalities who have changed their former country for this country only as farmyard beasts change one feeding-trough for another." His *Fear God and Take Your Own Part* criticized hyphenated Americans for hoisting the American flag below that of the country of their origin. Woodrow Wilson, a Democrat, had similar convictions: on May 16, 1914, he stated in Washington: "Some Americans need hyphens in their names, because only part of them has come over." Later he regretted, in a speech in St. Paul on September 9, 1919, that there "are a great many hyphens left in America." He added: "For my part, I think the most un-American thing in the world is a hyphen."

After World War II, the melting pot of Europeans was replaced by one of all races. Less and less was there talk of hyphenated Americans, for basically, there was no longer much reason to do so. Most immigrants, glad to be able to live in the nation with the highest standard of living, increasingly refrained from emphasizing their origin. Discrimination was prohibited by law. Nevertheless, America continued to be seen as a land of immigrants. In Maldwyn Allen Jones's book on immigration, published at the beginning of 1960, immigration was considered "America's historic *raison d'être* . . . the most persistent and the most pervasive influence in her development." In *The Uprooted: The Epic Story of the Great Migrations that Made the American People* (1951), Oscar Handlin even went so far as to assert on the first page "that the immigrants *were* American history." Higham's *Send These to Me* voiced a similar opinion. The evaluations of these scholars were supported by American presidents. In the year of his assassination, a book attributed to John F. Kennedy, *A Nation of Immigrants* (1963), was published. President Reagan often emphasized the significance of immigration. In 1985, his State of the Union Address especially praised an immigrant from Vietnam. Immigrants brought many a thing along with them. As P. J. Bailey wrote in *Festus: The Surface* (1, 340):

> America! half brother of the world!
> With something good and bad of every land.

For what, then, was America mainly praised and criticized?

3 Freedom and Manifest Destiny

Movements for freedom and independence and corresponding revolutions often brought forth enthusiasm. Edmund Burke's treatise *Conciliation with America* emphasized that the colonists merely claimed rights that were enjoyed by the people of England. The year of independence, Thomas Paine wrote in *The Crisis* that Americans fought in order to liberate a country and to make room for honest people. According to a letter of Horace Walpole, dated February 17, 1779, in America "liberty has still a continent to live in." His compatriot, the minister and moralist Richard Price, in his *Observations on the Importance of the American Revolution* (1784), praised "the revolution in favour of universal liberty which has taken place in America;—a revolution which opens a new prospect in human affairs." To him, the War for Independence "did great good by disseminating just sentiments of the rights of mankind, and the nature of legitimate government; by exciting a spirit of resistance to tyranny . . . and by occasioning the establishment in America of forms of government more equitable and more liberal than any the world has yet known." For Price, America demonstrated that "the members of a civil community are *confederates,* not *subjects;* and their rulers, *servants,* not *masters.*—And that all legitimate government consists in the dominion of equal laws made with common consent." Condorcet's *De l'influence de la Révolution d'Amérique sur l'Europe,* written in 1786 and published in 1788, called the Declaration of Independence a "simple and sublime exposition" of "rights so sacred and so long forgotten," adding that in "no nation, have they been so well known and so well preserved in such a perfect integrity" as in America. According to him Americans were "the only people with whom one finds neither maxims of Machiavellism established into political principles, nor, among the leaders, the . . . opinion that it is impossible to make the social order perfect and to reconcile public prosperity with justice." Later on, Friedrich Gentz lauded the legitimacy of the American Revolution and was happy to note that American government was a means for the protection of the rights of the individual. Tocqueville, influenced by the Founding Fathers, the authors of the *Federalist,* as well as by Justice Joseph Story, passed a similar judgment.

Americans were no less enthusiastic. Samuel Adams, one of the firebrands of the revolution, said of immigrants in Philadelphia on August 1, 1776: "Driven from every other corner of the earth, freedom of thought and the right of private judgment in matters of conscience direct their course to this happy country as their last asylum." The Declaration of Independence denounces infringements of the king upon the rights of individuals. It emphasizes that all men are created equal and have a right to certain unalienable rights such as life, liberty, and the pursuit of happiness, that governments are instituted among men to secure these rights, deriving their just powers from the consent of the governed. In his First Inaugural Address, George Washington stated that "the preservation of the sacred fire of liberty, and the destiny of the Republican model of Government, are . . . staked on the experiment entrusted to the hands of the American people." In his Proposed Address to Congress of 1789 he praised the Constitution because "no government before introduced among mankind ever contained so many checks and such efficacious restraints to prevent it from degenerating into any species of oppression." He anticipated "the sweet enjoyment of partaking . . . the benign influence of good Laws under a free Government" in his Farewell Address of 1796. Jefferson was of a similar opinion. His First Inaugural Address considered republican government under the Constitution "the world's best hope," the "strongest government on earth," and "the only one where every man, at the call of the laws, would fly to the standard of the law, and would merit invasions of the public order as his own personal concern."

Similar evaluations were made later on. In his lectures on public and private education Ralph Waldo Emerson stated that "America means opportunity, freedom, power." William Cullen Bryant wrote in "Oh Mighty Mother of a Mighty Race" that America meant freedom and peace for the downtrodden and oppressed of the earth. In "The Ages," we read:

> Here the free spirit of mankind, at length,
> Throws its last fetters off; and who shall place
> A limit to the giant's unchained strength
> Or curb his swiftness in the forward race?

In 1858, Lincoln stated in Edwardsville: "Our reliance is in the *love of liberty* which God has planted in our bosoms. Our defense is in the preservation of the spirit which prizes liberty as the heritage of all men, in all lands, every where." In 1887, James Cardinal Gibbons said in Rome: "Our country has liberty without license and authority without despotism." Woodrow Wilson saw America as a country in which "all men are entitled to the benefits of the law," adding that "America lives in the heart of every man everywhere who wishes to find a region where he will be free to work out his destiny as he chooses." To him, America stood "for the sovereignty of self-governing people" (speeches of December 14, 1906, April 6, 1912, and January 29, 1916). Sidney Smith in *Waterton's Wanderings* called America "This great spectacle of human happiness." In his New Year's greetings of 1931, Albert Einstein wrote: "I feel you are justified in looking into the future with true assurance, because you have a mode of living in which we find the joy of life and the joy of work harmoniously combined. Added to this is the spirit of ambition which pervades your very being, and seems to make the day's work like a happy child at play." In 1918, the House of Representatives in the name of the American people seconded William Tyler Page's words in *The American Creed:* "I believe in the United States of America as a government of the people, by the people, for the people; whose just powers are derived from the consent of the governed; a democracy in a republic; a sovereign nation of many sovereign states; a perfect union, one and inseparable; established upon those principles of freedom, equality, justice and humanity for which American patriots sacrificed their lives and fortunes."

These statements, to which many others could be added, show that America was mainly seen as a land of liberty. The words of the national anthem, "land of the free and the home of the brave," are telling: freedom comes first. In tune with this fact, it was praised by poets. "Sweet land of liberty . . . Let freedom ring," we read in Samuel Francis Smith's *America;* "For Freedom's Flag and Freedom's Land," in Bayard Taylor's *To the American People.* In *America for Me,* Henry van Dyke speaks of the "land of youth and freedom," and so on.

In principle, those who found freedom characteristic of America considered it something good. However, what was felt to be bad about America should also be stated. In November 1782 King George III wrote to Shelburne: "I cannot conclude without mentioning how sensibly I feel the dismemberment of America from this empire . . . did I not also know that knavery seems to be so much the striking feature of its inhabitants that it may not in the end be an evil that they will become aliens to this kingdom." His compatriot Sidney Smith, in his review of Seybert's *Annals of the United States* published at the beginning of 1820 in the *Edinburgh*

Review, asked, "under which of the old tyrannical governments of Europe is every sixth man a slave, whom his fellow-creatures may buy, and sell, and torture?" Robert von Mohl considered slavery, which until 1808 was immune even from amendments to the Constitution, a misfortune. Eighty years after abolition Gunnar Myrdal, in *An American Dilemma: The Negro Problem and Modern Democracy,* emphasized the black problem as one of American democracy. The black riots in the 1950s and 1960s as well as the fact that in the election of President Reagan nearly all the states voted for, and nearly all blacks against, him show that in spite of all civil rights legislation, that dilemma still existed in the 1980s. Existing discrimination as well as reverse discrimination continue to be considered regrettable. Arguments used prior to abolition can still be heard.

Other things were criticized. In his remarks on success Emerson denounced a shallow Americanism that hopes to come to riches by virtue of credit, to find out about the spirit through phrenology, to gain knowledge without studying, and to achieve mastery without apprenticeship. In 1968, *The Bitch-Goddess of Success: Variations on an American Theme,* quoted William James, who had denounced "the moral flabbiness born of the exclusive worship of the bitch-goddess SUCCESS. That—with the squalid cash interpretation put on the word success—is our national disease." Other well-known authors in that volume are Tocqueville, Henry David Thoreau, Walt Whitman, Charles Ives, John F. Kennedy, George F. Kennan.

Doubts about success in a large measure derive from the fact that it has been measured mainly in materialistic terms. This does not surprise, for America was seen as the land of materialism at an early age. With a Golden Age, Americans longed for gold and money, a prosperity in which, with an increasing supply of goods, one luxury after another was declared a necessity. When in 1798 the Duke of Rochefoucauld-Liancourt published a description of his travels, he mentioned that in America the quest for riches was the predominant passion. In Richard Parkinson's *A Tour of America* (1805) we read that in America all are out for money. G. W. Steevens, *The Land of the Dollar* (1897), depicted Americans as the most materialistic people in the world. In his description of the American scene, Henry James mentioned the "great American gold-rattling." In his discourse on America, Matthew Arnold in 1884 complained of American harshness, American materialism, and the absence of soul and sensitivity. When members of the Democratic party criticized the Fifty-first Congress for being a billion-dollar Congress, Charles Foster, the secretary of the Treasury under President Harrison, is reputed to have answered that America was, after all, a billion-dollar country. That answer was praised by Thomas B. Reed in the March issue of the

North American Review of 1892. After World War II, President Coolidge stated that "America's business is business." Laski (p. 46) wrote that this statement symbolized the public opinion prevalent up to that time. Even after World War I, he felt that what George Santayana called "genteel tradition" was "a very small element in the American tradition." This appears to be the case today. Success is still being measured by money-making.

Two men who counted for something at the turn of the century because they had a lot of money also had different opinions on America and, accordingly, different plans. Cecil Rhodes, the British empire builder and founder of scholarships that young Americans aspire to, hoped that America, the lost child, eventually would return to the open arms of Mother Britannia. By contrast, the American Andrew Carnegie, who built a steel empire in his country and donated libraries to many cities, was of the opinion that the grown-up, strong child sooner or later would take care of its old enfeebled mother. His thought points to something important: just as children want to show their parents that they know how to do things better, a microcosm will strive toward becoming a macrocosm, greater and more beautiful.

America was thought to influence England and even the world and to be a powerful example. According to Richard Price, American independence laid "the foundation . . . of an empire which may be the seat of liberty, science and virtue, and from whence there is reason to hope these sacred blessings will spread, till they become universal." To him, "next to the introduction of Christianity among mankind, the American revolution may prove the most important step in the progressive course of human improvement. It is an event which may produce a general diffusion of the principles of humanity, and become the means of setting free mankind from the shackles of superstition and tyranny, by leading them to see and know that nothing is *fundamental* but impartial enquiry, an honest mind, and virtuous practice" (*Observations on the Importance of the American Revolution,* pp. 4, 7). In his observations on the influence of the American Revolution upon Europe, written in 1786 and published in 1788, Condorcet thought that, in a few generations, America, by producing nearly as many men as all of Europe who would add to knowledge, would at least double progress and improve the lot of humanity. In Washington's Farewell Address we read that American institutions will be recommended "to the applause, the affection and adoption of every nation." On October 15, 1785, Jefferson wrote to J. Bannister from Paris that "an American, coming to Europe for education, loses in his knowledge, in his morals, in his health, in his habits, and in his happiness." He was of the opinion that Europeans could learn from Americans. Emerson agreed. In his lecture on character, he stated that the less America looked abroad, the greater would be its future. On July 4, 1821, John Quincy Adams regretted that when, in the assembly of nations, the United States spoke "the language of equal liberty, equal justice, and equal rights," it often was "to heedless and often disdainful ears." Five years later, George Channing asserted in the Kings Message of December 12, 1828, that the New World had been brought into existence in order to correct the equilibrium of the Old. When in 1825 Daniel Webster laid the foundation stone for the Bunker Hill Monument, he expressed the hope that his country may "itself become a vast and splendid monument . . . of wisdom, of peace, and of liberty, upon which the world may gaze with admiration forever." In Walt Whitman's "By Blue Ontario's Shore" we read that America has built for humanity. When Whitman sent Emerson his *Leaves of Grass,* he wrote that he had full confidence in the future: one had not overcome for centuries castes and fables in order now to stop. On April 7, 1912, Woodrow Wilson stated in Chicago that "America lives in the hearts of every man everywhere who wishes to find a region somewhere where he will be free to work out his destiny as he chooses." On May 17, 1915, he emphasized that "America . . . asks nothing for herself except, what she has a right to ask for humanity itself." Henry Wadsworth Longfellow expressed the American mission in the last lines of "The Building of the Ship":

> Thou, too, sail on, O Ship of State!
> Sail on, O Union, strong and great!
> Our hearts, our hopes, are all with thee,
> Humanity with all its fears,
> With all the hopes of future years,
> Is hanging breathless on thy fate!
> . . . .
> Sail on, nor fear to breast the sea!
> Our hearts, our hopes, our prayers, our tears,
> Our faith, triumphant o'er our fears,
> Are all with thee,—are all with thee!

These words point to America's manifest destiny to export and realize its values and to enlarge its territory. Originally, that concept was merely applied to the extension on the American continent—the westward movement of pioneers and conquerers. The Democratic party gave the idea of manifest destiny a prominent place when in the fall of 1844 the annexation of Texas was a major issue in the election campaign. In view of opposition to this annexation, John L. Sullivan in 1845 emphasized in the leading article of the July/August issue of *United States Magazine and Democratic Review:* "Our manifest destiny to overspread the continent allotted by Providence for the free development of our yearly multiplying millions." On January 3, 1846, Robert C. Winthrop defended title to Oregon on the grounds of manifest destiny in the House of Representatives. Following the Civil War, one no longer was content with mere extensions within the American continent. In the leading article of the *New York Herald* of April 3, 1865, James Gordon Bennett wrote: "It is our manifest destiny to lead and rule all other nations." Accordingly, President McKinley brushed off the annexation of Hawaii with the words "manifest destiny." The United States had become an imperialist power. Its manifest destiny manifested itself in the policy of the Big Stick toward Latin America and its participation in two world wars, the Korean War, and the Vietnam War, a war that demonstrated the enormous power of public opinion and the dependence of the elected government upon it.

There are many more examples for assertions of imperialism. When the new nation was merely on the margin of world politics, Jefferson wrote in 1815 to Thomas Leiper: "Not in our day, but at a distant one, we may shake a rod over the heads of all, which may make the stoutest tremble. But I hope our wisdom will grow with our power, and teach us that the less we use our power the greater it will be." On the other hand, there were Americans who believed in the principle, "My country, right or wrong." (Stephen Decatur, on the occasion of a toast to him in Norfolk in 1816; John C. Crittenden in a speech before Congress in 1846; Carl Schurz in an address to the Senate).

American imperialism has been dealt heavy blows, especially since the 1960s. Nevertheless, America's strength and importance in international relations is seldom questioned. Even if the United States today is relatively weaker than it was in 1945 and if its strength should decline still further, the values it stands for will occupy people's minds for a long time to come.

4 Unlimited Opportunities, Free Government, Liberal Variations

The United States has been praised as a land of liberty and criticized for being materialistic. In view of the fact that the Declaration of Independence with its emphasis upon the pursuit of happiness came about when Adam Smith propagated free enterprise, it is hardly surprising that a materialistic pursuit of happiness was considered a good aspect of freedom. No doubt materialism has its good sides. In my study in defense of property I emphasized at the very beginning that it is often difficult to draw the line between the idealistic and the materialistic, because the latter can be very much to the good—as for instance in the case of philanthropic foundations. I drew attention to the fact that languages connect material goods, private property, with what is good—that for instance *goods* in the sense of possessions and property correspond to the adjective *good,* that *property* corresponds to *proper, Gut* to *gut* in German, *les biens* to *bien* in French, and so on.

I also pointed out dubious aspects of materialism. Now, if American materialism is criticized but, on the other hand, seen by most people as a result of freedom, freedom must, as was maintained by Schelling, also be the freedom to do evil. A similar evaluation can be found in the writings of Kant and Hegel and in those of America's Founding Fathers, all of whom basically favored freedom. The latter, while considering people good enough to be trusted with self-government, felt they could not be trusted absolutely. The result was a Constitution that, in tune with the then prevalent concept of liberalism, divided democratic government and provided for checks and balances in order to check the danger of liberty as well as that of liberal popular power. A measured and modest desire for greater freedom could degenerate into an insatiable drive for ever more liberty to do what one felt like doing, whether it was desired by an individual or the majority.

America is not only the land of the free but the land of an ever greater quest for freedom. If this quest is called liberalism, then the United States can be considered the land of liberalism. Such an evaluation also follows from the mere fact that America is the land of liberty, of the free pursuit of happiness with its materialistic overtones. For this fact shows that its inhabitants are free to always act ever more freely to their own advantage. In the land of implied powers, this usually was not particularly emphasized. However, I want to stress it for the sake of clarity, for only clarity makes truth evident.

My own picture of America has been gradually formed since my childhood. At an early age I heard of the "uncle from America" who in the land of unlimited opportunities had amassed great wealth. Since I heard that again and again, I kept thinking about it and arrived at the conclusion that wherever opportunities are unlimited, there must be a great deal of freedom, because freedom is the opposite of limitation. Therefore, people who in America became wealthy as a matter of course had to be freer in that country than anywhere else in order to become rich. Since I heard only of rich uncles from America but not of rich uncles from other countries, and only of America as the land of unlimited opportunities but not of any other country with such opportunities, I saw America in a class by itself. Picasso is said to have expressed the desire to be able to paint like a child because a child, in his opinion, had a sense of what is essential. Perhaps I felt in my early years what most observers have considered the essential feature of America, namely, her liberty as leading to riches.

Later, in my youth, I discovered America as the New World in Goethe's poem, to which I dare adding my translation into English:

Den Vereinigten Staaten

Amerika, du hast es besser
Als unser Kontinent, der alte,
Hast keine verfallene Schlösser
Und keine Basalta.

Dich stört nicht im Innern,
Zu lebendiger Zeit,
Unnützes Erinnern
Und vergeblicher Streit.

Benutzt die Gegenwart mit Glück!
Und wenn nun eure Kinder dichten,

Bewahre sie ein gut Geschick
Vor Ritter-, Räuber- und Gespenstergeschichten!

For the United States

America, you have it better
Than our continent, the old,
You have no castles in ruins
And no basalts.

Your interior is not disturbed,
In a lively present,
By useless memories
And futile disputes.

Make use of the present with luck!
And should your children be bards,
May a good providence shield them
From stories of knights, brigands, and ghosts!

These lines were picked by my teachers, and I picked from them many a thing. The juxtaposition of America to the old continent with its old world of basalts and decayed castles made it the New Continent. Also, America was new because there was no remembering there, in fact nothing old, because one can remember only what is old. In America's interior everything existed in a lively and living present, which was to be used and taken advantage of with luck and fortune. Futile disputes of the past were water over the dam: let bygones be bygones. If these disputes were in vain, those taking place in the present were not: struggling in the pursuit of happiness, in that free enterprise symptomatic of, among other things, free trade, was in good order. Only the present counts and, in a large measure, is to be used for materialistic ends: for the pursuit of happiness here on earth, with steady speculations on what is profitable and what is worthless.

Later on, after the freely elected government of the United States, thinking only of present advantage, killed women, the aged, and children with atomic bombs in order to save the lives of American soldiers; afterward, American women, following their present desires, wanted to get their boys home, thus surrendering wide stretches of land in central Europe to Russia and the communists; after the Marshall Plan aided millions of hungry people and the Truman Doctrine prevented further expansions of communism, I read Thomas Mann's essay on Goethe and democracy. "'Lebendige Zeit,' das ist es" (the lively present, that's it), he wrote with respect to Goethe's poem on America. According to Mann, the German poet he admired the most was of the opinion that America was ruled by the quest for new things, by a lively curiosity, by the desire for soberly getting rid of a world sick with dull traditions that hinder life. In *Dichtung und Wahrheit* Goethe had described the American victory in the War of Independence as "an alleviation for mankind." In 1819, when he gave his collected works to Harvard University, he called the United States a "wonderful land" upon which "the whole world looks on account of a laudable legal condition which promotes unlimited growth." He asked Sulpiz Boisserée: "What would have happened if thirty years ago I would have gone to America with some friends and had never heard of Kant etc.!"

All this occupied my mind. During the previous years I had lived in Heidelberg, a city I have, ever since, visited as much as I could. In that location of American military headquarters, a city that attracted many American tourists, I had observed American men and women at close range—cheerful, naive people, without many problems. Their easygoingness stood in big contrast to the then existing *Lebensangst,* the serious outlook upon things shared by most Germans who after the war were deprived of the necessities of life. I became aware of American materialism, obvious in the free, or black, market. Members of the occupation forces bought flawless one-carat diamonds for thirty cartons of cigarettes, always intent to lower the price even further. There seemed to be no limit to the growth of their property by virtue of free trade. Obviously, the land of unlimited opportunities had been exported to Germany. In view of Goethe's indication that Americans had not heard of Kant, I asked myself whether what he called an alleviation for humanity in the last analysis actually boiled down to a shallow taking it easy irrespective of legal and moral inhibitions. This question also was prompted by Mann's comment that Goethe's remark on Kant reminded him of the introductory poem to *Westöstlicher Diwan:*

Dort, im Reinen und im Rechten
Will ich menschlichen Geschlechten
In des Ursprungs Tiefe dringen,
Wo sie noch von Gott empfingen
Himmelslehr' in Erdesprachen
Und sich nicht den Kopf zerbrachen.

There, in the pure and the right
I want to examine human races
In the depth of their origin,

Where they still received from God
Heaven's teachings in earthly words
And did not rack their brains.

Mann emphasized: "'And did not rack their brains.' That's it. Building bridges to America derives from the desire to get away from aged, tiresome complications, from too many thoughts, from a European world overburdened with spiritual and historical traditions and in the end threatened by nihilism, into a world bare of preconditions and full of naturalness, simplicity, even naïveté and careless youthful strength." He added that the sentence at the end of *Faust,* "To stand with free people on free ground," rang quite American. For Goethe, the future belonged to the man who lived for the day, whose "practical thinking" is directed toward the tangible, useful. It belonged to an activity that is not inhibited by pale thoughts.

The latter for Goethe obviously implied reproachful brooding, which often hinders activity. For on account of the imperatives of the day, practical thinking prompts Americans to vitally and colorfully think of moneymaking in the pursuit of happiness. During my sojourn in the United States, this fact became more and more obvious to me.

At Princeton, I attended a seminar given by Alpheus Thomas Mason. He held the chair that Edward S. Corwin and Woodrow Wilson, both of whom had an impact upon American government, had occupied before him. In his seminar, entitled American Political Thought, he introduced a new subject, which for over thirty years has been my most popular offering at Johns Hopkins University. In 1946, Mason published a bestseller, *Brandeis: A Free Man's Life*. When I attended his seminar in 1949, his anthology *Free Government in the Making* had just come out, addressed "To my students in American Political Thought, participants in a continuing symposium." The title fascinated me: *Free Government in the Making*. From it follows that free government is in the making all the time—obviously by those "doers," those activists, who according to Mason are predominant in American civilization. It was less clear what they did in particular and how they did it. For actually, the term *free government* does not really make clear what kind of a government it is. Is it one under which the governed are free, or one that is free to oppress them? This appeared to me the big question, leaving open the possibility of different, even opposing concepts of freedom. The American form of government turned out to be ambivalent. The concept of free government is the great American ambiguity, doing justice to America's reputation as the land of unlimited opportunities.

Statements by the Founding Fathers left little doubt that they conceived free government in the former sense. On the other hand, voices could be heard at their time according to which the democratic majority was free to impose its will upon the minority and upon individuals. The government preferred by Locke stood opposed to that desired by Rousseau. For a long time, Locke's idea was officially accepted. However, this changed. The United States developed from a country in which individuals were protected from the majority to one in which that protection decreased. At the end of the nineteenth century, the two interpretations of free government were about in balance. Herbert Spencer, favoring freedom of the individual, saw himself confronted by Oliver Wendell Holmes, an associate justice of the Supreme Court who in a dissent in *Lochner v. New York* (1905) wrote that the Constitution "does not enact Mr. Herbert Spencer's Social Statics." In the 1930s, things had gotten so far as to prompt the vice president of the American Liberty League and believer in laissez-faire, Raoul E. Desvernine, to liken Franklin D. Roosevelt's controls and regulations of the economy to those of Kemal Atatürk, Mussolini, and Stalin. Nevertheless, Roosevelt continued to represent the will of the majority vis-à-vis the wishes of individuals. To Roosevelt free government obviously meant to a large degree the liberty of the democratic government to restrict the behavior of individuals. Professor Mason saw in all these opinions "liberal variations." These words show the enormous range and the many meanings of liberalism in America. I was rather puzzled by this, for in Europe I had been used to a much narrower concept of liberalism, one that plainly aimed at the protection of the individual from the government.

On Mason's advice, I enrolled in Louis Hartz's seminar on American political thought at Harvard. It too made me aware that Americans subsumed under liberalism considerably more than did Europeans, even things which to Europeans are incompatible with liberalism. In 1955, Hartz published *The Liberal Tradition in America: An Interpretation of American Political Thought since the Revolution*. The cover of the paperback is telling. It shows two star-spangled banners waving with different strength—in opposite directions! The flagpoles are surrounded by the words, "a new concept of a liberal community that relates American politics and political thought to the mainstream of Western history." Here grew different, even opposite, movements, thoughts, and opinions out of the matrix of the development of the West! They all were ordered into the fold of liberalism. However, the latter's order appears quite disorderly because everybody obviously can run with the tide. In the first chapter, dealing with the concept of a liberal society, there are subtitles such as "Natural Liberalism" and "The Dynamics of a Liberal Society." The vagueness of the word *liberalism* is emphasized, as is its nebulousness on account of modern social reforms. Hartz added that even the Lockean idea of liberalism underwent changes as early as the Puritans. He spoke of the "American liberal world," its "natural liberalism," of liberalism as a natural American phenomenon, of the firm dogmatic liberalism of a liberal way of life, of "the secret root from which have sprung many of the most puzzling of American cultural phenomena," of the "absolute liberal faith." He wrote that in America there never has been a "liberal movement," a real "liberal party," because the American way of life is liberal anyway. He added that in American liberal society "the individualism of Hamilton is also a secret part of the Jeffersonian psyche," even though the two usually have been juxtaposed. Hartz spoke of "the counter resources a liberal society can muster against this deep and unwritten compulsion it contains." He called its problems "bizarre," pointed to its "magical chemistry," which he saw as the triumph of the liberal idea, and mentioned the utility of a liberal society in which many groups can thrive. He mentioned the wide variations of American liberalism, "America's irrational liberalism." The chapter ends with the finding that an analysis of American liberalism is not a happy undertaking because it "is likely to discover on occasion a national villain, such as the tyrannical force of Lockean sentiment." He was of the opinion that American liberalism cannot guarantee remedies for national weaknesses. Going on reading, one encounters titles such as "The Whig Dilemma," "The Atrophy of Whig Progressivism," "The American Democrat: Hercules and Hamlet," "Individual Fear: The Problem of the Majority," "Capitalistic Lust: Conscience and Appetite," "The New Whiggery: Democratic Capitalism," "The 'Discovery of America': Charm and Terror," "Rugged Individualism and State Power," "Progressives and Socialists," "Liberal Reform in America," "Socialism in the Wilderness," "The Triumph and Transformation of Liberal Reform," "The Strategy of a Deflated Whiggery," All this shows the tremendous scope of American liberalism, of "liberal absolutism."

Coming from abroad, I found this scope too wide even in the land of unlimited opportunities. For so far that land had implied to me only one in which people through their own efforts could get ahead without the government putting anything in their way and which permitted them to keep the rewards of their labor. I knew, of course, that this kind of liberalism also had its variations; that, for instance, Manchester laissez-faire went further than that of Erhard's social market economy; that liberalism appeared different in different countries under different conditions. On the other hand, all European liberals as a matter of principle emphasized the freedom of individuals from the state, however party programs might differ.

From the time of the founders of the United States into the twentieth century, the Constitution was interpreted in the sense of European liberalism. I therefore asked myself whether or not an interpretation of free government to the effect that the democratic majority is free to do all it desires, and thus free to oppress individuals, was a perversion of liberalism propagated as a liberal variation. For it often is only one step from variation to perversion. I could not very well imagine that the people's freedom to be left alone by the government was equal to the freedom of the government not to leave them alone. My thoughts were supported by Americans for whom absolute majority rule was incompatible with genuine liberalism and free government. They were further sustained by my German experience. Hadn't it been asserted in the Third Reich, following Hitler's criticisms of democracy, that National Socialism stood for a nobler and purer democracy than that of Western nations? And then, there was Nietzsche's thought of the revaluation of values, that brooding omnipresence in our time. Was the new evaluation of liberalism in the United States perhaps an attack on its traditional concepts, an attack considered timely in that country? And did that attack correspond to the second of Nietzsche's *Untimely Meditations,* turning against historicism? Did the traditional concept of liberalism, having prevailed for a long time in America, perhaps correspond to that "historical sickness," which according to Nietzsche would be detrimental to spontaneous life? Did it unjustly restrict the "plastic ability" of men, their creative freedom? Do we live at a time of reevaluations in which a new evaluation of free government in America could take place, just as a new evaluation of democracy was put forward under the Hitler regime? But aren't new evaluations devaluations of what has proved itself and for that reason has been honored?

My European respect for tradition made me answer the last question in the affirmative. This is reflected in my books on America. My *Federalist* (1960) shows that the classic commentary on the Constitution saw in a free government one under which the ruling majority was, for the sake of the protection of individuals, bound by laws. It emphasizes that the men who made the Constitution feared the majority and restricted it in favor of the individual by separations of governmental power and other limitations of the government. My *America's Political Dilemma* (1968) sees that dilemma in the march from limited to unlimited democracy. It points to the latter's despotic aspects and attempts to show how the United States increasingly drifted toward what its founders wanted to prevent, namely, absolute majority rule, something denounced in 1936 by Desvernine as democratic despotism.

Both books were published during the decade in which John F. Kennedy, his brother Robert, and Martin Luther King, Jr., were murdered, the very decade that the youngest president of the United States had heralded as the most glorious in the postwar period. At that time, I became very much aware of how, in contrast to the quiet 1950s under President

Eisenhower, America had changed, how change for the sake of change had become a principle and unlimited majority rule increasingly accepted.

This development was resisted by many liberals of the old school. They now called themselves conservatives because they wanted to preserve the traditional interpretations of free government and liberalism. On the other hand, F. A. Hayek, who ever since the publication of his bestseller *The Road to Serfdom* (1944) had been considered one of their spokesmen, emphasized in *The Constitution of Liberty* (1960) that he was not a conservative, but an "Old Whig." Here again, liberal variations were evident: Old Whigs were distinguished from New Whigs. And if Hayek in spite of his insistence that he was a liberal is claimed by American conservatives to be one of theirs, there can be little doubt that the latter, interested as they are in protecting the liberalism current at the time of the American Revolution and characterized by an emphasis upon the protection of the individual from the government, basically are liberals. However, since those pleading for an unrestricted freedom of the majority also advanced on the grounds of the traditional concept of free government, it is conceivable that their activities too could derive from that concept and that they could pose as liberals with a good conscience. This is not contradicted by the fact that their kind of liberalism is denounced by the believers in the older concept as degenerate. Degeneration shows a lowering of quality rather than a change of substance. Degenerate nobility is still nobility. Dadaism was considered degenerate art. Its place in the history of art cannot be doubted, whether it is judged favorably or not: als dada da war, war dada da. Even if new liberalisms are considered degenerations of liberalism, they still are liberalisms. Just as the new Whigs did not think they were degenerate Whigs, modern liberals do not consider themselves degenerate liberals. On the contrary, they see themselves as forward marching, progressive, and progressed liberals who live up to the liberal quest for ever new liberations and liberalisms. For if liberalism is a movement toward greater and greater freedom, those will consider themselves true and genuine liberals who discard traditional, old liberalisms as history, the way Nietzsche discarded history as something one studies and knows about but that, however, is atrophied and no longer can give anything to the living.

The argument that modern liberalisms derive from the concrete historical movement generally known as liberalism, a movement interested in the emancipation of individuals from superior powers, cannot easily be discarded. This movement began at about the time of the Reformation, which wanted to liberate individuals from the pope and his church. It continued in movements toward limitations on state power, culminating in the English, American, and French Revolutions, which were directed against absolutism and its mercantilist, Colbertist, and cameralist aspects. Then came the constitutionalism of the nineteenth century, in which concepts like Manchesterism, night-watchman state, and cutthroat competition flourished. This development shows that liberalism is not static. Religious freedom was followed by that of trade, of speech, of the press, of assembly, of association, and so on.

Although all the latter liberties imply emancipations from the government, due to the obvious expansionist trend inherent in liberalism it could not be precluded that sooner or later other types of liberty would follow, interpreting liberalism in the sense of an ever greater freedom of the ruling majority to do whatever it considered opportune at the time. The probability of such a development was likely to grow in view of the fact that the liberalism directed against absolute monarchy saw in popular government the best means for the protection of the individual from the state. From an early stage, liberalism implied the freedom of individuals from the government through their participation in government. And if for the protection of freedom from the government a form of government is chosen under which individuals are free to participate in that protection, then extensions of the suffrage to poorer parts of the population are likely to make these parts demand that the government do something for them even at costs to others. Basically, liberalism is anthropocentric, egoistic, egotistic, egocentric, and for that reason, often excentric. Under liberalism, everybody can first think of himself and take care of himself because he is closest to himself. Thus the freedom from the government, for which popular self-government appeared to be the best guarantee, could become the freedom of the self-governing people to do as they pleased at any particular time. The motto of the absolute monarch, *tel est Notre plaisir,* was replaced by the democratic *tel est notre plaisir.* Not capitalizing the word *notre* in the latter case looks like a mockery, given the fact that according to the principle *vox populi vox Dei* the democratic majority certainly is more powerful than the aristocratic and monarchical minority in the age of absolutism, much as the latter might have operated under the *gratia dei.*

Such a development was not surprising, especially in America. Already prior to independence the struggle in the various colonies between legislatures representing the people and governors appointed by the king had made it obvious that Americans saw in self-government the best means for the protection of their liberty from governmental power. After independence, the legislative assemblies of the newly independent states were more powerful than the elected governors and passed laws that favored the majority, often hurting the minority. Something similar later occurred on the national level.

The Declaration of Independence makes clear that governments are based upon the consent of the governed and that it is their purpose to protect human rights, including life, liberty, and the pursuit of happiness. The Constitution in a large measure was adopted to protect individuals from legislative encroachments. Its preamble makes plain that the blessings of liberty and the promotion of the general welfare are to be brought about by a popular government. Much as free government in the beginning may have been interpreted to mean the protection of individuals from the government, after extensions of the suffrage it was increasingly understood to imply the freedom of the elected ruling majority and to help that majority even at the cost of the minority.

Although in many respects liberal variations, which came about especially since the end of the nineteenth century, can be derived from the historical liberal movement that reached a climax in the American Revolution, one is reluctant to consider that movement their only source. Without doubt that movement brought forth many modern liberalisms in tune with it, of which it need not be ashamed. Extensions of the freedom of the press to radio and television, aspects of civil rights laws, and the rights of the accused come to mind. So do extensions of the suffrage. In these cases, the concept of liberalism prevalent at the founding of the United States brought forth liberalisms that can be considered well in line with it. It looks different when one realizes that the new concept of free government is hardly compatible with the old one. A government under which individuals enjoy freedom differs from one that is free to oppress them. And giving demonstrators and criminals so many rights that public security is seriously jeopardized is hardly compatible with the liberalism prevailing at the time of the adoption of the Constitution, which provided for a good balance of liberty and order.

Now if movements and desires that differ to a degree that they seem to be opposed to, and incompatible with, each other pose as liberal and are called liberal variations, then liberalism as their source must be something more comprehensive than the liberalism dominant at the time of the American Revolution. It leaves open the possibility that some liberal variants may lead to the destruction of others and that liberal values can be upgraded or downgraded. From such an endless sea of values one can easily arrive at an endless desert of values and, from there, to an absence of values. Since the absence of values is tantamount to value-freeness, liberalism as the source of all kinds of liberalisms with their often opposing and incompatible values must be value-free. And since what is free of values is purified from them, value-free liberalism must be pure liberalism. The source of American liberal variations is, therefore, not the liberal variant current at the time of the American Revolution. Rather, it is pure liberalism, which also is the source of later liberal variations. It is liberalism proper in distinction to what were considered proper liberalisms by those who in various liberal variants wanted to express their respective desires and plans. Perhaps one can find, as in case of the liberal Mill, indications of value-free, pure liberalism in the writings of liberals like Locke, Montesquieu, Smith, and Kant. Such indications, however, would be the exception. For all these liberals favored limited movements for the emancipation of individuals, inclined toward specific values and brought about by means of republican government. At any rate, all liberal variations, including the one generally cherished at the beginning of the United States, have their source in pure liberalism, in the liberal idea that is partially realized by them. This does not mean that the particular form of liberalism prevalent at the founding of the United States could not have spawned liberal variations opposed to it, as will be demonstrated later on. In that case, the most different liberalisms were promoted in America not only by the idea of pure liberalism but also by the concept of free government as generally accepted during its formative period.

As a result, there came about so many liberal variations in the United States that pure liberalism seems to be realized there to a larger degree than in other Western democracies, usually also known as liberal democracies. However, liberalism as a drive for freedom is not merely a drive toward dreaming of freedom, much as it may derive from that dream. It also is not just a quest toward emphasizing natural law, much as it may be based upon that law. Liberalism is the drive for the possibility of free action, and the struggle for specific aspects of freedom so far has been one for specific positive, enforceable rights. Therefore, pure liberalism is the drive toward pure, unlimited, enforceable freedom and as such one toward unlimited opportunities. America being the country in which pure liberalism has been realized the most, we may conclude that America offers more opportunities than any other nation. As the land of pure liberalism, America is the land of unlimited opportunities—in a wider sense than sheer materialistic advancement. Although it is difficult in a society known to be materialistic to separate moneymaking and unlimited opportunities, the latter go beyond mere moneymaking. Unlimited opportunities are not necessarily tied to moneymaking and are thus free of it—and therefore purer, more genuine, and unlimited. Although as something real these opportunities are not absolutes (the realization of the absolute is rare), they still are closer to the absolute, the purely unlimited, than they would be if they existed only with respect to material advancement. The busy American is simply the working American, the doer.

This busy man in business, this businessman, need not necessarily be an original mind, an inventor, in order to be admired. It will do if, like Thomas A. Edison and Henry Ford, he can apply with exceptional brilliance ideas that others have conceived, make something of them, and become an industrial tycoon. Also he can, in liberal fashion, discard moral or even legal inhibitions as long as he gets somewhere. One cannot read about the methods by which John D. Rockefeller established his supremacy in the oil industry without seeing a long trail of bribery and corruption, thuggery and suicide. Laws then appear less as something to be honored than as obstacles that have to be circumvented by finding loopholes. The dubious procedures used by Joseph P. Kennedy to amass a fortune did not prevent him from moving up into the oligarchy of Boston, from becoming American ambassador to the Court of St. James. Furthermore, the voters of Massachusetts had no inhibitions against electing his son John to the U.S. Senate in spite of the fact that his election campaign obviously was financed by his father. The same is true of the voters of the whole United States: in 1960, they sent John Kennedy to the White House after, on July 4, he reminded them of the New World tradition to get busy creating new things: "It is time for a new generation of leadership, to cope with new problems and new opportunities. For there is a new world to be won."

5 The Business of America Is Business

The multiplicity of opportunities in the United States cannot blind us to the fact that those with a materialistic orientation make up most liberalisms. Moneymaking still plays a big role. "Nothing succeeds like success," is a generally recognized saying. And success is mainly measured by income. Few criticize it as something materialistic. It is considered a god rather than a bitch-goddess. Even professors, who should publish their findings simply for the sake of scholarship, are very much interested in making money. "The business of America is business," said Calvin Coolidge, president from 1923 to 1929, during the Golden Twenties, which were characterized by free enterprise. His first name is telling. Max Weber's well-known treatise on the Protestant ethic and the spirit of capitalism (1905) emphasized that the ever growing quest for acquisitions is especially strong among Calvinists. And their influence has always been very strong in the United States. Notwithstanding many movements toward social reform, America has remained a country of entrepreneurs. Even after World War II, when the ideas of John Maynard Keynes were quite popular, one held on to the principle of free enterprise. This explains the success of F. A. Hayek's book against the socialists of all parties. Although it was translated into many languages, it enjoyed its greatest popularity in the country of its origin. It corresponded to traditional American inclinations toward the free market, already evident prior to the publication of Adam Smith's bestseller on the wealth of nations, a work which, published as it was in 1776, became in a way the guiding star for the basically free and independent American way of life. The spirit of capitalism, being one of free trade and free activity, is one of mobility, often considered the alter ego of the liberal movement directed against mercantilism. Trading and changing is a liberal motto, which in the United States has always been held in high esteem. It is imbued with the spirit of activity: the freedoms to trade, to act, and to change constitute a liberal triune probably more praised in America than anywhere else.

The sentence, "The business of America is business," indicates that in the United States more than in any other nation business is the way of life. After World War I, when America emerged from its debtor position to become the world's biggest creditor nation, one obviously wanted to emphasize that business and businessmen had made America great and would continue to do so. Perhaps Coolidge also thought of the busy American in a more general way, for business is not only applicable to economic matters. Although it will usually be connected with those, it is used in the broader general sense of being busy. "Let's get down to business," can simply mean "Let's deal with the subject matter now." If an American feels someone interferes in what he is doing, he may assert his individualism by saying, "That's my business" or, more strongly, "That's none of your business," "Mind your own business," even using the expression "goddam business."

It hardly is possible not to be aware of the big role the economy plays in American life. American cities stand out in their regions mainly on account of their economic significance. Chicago overshadows all other cities of the Middle West, Los Angeles those on the West Coast, including beautiful San Francisco with its rich traditions. In Texas, business centers such as Dallas and Houston are more important than the capital, Austin, home to the university of that state. In Michigan, Detroit with its industry far overshadows the university town of Ann Arbor or the capital, Lansing. Things are not different on the national level. For a long time, Boston was considered the intellectual capital of the nation, and Washington always has been the seat of the federal government. Yet New York is more important because it is the center of the business world. There probably is no other place where business life is so overwhelmingly obvious in just four avenues running parallel and in proximity. Nowhere else can there be found the kind of agglomeration of luxury residences of rich businessmen as on Park Avenue, nowhere such a concentration of advertising agencies as on Madison Avenue. Fifth Avenue boasts more department stores than any other street in the world: it is a veritable fairyland of supply in all seasons—not only before Christmas, when it seems to outdo itself. The enormous business complex of Rockefeller Center with its skyscrapers seems to dwarf the neo-Gothic St. Patrick's Cathedral facing it, although nowhere else in the big city as in this cathedral did I relax as much, did I feel as safe from the business world and its activities. The Empire State Building, for a long time the characteristic feature of New

York City, makes Fifth Avenue look majestic. Looking from the ground toward its top, one is surprised that one building contains as many offices as it does. Then surveying the city from its observation tower, one notices from year to year ever new impressive buildings, especially on Sixth Avenue, where one skyscraper after another were built in a short time. That avenue is also called Avenue of the Americas in honor of all the nations of the Western Hemisphere. Its grandeur honors the spirit of enterprise in the United States of North America. The straight lines of the avenues mentioned appeared to me symbolic of the thrust of an unlimited liberal trade in which many an individual established himself only to see his business pushed aside by others in the competition inherent in a free trade which in the land of liberalisms seems to be unlimited.

The importance of the economy for American life is obvious in the media. The enormous editions of dailies like the *New York Times* and the *Los Angeles Times* are overshadowed by that of the *Wall Street Journal,* which concentrates on economic matters. There are thousands of radio and television stations, which—as do the newspapers—compete for the support of the business world. However, whereas in the press advertising as a matter of principle is separated from the rest of its offerings and does not interfere with its articles, the situation is different in the case of radio and television. Usually, when things are about to get interesting, the transmission is interrupted by advertising. This often is irritating, but few people seem to mind. It obviously achieves its economic purpose, because the audience is all eyes and ears whenever it tunes in. We are faced by carefully calculated, smart business tactics of presentation. Given the fact that such interruptions are relatively rare in the press, are frequent in radio, and even more so in television, one can speak of an escalation of interruptions. Although interrupting is usually considered bad manners, it would probably go too far to speak here of an escalation of bad manners that came about with technical development. The abundance of advertising, which obviously pays off, is generally accepted. In tune with the respect for money, it is considered the good right of sponsors to interrupt at their pleasure transmissions that they finance and make possible. One is quite willing, although not perhaps enthusiastic, to pay this price for the freedom of the media. According to the First Amendment of the federal Constitution (Article 1 of the Bill of Rights), that freedom is protected from infringements by lawmakers. For some time now, it even has been considered a preferred freedom. To most Americans, freedom still means, above all, freedom from governmental power. The power of the media appears less dangerous, although it is known that the media are controlled by those financing them through advertising—that is, by business enterprises.

The latter are mainly interested in pleasing the public and in selling their goods. Thus radio and television shows and the print media usually are judged by the size of their audiences. Quantity counts more than quality. Programs and articles are planned with a view to the number of readers, listeners, and viewers, just as party platforms are adjusted to vote-getting. This is obvious not only in the case of amusing entertainments, which head television offerings. Show business also brings serious and disturbing things, especially if it is sensational enough to attract a large audience. This is not surprising in the land of the thriller. Thus the "Holocaust" television series in the spring of 1978 (which to my mind set the reconciliation of Germany and the Untied States back many years) was in a large measure motivated by the speculation that this horror show of nearly ten hours would prevent the National Broadcasting Corporation's audience from shrinking further. Little thought was given to the harm it could do to American-German relations. When in 1985 President Reagan, with a view to improving these relations, wanted to visit the German military cemetery in Bitburg, the media tried to talk him out of it. Fritz Ullrick Fack wrote in the leading article of the *Frankfurter Allgemeine Zeitung für Deutschland:* "President Reagan had the right instinct when he wanted to go. But a powerful publicistic machinery in his country cherishes revenge into the seventh generation and is grateful for every opportunity to dig out the horror picture of the bad German in order to open old wounds. Those running it do not even care to sort the dead and to make the President a puppet. Here a thirst for power is intertwined with the business interests of an entertainment industry to whom the 'nazi theme' always is welcome. No trace whatsoever of differentiation and responsibility."

The question also has been raised whether or not economic interests prevented a differentiated, responsible reporting on the Soviet Union. The might of that nation caused many Americans a great deal of anguish; news that lessened that fear, therefore was welcome. Therefore, what would be more opportune than bringing such news? Customers buy what they like—what they like to read, to hear, and to see. Thus the media were likely to emphasize the difficulties facing the Soviet Union rather than its successes. Dissidence, alcoholism, economic problems, losses in Afghanistan (which was depicted as a Russian Vietnam), as well as divisions within the communist bloc that put in doubt the leadership of the Soviet Union, they all made good copy. A great hope, underlined by the media, was that Russia would be preoccupied with the emerging China and, as a result, would leave the United States alone. There was even talk of an alliance between America and China against Russia; and thus the American public could be lulled into feeling secure. I never encountered in the media the suggestion that America might be invaded. Rather, they emphasized that the "splendid isolation" America enjoys to a greater extent than England makes universal conscription unnecessary. This also goes over well, because exempting young people from military service allows them to take advantages of the opportunities of civilian life at an early age.

Worries are not only alleviated in the media by programs that, in liberal variety, have something for just about everybody. Advertising interruptions of these programs, too, are conducive to making people feel good. The direction of thought is interrupted by this diversion. The oversupply of goods and shows outside their homes—in markets and supermarkets, stores and department stores, movie theaters, musicals and operas, is made plain to Americans in their homes by the media in a way that is more imposing and more pestering than the advertisements they receive in the mail. The ads make glowing predictions. Attention is diverted from the everyday to the beautiful moment. They can bring about a veritable euphoria. Something praised for being worth its price appears to be worth praising. The potential customer is faced with advertisements of such a multiplicity of opportunities of investments, purchases, and enjoyments that he thinks he is in a Utopia, in a Golden Age. John F. Kennedy (who for some time was a journalist himself and was liked by the media) hit the right chord when, reminiscent of the Golden Twenties, he predicted the Golden Sixties. Praise often lets us forget price. Praise of one thing follows that of another, and all of this leads to an almost drunken belief in opportunity. As the research of public relations firms obviously has found, interruptions by advertisements are welcome diversions for most people, even though they may nauseate some. After all, they show the abundance of the American way of life. Thus the media (and especially television, with at least one set in about every home), with their many interruptions showing people a veritable mass of opportunities, are characteristic of the American way of life. Interruptions and opportunities point to something new, a breaking away from the old. Opportunities bring relief from the old. Each interruption brings something new, shows new opportunities.

6 Coming and Going, Pursuit of Happiness, Changing

Coming and going in the business world, in the media influenced and financed by it, coming and going in many other respects: America is the land of coming and going, the land of ever new arrivals and farewells. One says good bye rather than auf Wiedersehen, au revoir, arrivederci, hasta la vista. One takes leave from what one wants to leave behind and forget. At the end of my critique of pure liberalism I wrote: "For better or worse people under the banner of pure liberalism will again and again take new liberties, for it is of the essence of liberalism to dissolve ties with the old in order to solve the new." This fact revealed itself to me especially in America. Perpetual comings and goings show America as a nation of a far-reaching liberalism.

America appears to be less a country of happiness but, as is said in its Declaration of Independence, of the *pursuit* of happiness. People pursue happiness by taking advantage of possibilities and opportunities. Consequently, people's happiness consists not so much in the enjoyment of what they have, of something concrete and limited, but in the sheer unlimited possibilities of going after new things. What has been achieved is nothing but a stepping-stone to achieve more. What has been created is the point of departure for creating more, and so it goes on and on in a never-ending drive for more and more. Achievement is the matrix of what is to be achieved, just as capital is the source of new capital. This demonstrates Weber's thesis of Calvinist ethics, which is especially strong in English-speaking countries. Perhaps it goes too far to equate Calvinism with capitalism. On the other hand, there can be little doubt that both complement each other. Marx, after emigrating to Calvinist England, wrote *The Capital* there, next to the *Communist Manifesto* probably his best known work. The England of his time was the first industrialized nation, the first land of capitalism. Likewise, New England is that part of America that, strongly influenced by Calvinism, was first industrialized and capitalized: here, too, Calvinism and capitalism intertwined. In turn, that stronghold of capitalism and Calvinism influenced, due to its intellectual and industrial strength, the rest of the United States. With growing industrialization, America became a land of Calvinism and capitalism, of calvincapitalism, of capitalcalvinism, if I may say so. When Calvin Coolidge—Keep Cool with Coolidge was a saying at his time, which reminds one of cool business calculation—remarked that America's business is business, this truth was coming from a Calvinist businessman who had advanced to the highest office of the nation. He symbolized the combination of Calvinism and capitalism, which can be considered the formula of American business—as something typically American. *Nomen est omen:* Just as John Calvin coolly calculated his teachings of predestination, of the morality of getting rich and of riches, and just as his views made Geneva and Switzerland the home of banks and business enterprises, Calvin Coolidge considered America a land of cooly calculating, deducting, adding, sometimes miscalculating businessmen.

Now the pursuit of happiness that Jefferson emphasized at the beginning of the new nation does not point to a mere never-ending activity and businesslike pursuit of happiness. It can be argued that this concept makes plain that happiness is the end, its pursuit nothing but a means to achieve it. As a matter of fact, many Americans are content with the mere enjoyment of what they have, as Thorstein Veblen wrote in *The Leisure Class* (1899). Many of them work toward early retirement. But although their number has increased since World War II, these still are the exception. Others, living in prosperity and luxury without working or ever having worked, just indulge in enjoying life. The broad masses occasionally hear of their dolce vita through scandals. However, even they are still the exception. Even among them there are many who keep on speculating as if they cannot resist making money, as if driven by an invisible hand—which brings to mind the one Adam Smith mentioned. Furthermore, America's rich are not only interested in economic wealth: the examples of the Roosevelts, Rockefellers, and Kennedys demonstrate that they are out for political power.

In America, there is no end to the pursuit of happiness. One American hero is Horatio Alger, who believed that the persistent pursuit of happiness must be crowned by success in the land of unlimited opportunities. This leads to the formula *Pursuit → Success.* The American ideal is still seen in Russell H. Conwell's urge, "Get rich, get rich," which was first emphasized in his lecture "Acres of Diamonds" (1861), held at a time when Spencer's social Darwinism began its victorious march, when the outbreak of the Civil War signaled the victory of the industrial, Calvinist-capitalist North over the agrarian, feudalist South. Conwell repeated his lecture, in a marathon probably never seen before, more than six thousand times, obviously to the delight of his audiences. Its message is that in America every place has its diamond mine and that, wherever you are, there is an opportunity to get rich. Following Calvin, this Baptist preacher accepted the equation *Virtue = Wealth* and thus furthered the American inclination toward considering material well-being as a sign of the grace of God and man's likeness to God, even of his own godliness. Conwell pointed to what Mark Twain called the Gilded Age.

Conwell's lecture urged the pursuit of happiness rather than the mere enjoyment of static prosperity or happiness. His persistent urge toward greater and greater riches reinforced the doctrine of laissez-faire and the gospel of wealth. It left little doubt about the importance of getting rich. Holding public office was "*prima facie* evidence of littleness . . . under our form of government," he told the young men in his audience. "If you only get the privilege of casting one vote, you don't get anything that is worth while. . . . This country is not run by votes. . . . It is governed by the ambition and the enterprises which control the votes." Thus money-makers in their never-ending mobility were the masters of politics. In 1900 Bishop William Lawrence of Massachusetts supported Conwell, emphasizing that the pursuit of happiness is more important than achieved well-being. For him, as for Calvin, "Godliness is in league with riches," and in "the long run it is only to the man of morality that wealth comes." Efficiency as a means of becoming rich was decreed by the laws of nature and of God.

Half a century later Alpheus Mason wrote in the foreword to his *Free Government in the Making* that the activist, the doer, is typical in America, and he adhered to this idea in later editions. It is in tune with the opinion of Louis Hartz, who in his book on the liberal tradition in America, when first mentioning Horatio Alger, remarked that even the crash of 1929 did not really shatter the brilliance of his image. This fact has been confirmed by other authors as well as by my own observations. America as the land of the pursuit of happiness is, above all, one of the drive for happiness, not one of the mere enjoyment of what has been achieved. Laissez-faire liberalism is still predominant, much as it may have come under attack by other liberalisms. The argument that pursuit is only a means for the attainment of happiness and therefore must be subordinate to its end can be countered by saying that the means simply has become more important than its end. History has known such elevations and dislocations. We need think only of the English principle of pure patriotism, as expressed in the words, My country, right or wrong. Thus with the slogan, Everything for Germany, the National Socialists advised the German people not to just think of themselves to the detriment of the Reich. Furthermore, the argument that the pursuit of happiness is a mere means, whereas happiness is the more important end, can be countered by the remark that the pursuit of happiness and happiness itself are not actually different things but are one and the same. This can be interpreted in the sense of both the drive for happiness and the enjoyment of happiness. Aside from that, it is possible to see in the drive itself that enjoyment and to see that America's happiness consists in a never-ending pursuit, in a never-ending hunt, for happiness. America would thus emerge as the land of fortune seekers who are possessed by a drive for the new, a drive that also is characteristic of liberalism.

Be this as it may, the pursuit of happiness, a concept of liberalism, is not just materialistic, much as the materialistic may dominate it. This can be seen in many respects. Herbert von Borch's *The Unfinished Society* saw America as a land in which there always is something to change, to complete, to improve, one of steady progress. All this corresponds to the pursuit of happiness. However, an examination of examples of that pursuit still shows that they all are more or less materialistically oriented. It was this basic American orientation that prompted me in the preceding pages to let remarks on American business life and its control of the media by means of economically oriented advertising precede statements on the pursuit of happiness, even though both business life and the pursuit of happiness, as well as other features of America, can be subsumed under the latter comprehensive concept. It is the best-known concept of the Declaration of Independence, which emphasizes the rights to "life, liberty, and the pursuit of happiness." This triune of Americanism and liberalism fascinates on account of its breadth and logic: one lives to be free for the pursuit of happiness; one is supposed to live, to be free, to pursue happiness. When Jefferson spoke of happiness he probably had in mind, as did most of his countrymen, what Locke did in his *Second Treatise of Civil Governments,* usually considered the source of the Declaration of Independence. Locke spoke of "life, liberty, and property," of "life, liberty and estate." Jefferson thus probably used "happiness," although perhaps not exclusively, in a materialistic connotation, equating possession and property. The happy American is one who is running after, and enjoying, possessions and property. His happiness grows with his riches in the goods of this earth.

These goods, above all else, enable him to "have fun." Fun is so important an aspect of the pursuit of happiness that Lerner considers it the "reigning moral deity" (p. 675). For generations American children have read the funnies, and so do the young and adults. One always is out for fun. Let's have fun, is the motto; We had fun, the satisfied comment. This often goes so far that foreigners think American are *funny* in the sense of *poor taste.* Memorial Day is not an autumn occasion of silent remembrance of the dead. Rather, it initiates with cheerful celebrations the beginning of summer. Honoring those killed in action by placing wreaths has become more or less marginal. The traditional Memorial Day of May 30 was shifted to follow a Sunday in order to prolong a weekend, making it into the Memorial Day weekend, during which people can amuse themselves at their pleasure. I often observed it in Washington. About a hundred thousand people gather in a picnic atmosphere in front of the Capitol to enjoy presentations by athletes, clowns, and musicians. The musical program, amplified by loudspeakers to an often ear-splitting level, extends from jazz and pop to Bach and Beethoven, played by the National Symphony Orchestra. One has fun, has liberated oneself from thinking of the dead. In 1984 Neil Postman published a book on how America amuses itself to death.

Next to the pursuit of happiness, other American characteristics to a large extent are of a materialistic nature. Change is desired for the sake of material gain. For most Americans the quantity of their possessions is the symbol of their quality. The country itself seems to be symbolic of change. The United States is not a unitary nation in which the same laws apply everywhere. They are a federal state composed of fifty member states, all of which have their own laws. For under the federal Constitution only a few and defined powers are delegated to the national government. The rest remain with the particular states. There is truth in referring to the United States simply as the States. America's federal character invites change and makes plain that the American way of life with its pursuit of happiness is one of change, one urging change for the sake of improvement. On September 25, 1971, the *New Yorker* ran a telling cartoon: a recreation vehicle speeds along the highway, prompting an observer to utter the sarcastic remark: "Aye, 'tis said when New York's sales tax jumped to seven per cent he slipped across the line into Connecticut. And when Connecticut passed its tax package he fled to New Hampshire. And now, the legend goes, he flees from state to state forever." Americans move from state to state in order to improve their lot.

They also move from city to city, from the countryside to town, and from town to countryside. For a long time America has been the country of moving back and forth. Even in colonial times Governor Dunmore remarked that the settlers acquired no attachment to place but that wandering about seemed engrafted to their nature and that they imagined that lands farther off were better than those upon which they had settled. Crèvecoeur also noted that fact, as did Tocqueville. The latter's contemporary Michael Chevalier wrote in the 1830s that America's most suitable emblem was the locomotive or the steamboat. Domingo F. Sarmiento, the Argentine scholar and later president of his country, was impressed during a visit to America by its railroads and many hotels. He stated that Americans were on the roads like ants. Francis Lieber said he felt during his time in America as if he were tied to the wing of a windmill and concluded that there were stationary nations and moving nations, and that movement was America's historical task. The picture has not changed to this day. From Charles Dickens to Harold Laski, from Tocqueville to Siegfried, from Lieber to Rudolf Heberle, the United States has been seen as a country in motion. The locomotive and the steamboat have been replaced by the automobile and the airplane. In the *New York Times* of February 16, 1965, Russell Baker wrote on "The National Motion Sickness." George W. Pierson's book, *The Moving American,* saw moving around as the characteristic feature of his country. At the end he emphasized that "American society with its institutions and its culture, and the American personality with its generosities and shortcomings, its temperament and style, have been marked and shaped by the almost uninterrupted experiment of migration. And our history, to a degree, has been that of Americanization by Motion."

This motion first became evident in the westward movement. In the eighteenth century, Bishop George Berkeley, the Irish metaphysician, prophecied, "Westward the course of Empire takes its way." John Quincy Adams, who preceded Jackson in the White House, stated, "Westward the star of Empire takes its way." Both could have complemented the concept of empire (*imperium*) by that of property (*dominium*), because those moving west, whom Crèvecoeur called pilgrims to the West, thought less of the extension of the American empire than of the improvement of their economic condition. Also, Horace Greeley thought of the latter when he urged: "Go West, young man, and grow up with the country. . . . Ioway—that's where the tall corn grows." A. D. Richardson wrote in *Beyond the Mississippi* (1867) that America was a bivouac rather than a nation, a grand army moving from the Atlantic to the Pacific, and pitching tents by the way. This did not change in the twentieth century. According to the census of 1930, three times the number of people born east of the Mississippi lived west of it. Only a third of those born west of that river, lived east of it. Still today, people move west, especially to California, often to the dismay of those living there. Oregon invites tourists for visits but discourages people from staying there. "Visit our state, but please don't stay!" it says on billboards. "America is West and the wind blowing," we read in Archibald MacLeish's *American Letter for Gerald Murphy.*

Aside from the wide western plains, larger towns were also magnets. The motto "Westward ho!" was complemented by "going to town." People moved from the country to the town, from the town to the city, from that to the metropolis. Often shortcuts were made, and one or two of these stations were omitted in order to advance faster. America is the land of urbanization. By 1930 the better part of the population lived in an urban environment, by 1970, four out of five Americans lived in cities. The riots in the 1950s and 1960s, which mainly affected the big cities (causing Edward C. Banfield to write *The Unheavenly City*) brought about an exodus into the suburbs. However, as the situation in the big cities improves, people have been moving back. The process of urbanization is continuing.

Aside from the migration to the West and into the cities, there has been a third major type of migration, that from state to state, town to town, farm to farm, and so on. This migration may well be more important than the other two. It is so big that it defies classification. Whenever I tell Americans that as a refugee from Silesia I had no home town in which I could meet many of those with whom I grew up, they usually just shrug their shoulders and answer that most Americans do not have a home town either and that, when they return to the place where they grew up, they seldom meet old acquaintances, because most of them have left. To me, America today appears the same as seen by Sarmiento, an anthill in which, however, on account of enormous increases in the population, there is now much greater motion than in 1847. Given all this mobility, one thinks of the words of Faust: "Such a crawling about I should like to see, to stand with free people on free ground!"

Had Goethe come to America, he perhaps would have written, "to *move* with free people on free ground." An anthill brings to mind productivity. American mobility can perhaps mainly be seen as prompted by the desire to produce, and the latter as predominantly motivated by material considerations. "Westward ho!" smells of fresh enterprise and symbolizes the spirit of the entrepreneur. "Going to town" is tantamount to being successful. Moving from one place to another is motivated by the hope of finding a better job. America is the country of the job and of changing jobs. It shows an amazing professional flexibility. The latter is so great that in a way it makes a farce of the idea of profession, let alone that of what Max Weber named a "calling," which, following Johann Gottlieb Fichte, he hopefully attributed to scholars. For in his lecture on scholarship as a calling, Weber saw in the calling of the scholar something similar to Fichte's destiny of the scholar: a not being able to act otherwise, an obligation to serve a specific task and the truth with unending devotion in order to humanely serve humanity and humanitarianism, which even death cannot prevent.

Thus we read in Fichte's Jena remarks on the destiny of the scholar at the end of the third and fourth lectures: "Oh! This is the most sublime of all thoughts: if I assume that task, I shall never finish it; therefore, much as my assumption of that task is certainly my destiny, I never can cease *to act* and therefore can never cease *to be*. Whatever is called death cannot put an end to my work: for my work shall be completed and it never can be completed. Therefore my existence is without an end—and I am eternal. By taking over that task I have claimed eternity. I daringly lift my head up toward the threatening chain of rocks, the roaring waterfall, the clouds swimming in loud lightning and thunder, and say: I am eternal and brave all your might! Fall all down on me, and you, earth and sky, mix in wild tumult! And all you elements—foam and get mad and grind in a wild struggle the last piece of sundust of the body which I call my own;—my will alone with its firm plan shall coolly and defiantly soar over the ruins of the cosmos; for I have obeyed my destiny, which is more permanent than you are; it is eternal and I am as eternal as it is. . . . I am called to proclaim the truth. My life and fate do not matter; the effects of my life matter enormously."

Now one can well imagine that American pioneers who civilized wild stretches of land and defied the threatening Rocky Mountains, the roaring waters of the Mississippi, and other hardships in a tough fight for survival, daring adventures in the search for gold and in the pursuit of happiness, took many a risk. The opening up of America is an ode of courageous enterprise. On the other hand these pioneers hardly possessed the kind of sense for immortal activity Fichte attributed to the scholar. Rather, whatever they engaged in was directed toward practical and tangible ends. They were interested less in eternal truths than in early visible successes. This is still the case today, and so it is with most people in other nations. Certainly Fichte had not expected it to be otherwise. He knew only too well that just a few have a calling for scholarship.

However, with respect to mere profession, America is probably unique. Next to scholars, Fichte saw the necessity of other estates, of professions that lead to a certain standing in society, to which people proudly belong for a lifetime. This kind of belonging, considered proper and honorable, has for a long time been highly esteemed in Germany and other nations. In America, a different attitude has always prevailed. America stands for the classless society, and many foreign observers have criticized it on this ground. Equality of condition—and with it more equality of opportunity than, for instance, existed in France at the time of Tocqueville and Marx—brought about the basically classless society that exists today. One wonders what Marx would have written had he gone to America instead of England. Derived from equal conditions and opportunities for all, the classless America, free as it is from conceits on account of rank (which does not necessarily mean an absence of good manners), is the land of jobs and job-hopping.

There is a difference between a profession in the European sense and a job in the American. It roughly corresponds to the difference between a statesman and a politician, a strategist and a tactician. For the good of his country, the statesman plans long range. He is willing to put up with political setbacks and to sacrifice personal desires for the national interest. The politician wants, above all, political victories, even of short duration. Always out for recognition, he politically manipulates politics for his own interest, which he depicts as that of the state. The statesman makes grand politics, the politician, little and petty politics. Basically, the statesman is constant, the politician flexible. Now if one sees, with Clausewitz, war as the continuation of politics by other means, then in times of war the strategist corresponds to the statesman and the tactician to the politician. The strategist plans long range in order to win the war. General Douglas MacArthur said upon his dismissal by President Truman that "in war there is no substitute for victory." According to Lenin, who was interested in the final victory of communism, the strategist is ready to make tactical retreats even if they are considered defeats. On the other hand, the tactician wants to win every battle, even if in the end he loses the war. He is interested in the success of the hour and its rewards.

The contrast is similar between the job and the profession. The profession demands a lifelong commitment. He who enters a profession does so long range and is willing to sacrifice to it. The profession gives status and honor—celebrated in, for example, Wagner's *Meistersinger.* Those who have their profession, and believe in it, frown upon changing it—considering change an admission of having failed, a sign of professional vagabondage, of faithlessness. One speaks of professional honor. One does not speak of job honor. Change is characteristic of the job. A job usually is taken and performed with a view of soon taking another one preferably with higher pay. Rather than sacrificing to the job, one sacrifices the job, even for an odd job one does not like, hoping to soon exchange it for another job or odd job. The job is a dollar relationship rather than a humane obligation.

Perhaps the many meanings of the word *job* are indicative of the many jobs Americans have. The German *Duden* defines *job* (after the words "Job, comp. Hiob") as occupation, remuneration, position. A jobber is a trader in the London Exchange who makes business deals only in his own name. According to *Webster's Fifth Collegiate Dictionary,* the origin of the noun is uncertain. It means "a piece of work; specif. any definite work undertaken in gross, esp. for a fixed price; also, a piece of work of the small miscellaneous kind taken as it comes from the public. The material thing on which work is being done. A piece of business done ostensibly as an official duty, but really for private gain. Any affair, circumstance, or event. A situation or employment." As a verb the word *job* has the following meanings: "To do odd or occasional pieces of work for hire. To seek private gain under pretense of public service. To buy and sell as a broker;

to deal in as a middleman. To sublet (work); as, to *job* a contract. To make a job of (a matter of public trust or duty). To hire or let by the job or for a period of service." As can be seen, there are a great many definitions in the abridged *Webster's*. Still more can be found in the unabridged dictionaries. However, the original and actual meaning of the word *job* is not as uncertain as its origin, much as it may mean all kinds of things. Without doubt, a job is something temporary, taken for rewards, something one is not as much attached to as one is to a profession. Although a profession also enables one to make a living, it is less exclusively interested in rewards, especially monetary ones. Perhaps it is significant that the *Duden* let the word *job* in the sense of "Hiob," the prophet, precede that word in these senses of work, whereas *Webster's* does it the other way around. Does the institution of the job bring bad news?

America is the land of changing from place to place, from job to job. It also is a place of changing marital partners, of divorce. In 1915, there was one divorce in a thousand marriages; in 1940, two divorces; in 1969, three; in 1972, four; in 1976, five. In 1915, for every ten marriages there was one divorce. In 1944, the ratio was 11:3; in 1972, 11:4; in 1976, 10:5. Today, yearly divorces are about half of yearly marriages.

Among the changes made for the sake of new possibilities in the liberal pursuit of happiness but not prompted by material considerations are those of a religious nature. A person coming to America from Europe is struck by its great variety of Protestant churches. The first immigrants from England brought along their sects. Many left the old country because they felt oppressed by the Anglical church. Where, as in Massachusetts, a Puritan theocracy was established, protests soon arose against the church monopoly sanctioned by the state. It was argued that, since one had left England for the sake of religious freedom, one could not then very well stay in Massachusetts, given its religious intoleration. Roger Williams (1603–82), an early advocate of religious freedom, felt that way. He had begun his pulpit career as an Anglican, turned to Separatism, and ended as a Seeker without ever being certain that he had gained the absolute truth he sought. Cotton Mather called him "a certain Windmill, whirling round with extraordinary violence." Williams moved to Rhode Island, where religious freedom was guaranteed by the government.

Williams's advocacy of religious freedom was shared by others. The First Amendment to the federal Constitution provides first of all, that "Congress shall make no law respecting an establishment of religion." Like Williams, many of his compatriots were uncertain which religion was the right one. Therefore, there came about a great number of religions and sects, which were divided and subdivided and which often merged with other religious groups. Preceding Hobbes, Richard Hooker had been deeply disturbed by the many sects in England. Yet the number of Protestant groups and groupings in the England of his time was small compared to those that came to be in the land of unlimited opportunity. Given the nature of America's many possibilities, this is hardly surprising. Neither is something else: although one could imagine that all this splitting up into religious groups is due to, and will result in, a certain fanaticism, preventing people from leaving their sects and, even more, from moving from one sect to another, this is not at all the case. The quest for liberty is too strong. Again and again people convert from one group to another. This does not just happen among Protestants: it takes place in others, Christian and non-Christian alike. The privatization of churches led to their deprimatization. Once the state church lost its privileged position, everyone could consider his own church privileged and freely choose whatever church suited him the best, for whatever reason, for the choice was not always determined by religious considerations. America, where religious freedom was first recognized by a government, became the land of freely switching church affiliations. The work of the pragmatist William James, *Varieties of Religious Experience,* fits the United States better than any other country. Since, in addition, immigrants from the whole world brought a great number of religions to the country, conversions were increased to an extent that one can, in tune with liberalism, call the United States a land of converts.

That characteristic feature of America, mobility, is especially obvious in the four aspects described above: territorial, professional, marital, and religious. They are the American mobility quaternion. People move from place to place, job to job, man to man, woman to woman, church to church as they like and as often as they can. They proceed from one belief in the pursuit of happiness here on earth to another, from one belief in salvation hereafter to another. USA: this abbreviation symbolizes the fact that things are next to one another, come one after another, that the center is lost. The USA is the land of perpetual ongoings, which many consider progressive.

All these movements, whether they are materialistically motivated or not, demonstrate assertions of individual liberties for the sake of more freedom, show pure liberalism at work. The individual moving west was not lured just by the (liberating) gold of California or by the ears of corn that could be grown on a homestead he could freely acquire. He also was attracted by the less restricted, purer, wilder freedom of the Wild West, where there were only a few laws and thus few restrictions. If he moved into a city, he was not motivated just by the prospect of (liberating) higher wages but also by other aspects promising greater freedom: he felt unobserved and had, after his working hours, his own spare time. The city makes for freedom. Moving from job to job occurred not merely for financial reasons. People also wanted to liberate themselves from their old occupations. They enjoyed their freedom to look for new jobs. Those who divorced wanted to escape from the restrictions of marriage and, often, financial misery. Religious converts desired to be free from the church they belonged to and, sometimes, sought a higher social status—for there is social status among religions in America, where the Episcopalians probably rank the highest.

The pursuit of happiness, which, generally speaking, is characterized by mobility and change of one kind or another, is more or less, but not exclusively, of a materialistic nature. Likewise, the quest for more freedom can be detected behind material motivations. One need not be familiar with Marx to be aware of the connection between freedom and material well-being. He who had *dominium,* had the *ius utendi, fruendi, abutendi.* He was, as far as his property was concerned, to a large degree sovereign—that is, free. He often would also possess *imperium* and thus was the freest individual in the realm of his property and jurisdiction. This can still be seen in some parts of the world today. In America, Alexander Hamilton emphasized that political power follows property. The powerful are free, and the most powerful are the most free. If economic strength leads to political power and if power means freedom, greater economic strength must bring more freedom. Thus the far-reaching mobility characteristic of the United States shows the land of—especially economic—opportunity as one in which the drive for freedom is especially strong, liberalism has been realized the furthest, and pure liberalism has been more nearly approached.

It is not surprising that Americans want to retain their old opportunities and advantages even after the closing of the frontier in the West, after cities became crowded, after work opportunities diminished, and after the possibilities of mobility were reduced. People do not want to be worse off; they like to have it better. Men do not want to be less free; they desire more freedom. Americans moved from place to place, job to job, and so on in order to enjoy more freedom, especially with respect to financial advantage. In view of this, in their liberal drive for greater possessions and thus more liberty they continue to try to reach their goal in spite of curtailed mobility. With that in mind, they join associations, or organize unions, clubs and parties, or in a less formal way, go along with the ruling majority. Their mobility is not thereby restricted, as it might seem at first sight. Much as one may be organized in an association, one still is free to leave it or to change to another one. And it is always possible to belong to the majority if one changes oneself accordingly. Thus the principle of mobility is being maintained even after individuals combine in associations or other groups. Although in many respects a member of an American association will feel tied to it and obligated by its statutes, his sense of attachment is usually weaker than that of members of associations in other Western democracies, where liberalism has not been accepted to the extent it has in the most Western of Western democracies. In individualistic America the individual basically always remains an individual, whatever group he may belong to. His ties to the group usually are so loose that they do not particularly restrain personal interests and certainly do not eliminate them. In the land that Tocqueville saw as one of joiners, the egoistic, egotistic, and egocentric nature of liberalism prevents a far-reaching integration of the individual with the group. This is not surprising. As many Americans are leaving their churches, they can be expected to leave worldly associations to an even greater degree, especially if material advantages can no longer be expected from membership—since such associations are joined mainly for economic reasons. Americans are Rotarians not just in the sense of belonging to Rotary clubs but in the one of rotating, or turning around, for personal advantage. In principle, Americans do not really know loyalty to associations but only to themselves. Americans are mobile and want to remain mobile.

The United States of North America was the first nation that introduced a businesslike abbreviation for its name: USA. (The second was the Soviet Union, with USSR.) Ever since, the USA became known as the land of abbreviations. I have noted above that the abbreviation USA shows a next-to-one-another, a one-after-the-other, symbolizing the idea of permanent progression. Still more comes to mind. To the uninitiated, these are three unconnected, meaningless letters, which seem to be arbitrarily thrown together. Each one maintains its own individuality. The *U* is open on top, the *S* at the left and right, the *A* at the bottom. This can be seen as a symbol of the United States being open to influences from all directions and influencing others in all directions. Is this abbreviation symbolic of receptivity from the north, west, east, and south, for giving to all, irrespective of where they live? Does it indicate God's own country's willingness to listen and to see, to open itself up, to beam out American values, to give to the world? Everything is open, except for the upper part of the *A* and the lower part of the *U*. However, these small parts can be considered exceptions to the rule that the USA basically is an open society perpetually in search of the new.

However, Americans do not enjoy peace, much as they want to be left alone to pursue happiness. America is still restless, for Americans seem to find satisfaction only in being, above all, active in accomplishing new tasks. This attitude seems to be indicated by the word *America*. That word begins with the letter *A*, the first of the alphabet. *A* thus stands for a beginning. If one furthermore takes into account that the letter *A* concludes the word *America*, the end appears as a new beginning, a never-ending beginning. *Nomen est omen:* the most Western of Western democracies appears as a land of never-ending innovation, a result of a never-ending drive for more liberties. And the driving force of America is its people, to whom we now turn.

In the preceding pages I concentrated on what appear to me the essential aspects of the United States of North America, the USA, the US or, what its citizens like to hear and to say most, America. I plan to do the same with respect to the American people. At the end of my study on America's political dilemma, I wrote that Americans basically are like other people. This is not surprising in view of the fact that they are descended from many nations. On the other hand, each people has its own characteristic features, as has been emphasized by Montesquieu as well as, in our days, by Salvador de Madariaga, *Portrait of Europe*. Thus it is probable that in a nation often identified with the New World there came about, after a colonial period of nearly three-hundred years and over two-hundred years of independence, certain peculiarities. Of course, the latter are not shared by all Americans to the same degree, if shared at all. For as a result of the varied ethnic composition of the American people, what is homogeneous will, hardly less than in the case of other people, be accompanied by the heterogeneous and pluralistic.

In my opinion, these peculiarities to a large extent derive from the fact that America is a nation of emigrants, immigrants, and their descendants.

II

American People

7 Emigrating, Immigrating

Unlike any other people, Americans are determined and formed by emigration and immigration. In the New World, there came about a New People.

With the discoveries of the globe, modern times became those of emigrations and immigrations. France, Great Britain, Holland, Portugal, Spain, and later on Germany and Italy, became colonial powers. Yet wherever their citizens emigrated, no country was as much their destination as the United States, which became a country of emigrants and immigrants. With few exceptions, immigrants formed but a small part of the original colonial populations. Natives predominated, irrespective of whether the flag followed the trade or vice versa; they were not pushed back or, as happened in the United States, severely decimated.

I am always struck by the fact that in most countries of Latin America nonwhites predominate. The North American melting pot is predominantly of white people and cannot compare with that of Brazil, which is composed of all colors. From Paraguay to the Rio Grande del Norte, Indians are numerous. They brought about powerful movements in both Mexico and Peru, to which victory was not denied. In the Caribbean, blacks are an important part of the population, and some states in that region are ruled by them. Outside the Western Hemisphere, blacks are numerically predominant in South Africa, and they rule in former Belgian, English, French, and Portuguese colonies. The traditional British policy of divide and conquer proved unable to prevent the unity of India and its sovereignty despite its large population. The French *mission civilisatrice* could not prevent the growth of the original population. Things were similar under the Dutch, German, Italian, and Portuguese systems.

The situation in Australia and Canada can be considered exceptional. The natives were pushed back, it is true, but their populations were not determined by emigration and immigration to the degree that the population of the United States was. The number of immigrants in these subcontinents remained relatively small. Furthermore, most of them had strong ties to Great Britain, and they kept these, together with their British citizenship; things thus remained basically British. I do not consider Argentina an exception. While in Ibero-America, Argentina is together with Uruguay the country with the lowest percentage of Indians, there still live there, especially in Patagonia, aborigines with full rights of citizenship. In contrast to the United States, where Indians were decimated under freely elected governments at the urging of white immigrants and their descendants, the extinction of Indians in Argentina was promoted mainly by the cruel dictator Rosas, who in the nineteenth century saw to it that Indians would fight Indians in a civil war.

The fact that in the United States Indians were decimated by free immigrants and their descendants under the aegis of free government as they were in no other country indicates that this occurred in the name of liberty and the drive for more liberty and that we are confronted by a specifically American aspect of liberalism. The fact that the westward movement as well as other movements inside the USA resulted in steady emigrations prompts the question whether or not emigrants have a greater drive for liberty than others. We must examine the relation of emigration to liberation. Furthermore, it must be asked whether or not among Americans, being descended from emigrants, the drive for more freedom is greater than it is with other people, whether Americans approach pure liberalism more nearly than others do.

The history of mankind is one of the drive for freedom, of emancipation through emigration—the close relationship of emancipation and emigration should not be overlooked. To both, the idea of greater freedom is basic. In Roman law, *emancipatio* meant the emancipation of the son from the supervision of the father by means of *mancipatio* and *manumissio*. Later on, *emancipation* came to mean the liberation of slaves. Lincoln became known as the Great Emancipator. Today, the emancipation of women means their liberation from male dominance. In America, where this emancipation was pushed forward first by the suffragette movement, it led to the replacement of *chairman* by *chairwoman*, of Princeton *man* by Princeton *woman*, and to the refusal of the first female astronaut to accept a bunch of flowers upon her return from space. Emancipation also is understood to mean liberation from all kinds of discrimination, that is, liberation in general. The word itself means liberation from the hand that exercises control, be it that of the paterfamilias, the slave owner, or the public—the *öffentliche Hand*. With the growth of the drive for freedom, words have become liberated from their original meaning and their application extended.

Churches have left little doubt that free people are bound by their dogma and by God. As did other authors before them, Kant and Hegel emphasized that free men also were bound by morals, by the state as the reality of the moral idea. In the first volume of his work on America, published shortly after the death of Hegel, Tocqueville stated, especially in chapter 17, that in the United States morals and religion were greatly respected. He emphasized that people ought to be moral, religious, and modest in relation to their freedom. Ever since Kierkegaard, Marx, and Nietzsche, the thought of pure emancipation, one not inhibited by moral, religious, and other values, has steadily gained ground. Since Freud, it has also advanced in the unconscious. Where external powers oppose official emancipation, there is inner emancipation, as can be concluded from the correspondence between Thomas Mann and Frank Thieß following World War II. They are based upon the old truth that thoughts are free. Even the most cruel tyrant cannot control what people think. People can have all kinds of thoughts and in that respect liberate themselves from oppression.

The correspondence mentioned concerned emigration. It juxtaposed those who fled dictatorships and emigrated to other nations with those who, for good or ill, continued to live under tyrants. Toscanini versus Furtwängler, Mann versus Thieß, and so on: the few who could afford to emigrate versus the many who could not. Thieß defended those who stayed in the Third Reich, writing that, aside from an emigration to foreign lands, there was an inner emigration. He thus extended the ordinary meaning of *emigration.* In his lecture on Richard Wagner's *Ring des Nibelungen,* Mann identified being abroad with misery (*Ausland* = *Elend*). Perhaps he was not happy in Los Angeles; certainly his brother Heinrich wasn't. Otherwise, the author of *Death in Venice,* with its Wagnerian overtones, would not have spent his last years in Zürich. Many a person who survived Hitler in Germany believed that the misery of those who remained in Germany under despotism may well have been greater than that of those who took off. In view of the martyrdom of some, this opinion probably is right. Those living under a tyranny are the survivors of a liberty killed by despotism. Under the Third Reich, their misery probably was greater than that of subjects living in the age of absolutism, enlightened as it may have been. Men like J. J. Winckelmann, Georg Hamann, and Herder were content with restricting their writing to aesthetics, religious pietism, and ethnic cultures. The cruelty of dictatorship does not result only in desires to emigrate abroad; it also brings about inner emigration.

Although inner emigration grows with oppression, it can also exist without it. In Kant's *Bemerkungen zum muthmaßblichen Anfang der Menschengeschichte,* we read: "It certainly is most important *to be content with destiny* (much as it has destined us in our earthly existence to such arduous roads): partly in order to still muster courage in spite of difficulties, partly to prevent us from blaming fate as an excuse for overlooking our own guilt in all these evils and for omitting remedies through self-improvement."

When this was written, the liberal movement was fighting for official recognition, which Kant did not live to see. He also did not experience the publication of *Faust,* the coming of Manchester liberalism, and cutthroat competition in the United States. The latter arrived only after liberalism had become established under constitutionalism, for with the official recognition of a movement its excesses grow. From Kant's statement one could get the impression that he not only resented censorship under the successor of Frederick the Great, something he had denounced in the foreword of his *Streit der Fakultäten,* but he spoke of evil in a quite general way, of the arduous road man is destined to travel on earth, and he advised not to lose courage. He asked whether evil is not due to ourselves and urged self-improvement. All this can be connected with Kant's liberal request to ever growing enlightenment for the sake of gaining greater freedom and the emancipation of man. Perhaps the philosopher from Königsberg who knew man and human nature and who, late in his literary career—at the end of his *Anthropology*—spoke of the cursed race to which we belong, wanted to state that evil rules man, that men should try to master evil, that they probably would not succeed in doing so because destiny, after all, had provided such an arduous road for them. Be this as it may, after *Faust,* Manchester liberalism, and cutthroat competition there can hardly be any doubt that human beings, basically, are discontented. They are restless; nothing lasts for them. Men discard things, whether or not this action throws them into a difficult situation or even damns them. There always exists the danger that human restlessness will degenerate into lawlessness. This has been asserted not only by Marxists denouncing capitalists, for *homo oeconomicus* is only one, although prominent, species of *homo sapiens.* He is not man as such who, while usually knowing what is to his advantage, often will be wise enough to be modest. Hobbes saw in man the *lupus;* this wolf, out for prey, as well as the more modest man, will tend toward emigration, be he living under a liberal or a despotic regime.

Much as emigration may make men forget the evil surrounding them, it still demonstrates the misery of their situation. Little as we know animal psychology, there is reason to believe that animals are more easily contented than humans. Even beasts of prey hunt only to still their hunger. German marmots store food in order not to go hungry. Perhaps it was this modesty that prompted Nietzsche at the end of *Zarathustra* to let "all these higher men," including two kings, a pope without a job, a terrible sorcerer, a voluntary beggar, a wanderer and his shadow, an old soothsayer, the most conscientious of spirit, and the ugliest man, lying on their knees like children and faithful little old females, to worship a donkey—the animal that—in spite of his occasional stubbornness caused by humans pushing him—is said to be patient, enduring, and modest. The donkey, so Nietzsche tells us, says yes (*ja*, or ee-ah) to everything, puts up with hardship, carries our burden, and goes through the world unassumingly with his grey color clothing his virtue and concealing his spirit and his wisdom. A thistle tickles his heart when he is hungry, and only then.

By contrast, man is haunted by the wheel of Ixion, which prevents his being content and causes him to desire more. He tries to escape his present condition, to emigrate from the status quo. Should an emigration to another place prove to be impossible or uncomfortable, he seeks inner emigration. He tortures himself with speculations on how he may improve his lot. Man is full of thoughts but hardly thinks of thanks. Calculating dreaming can even be found in the child. It does not cease later on, when education and pseudoeducation seem to offer more opportunity. In old age, doubts concerning the success of one's life often result in the desire to still get as much done as possible before the end comes. Indifference can be traced to inability rather than to an absence of desire. Those thrown into space, status, and time want to escape their fate, which they consider damnation. However, following each escape they find that their new existence with its achievement does not let them rest, either. They emigrate on and on. With his steady emigration man demonstrates the nonbeing of being, that beings here and there are nothing but temporary phenomena, calling for never-ending desires to be somewhere else. He is condemned to live for the moment but never wants that moment to remain, on account of that moment's beauty. Man is being driven in the present, which, however, is so short it hardly exists. He is aware of it only because he wants to escape it. He only accepts it as a jumping-off place to new advancement. By his very nature, man is an emigrant, whether he goes abroad or goes from one situation to another, or goes off into some inner emigration. He is likely to do all this not just under a despotic, but also under a liberal, regime.

As with the word *emancipation*, the meaning of *emigration* has also broadened. In the latter, the possibility of broadening was indicated early: in Rome, *emigratio* meant going away from a place, to emigrate, but also to transgress writings and rules. While today, *emigration* is generally understood to mean moving to another country, which for the emigrant is a new country, it also points to an extended function of emigrating. The scholar searches for new land. He is not content with what is known, whether or not it is put down in writing. He wants to get away from it, to make the unknown known, to go beyond what is put down in writing and rules, to go on to new land. Similarly, ordinary people will desire to go beyond what is known to, and binding upon, them in order to get to new shores, be it by emigrating abroad, by making changes at home, or by inner emigration. All this need not be motivated by external pressure. There is an inner voice in man, which does not tell him just what is noble, fair, just, and good but, also, what is yet unfinished, what can be improved. This voice, much as it is one of the conscience, is always out to broaden knowledge—the knowledge, among other things, of how one can improve one's lot. Man fears the despotism of men ruling him, but he also escapes the despot inside himself that tries to make him accept the status quo.

The kinds of emigration mentioned show through their variety that they are nothing but aspects of a general concept of emigration. This is underscored by the fact that they appear in different ways because different individuals evaluate them subjectively, seeing and emphasizing in them different phenomena. Emigration thus resembles emancipation, which is concerned with different kinds of liberation that usually produce limited aspects of freedom and only partially approach pure freedom.

For men, emigration is a means for emancipation. People emigrate from a desire for freedom. Therefore the desire to emigrate is greatest with those who drive toward more freedom par excellence—namely, liberals. The more liberal a person is, the greater his desire for emancipation from the status quo. Egoistic, egotistic, and egocentric as the individual is, he also is a social being, interested in pursuing his inclinations unhindered and at peace with others. The individual engages society for his safety, to communicate, and to find consolation. He needs the state, be it that of Hobbes, Locke, Rousseau, Kant, Hegel, or Marx, to secure his life, liberty, and property. He is born into a society, grows up in it, and generally has ties to it, which diminish from the smaller to the larger group. He is, first of all, tied to his family, then to his place of residence, and finally, to his nation. Rousseau accused the so-called citizens of the world of attempting to shun their national duties.

The wheel of Ixion turns toward emigration for the sake of emancipation. However, this desire often is neutralized by the desire to remain, because the latter is more convenient. People like what is simple and try to avoid what is complicated. Someone unhappily married will remain married out of convenience. If he holds a job he does not like, he will often keep it for the same reason. If he does not like conditions in his country, he nevertheless will be reluctant to go abroad, into potential misery, and will content himself with inner emigration. In many respects the individual is like a thing: an external push is necessary to move him. Although he may not like a situation, he will prefer inner emigration to a change of place. Man is a careful, striving being; he carries his worries with him for a long time before revolting and turning an inner emigration into an external one.

On the other hand, he can—especially if he is liberal and thirsting for emancipation and liberty—be dissatisfied to an extent that he will not be content with inner emigration. In that case the tendency toward convenience will give way to one toward liberty, even at the cost of uncertain risk. The marriage is dissolved, the job changed, the country left. The drive is stronger than the inclination; the quest for freedom vanquishes that for convenience. This is reflected in the characterization of history as a drive for freedom and emancipation, that is, a drive for liberalism in contrast to conservatism. The conserving nature precludes history, with its characteristic movement. If inner emigration is greater for liberals than for other people and if it grows with their liberalism, it will be the greatest for those who dare make the step from inner emigration to outer emigration. The risk of emigration probably grows with the size of what is left and reachable. For a marriage partner seeking divorce, the risk is likely to be smaller than for someone changing his profession, although the latter in most cases will be able to inform himself about what he is going to face. Emigration to another country is the most uncertain; its risk grows with the diversity of the foreign culture.

Locke, considered the ideologue of the American Revolution, emphasized that people have the right to rebel against a despotic government in case of persistant unbearable oppression. Therefore, inner emigration first, and then an external one, for rebellion is emigration inasmuch as those rebelling want to get away from their government. Locke, in his *Second Treatise,* saved his remarks on the right of rebellion, considered by many to be the most important statement of his political philosophy, until the end, as if he planned them to remain the longest on the reader's mind.

Those fighting for American independence two generations later took up Locke's thoughts. Some passages of the Declaration of Independence on liberties seem to be simply copied from Locke. From that it follows that prior to the American Revolution and the emigration from the existing government there was an inner emigration. We first read that governments are instituted to secure the unalienable rights of man, that "whenever any Form of Government becomes destructive of these Ends, it is the Right of the People to alter or abolish it, and to institute new Government, laying its Foundation on such Principles and organizing its Powers in such Form, as to them shall seem most likely to effect their Safety and Happiness." And then we read: "Prudence, indeed, will dictate that Governments long established should not be changed for light and transient

Causes; and accordingly all Experience hath shewn, that Mankind are more disposed to suffer, while Evils are sufferable, than to right themselves by abolishing the Forms to which they are accustomed. But when a long Train of Abuses and Usurpations, pursuing invariably the same Object evinces a Design to reduce them under absolute Despotism, it is their Right, it is their Duty, to throw off such Government, and to provide new Guards for their future Security." Thereupon one reads: "Such has been the patient Sufferance of these Colonies, and such is now the Necessity which constrains them to alter their former Systems of Government. The History of the present King of Great-Britain is a History of repeated Injuries and Usurpations, all having in direct Object the Establishment of an absolute Tyranny over these States." After a long enumeration of the king's oppressive measures there come the words: "In every stage of these Oppressions we have Petitioned for Redress in the most humble Terms: Our repeated Petitions have been answered only by repeated Injury. A Prince whose Character is thus marked by every act which may define a Tyrant, is unfit to be the Ruler of a free People."

Speaking of "these States," the declaration of independence from tyranny indicates that the former colonies have become sovereign states. The American Revolution thus was not just a rebellion in the sense of Locke who, in defense of the Glorious Revolution, merely justified rebellion within a state in which the rebels were going to continue to live. The Americans objected to their remaining part of the British Empire, and they led the thirteen colonies out of the English realm. If one is of the opinion that Locke's rebellion or the Glorious Revolution were no real emigrations because in both cases people did not move from one place to another, one assumes too narrow a concept of emigration. However, in view of inner emigration, such a concept is no longer sufficient. Furthermore, as Alexander Rüstow has shown in *Ortsbestimmung der Gegenwart* (1950–57), a place is not just something territorial. It can mean a certain way of being, an *état,* which can exist in a certain state, *Etat,* but is not necessarily tied to it. Thus if emigration simply means leaving an existing condition, then the American Revolution definitely was an emigration: the inhabitants of thirteen colonies left the state of oppression in order to move into a state of greater freedom. Aside from that, they emigrated en masse from the state of Great Britain into the states of Massachusetts, New York, New Jersey, and so on, and later, with the adoption of the Articles of Confederation in 1778, into the United States of America. In the American Revolution, a state, Great Britain, was left to an extent not experienced before. (In the United Netherlands, the number of inhabitants as well as the size of territory was smaller.) The American Revolution thus showed the greatest of all emigrations.

In his first speech as president, which was under the specter of secession, Lincoln said: "Union is perpetual . . . much older than the Constitution. It was formed in fact, by the Articles of Association in 1774 . . . matured and continued by the Articles of Confederation in 1778. And finally, in 1787, one of the declared objectives for ordaining and establishing the Constitution was 'to form a more perfect Union.'" This was stated by a politician who more than his predecessors emphasized the idea of the one nation and of national democracy under a strong president. Lincoln probably was motivated by the desire to save the Union and for that reason even took the liberty of transgressing provisions of the Constitution. For that shrewd politician, saving the Union was central at that time.

In analogy to Lincoln's words, a political scientist may say without being motivated by any particular desire that America was expecting emigrants from the beginning. The original colonists came from abroad. The revolutionaries of 1776 were immigrants or their descendents. Later on, emigrants after emigrants arrived, by the few and by whole waves, down to our day. They made the United States the land of immigrants *par excellence* and the American people an immigrant people. The arrival of slaves does not contradict this fact, for the borderline between voluntary and involuntary emigration usually is drawn only between emigrants and refugees, although it too is difficult to draw and appears to be artificial. Coming voluntarily or involuntarily cannot change the fact that one comes. Only the Indians, the least significant part of the American population, did not immigrate into America. On the other hand, they moved from hunting ground to hunting ground within America, from prairie to prairie, nomads as they were—in contrast to the Indians south of the Rio Grande.

In the official census of 1980, which counted 231 million inhabitants, Americans declared their origin as follows (in thousands): English, 49,598; German, 49,224; Irish, 40,166; French, (without Basques) 12,892; Italian, 12,184; Scottish, 10,049; Polish, 8,228; Dutch, 6,304; Swedish, 4,345; Norwegian, 3,454; Russian (without Ukrainians, Ruthenians, White Russians, and some other ethnic groups), 2,781; Czech (including those who reported being Czechs, Bohemians, Moravians, or Czechoslovakians), 1,892; Hungarian, 1,777; Welsh, 1,665; Danish, 1,518; Portuguese, 1,024; Lebanese, 295; Armenian, 213; Iranian, 123; Syrian, 107; Arabic (generally), 93; Afro-American 20,965; African (generally), 204; Chinese, 894; Philippine, 795; Japanese, 791; Korean, 377; Eastern Indian, 312; Vietnamese, 215; Jamaican, 253; Haitian, 90; Mexican, 7,693; Hispanic, 2,687; Puerto Rican, 1,444; Cuban, 598; Dominican, 171; Colombian, 156; Spanish, 95; Ecuadorian, 88; Salvadoran, 85; Hawaiian, 202; American Indian, 6,716; French Canadian, 780; and Canadian, 456.

However great the differences among the ethnic parts of the American people may be and whatever consequences they may have for the nation, the census shows that Americans are descended from other nationals, that they are composed of emigrants and their descendants. There also cannot be much doubt that emigrants went to the land of liberty desiring liberty. Vergil wrote: "Exilioque domos et dulcia limina mutant Atque alio patriam quaerunt sub sole jacentem" (For exile they leave home and familiar gates, looking for a land under other suns; *Georgias,* 2, 511). Those going to America thought it to be the land of the free under the sun of liberty:

> From the vine-land, from the Rhine-land,
> From the Shannon, from the Scheldt,
> From the ancient homes of genius,
> From the sainted home of Celt,
> From Italy, from Hungary,
> All as brothers join and come,
> To the sinew-bracing bugle
> And the foot-propelling drum;
> Too proud beneath the starry flag to die, and keep secure
> The liberty they dreamed of by the Danube, Elbe and Suir.
>
> John Savage, *Muster of the North*

Often people did not leave the old country with an easy heart. In Oliver Goldsmith's "Traveller" (407) we read:

> Beheld the duteous son, the sire decayed,
> The modest matron, and the blushing maid,
> Forc'd from their homes, a melancholy train,
> To traverse climes beyond the Western main.

One went into the uncertain. The Wild West began with the crossing of the Atlantic. Those arriving did not have it easy in America. R. H. Schauffler, describing immigrants on Ellis Island, wrote in "Scum of the Earth":

> At the gate of the West I stand,
> On the isle where the nations throng.
> We call them "scum o' the earth."

Only too often those arriving were seen as the scum of the earth. Nevertheless, they defied adversity by striving for freedom.

The idea of the scum of the earth does not just indicate that among those arriving there were down-at-the-heels people and criminals and debtors seeking freedom from criminal and civil prosecution. It also points to underdogs such as those who after World War II were refugees in West Germany, people who had lost everything and were looked down upon by those who had been able to keep everything. They no longer were content with inner emigration. *Beati possidentes:* all too often they arrogantly frown upon the have-nots. And most immigrants were have-nots, not just in material goods but also in education. The so-called brain drain came only after World War II.

It will be asked whether or not the uneducated emigrants thought of inner emigration in view of the fact that this concept came about only after that war. The answer is that education is not a prerequisite for common sense and natural feeling. Often the uneducated are the unadulterated. The drive for freedom is so basic and so innate in man that it can come forth in everybody. Even the most primitive human being knows how to put up with his fate, how to patiently endure things without any hope for material gain. He may well know how to do this better than others, for he did—and had to—learn it in the ranks when life was miserable for him. He experienced all that before he pondered his lot and worried over it and thought of emigration in order to liberate himself from misery. There is a certain melancholy in the song, "Muß i denn, muß i denn zum Städtele hinaus." How much greater must be the melancholy among those who, unlike drafted soldiers, know they won't return after a year's conscription, who do not know whether they will ever again see what has been familiar to them. As was pointed out in Higham's *Sent These to Me,* many a person sadly left his *shtetl* in eastern Europe—and not only there.

It is open to doubt whether or not those going abroad are more courageous than those who stick out adverse conditions at home. On the other hand, inner emigration is more difficult to prove than external emigration. It will always be a question whether those maintaining they went on an inner emigration actually did so, suffered heroically as much as they claim, and did want to liberate themselves from the hardship surrounding them. By contrast, a certain courage for the sake of freedom cannot well be denied to those going abroad. The love of freedom is distinguished from the drive for freedom. The love of freedom is possible without the drive for freedom, whereas the drive for freedom cannot exist without the love of freedom. One may love liberty without desiring more of it. However, if one desires an extension of liberty, one must also love it. Someone preferring inner to external emigration without doubt can love freedom. It is another question whether or not his love of freedom is so great as to make him drive for more freedom to the extent of physical liberation from his unpleasant environment. Often, that drive will not be so great that the individual dares to make it publicly known, be it by informing others or by emigrating. On the other hand, the emigrant demonstrates his drive for more freedom to the whole world. His courage vis-à-vis a government permitting free emigration need not be great; his courage in facing the uncertainties awaiting him in the foreign land certainly is.

Emigrants have conceived of freedom in different ways. To criminals, it meant freedom from punishment; to debtors, freedom from creditors. Others saw in liberty mainly freedom from military service, from censorship, from a state church. Most people, however, hoped for liberation from economic misery. Often emigrants were motivated by combinations of different interpretations of liberty, and many of these interpretations were exported by them to America. Whenever the United States is called the land of liberty, the word *liberty* is understood to mean the general comprehensive concept, comprising all types of liberty that can be found in the United States—that is, innumerable ones. And whenever the national anthem praises the land of the free, it means to convey the idea that Americans are free and can be free any way they want. This corresponds to freedom as such, or pure freedom, according to which individuals can do as they please.

The literature on emigration has emphasized the hardship of the voyage. Yet on the high seas, freedom can be appreciated in a grandeur which cheers up the human mind. The individual, after having made up his mind to emigrate as a result of desires for the concrete, more or less narrow aspects of freedom, became aware of further aspects of freedom on account of the conditions and formalities of passage. He did so due to his small berth aboard ship. On the other hand, he may have become aware that freedom means more than just his own peculiar narrow understandings of it. On the high seas one can become acquainted with the greatness of the world and of freedom, for the sea is an overwhelming symbol of the colossal and the evermore. In its breadth and width men feel deserted and lost, like a ship tossing and pitching on waves. But just as the boat in its free course moves toward new shores, men will want to imitate it and to conquer the elements. The sea is the great freedom, the *Große Freiheit,* as Hamburg, an important port of emigration, named a street close to the harbor. Like the sea, freedom is both ugly and beautiful, showing itself in mildness and wildness. The waves of the sea show particles of the great whole. The great and the sublime make our own littleness evident. Everyone can be conscious of this fact even if he is not familiar—and most emigrants probably are not—with the aesthetics of a Burke, Kant, Loti, Friedrich, or Turner. As a matter of fact, this unfamiliarity may even increase this consciousness because the uneducated, being the unadulterated, are perhaps the closest to nature, to what is natural. This was indicated not only by the Sermon on the Mount and asserted by Rousseau; even the most simple and naive can see their own smallness as well as the littleness, even pettiness, of their concept of freedom—and in the bigness of the ocean, the largesse of freedom and of the world. They can hope for new liberties in the New World. In the waving waves they can see the beating hearts of emigrants anxious for specific aspects of freedom, and in the infiniteness of the sea, freedom as such, that Great Freedom comprising all its particular aspects, a freedom they hope to approach with their approach to the new land. The New World could appear to them as something where there perhaps could be found more than just the liberties they originally expected.

With the crossing, the emigrant's dream of freedom comes closer to its realization. Upon his arrival, he might, after the deprivations of the voyage, have the elevating feeling that he has made it—and will make it in the future. As was shown above, America for a long time was seen as the home of those seeking liberty. After the French people donated the Statue of Liberty, created by Frédéric-Auguste Bartholdi, to the American people as a token of friendship, many emigrants were enthusiastically touched by the verses of Emma Lazarus inscribed on the statue, which likened America to the Colossus of Rhodes, one of antiquity's seven wonders of the world:

The New Colossus

Not like the brazen giant of Greek fame,
With conquering limbs astride from land to land,
Here at our sea-washed, sunset gates shall stand
A mighty woman with a torch, whose flame
Is the imprisoned lightning, and her name
Mother of Exiles. From her beacon-hand
Glows world-wide welcome; her mild eyes command
The air-bridged harbor that twin cities frame.

"Keep, ancient lands, your storied pomp!" cries she
With silent lips. "Give me your tired, your poor,
Your huddled masses yearning to breathe free,
The wretched refuse of your teeming shore.
Send these, the homeless, tempest-tost to me,
I lift my lamp beside the golden door!"

With their arrival in the New World, emigrants became immigrants. Yet in spite of all the immigration, the word *immigrant* was not known for a long time. Up to about the adoption of the Constitution, one spoke of emigrants, only. Immigrants were called emigrants by people like

Crèvecoeur and Thomas Paine. In 1789 Jedidiah Morse's patriotic *The American Geography* mentioned "immigrants" from Scotland, Ireland, Germany, and France living in New York (p. 253). In 1809 a traveler stated that perhaps *immigrant* was the only new word which on account of what happened in America had to be added to the English language (Mitford M. Mathews, ed., *A Dictionary of Americanisms on Historical Principles,* 1951).

However, the idea of emigration was not gone with immigration. It would be wrong to assume that with the arrival in the new country basic changes came about in the character of the newcomers. Immigration was primarily concerned with the legal status of the immigrant rather than his individual nature, immigration authorities later on being subordinated to the Department of Justice. As was said, it was characteristic of his nature that the emigrant was not satisfied with inner emigration, that in a clear demonstration of his drive for more freedom he was not reluctant to bring about an open break with his environment. He thus showed a critical spirit driving for liberty, which probably was inherited by his descendents. Someone tending toward criticism will criticize until he is liberated from any cause to criticize. And since due to the human desire for freedom there will be criticism as long as men are not absolutely free, they will continue to criticize until they enjoy pure freedom.

In contrast to other nations, naturalization in America did not really change the emigrant's nature too much. Americanization merely meant that the immigrants were received into a society composed of emigrants and immigrants and their descendents, into a milieu that actually was not too different from their own emigrant-immigrant milieu and its corresponding outlook. Since that outlook leaves no doubt about the drive for greater freedom, that drive is likely to persist even in those born in the United States, the "true born Americans," and even more so, since it is kept alive by new immigrants. Thus Americans probably are more oriented toward liberalism than other people. There is in the American nation an emigration mentality the like of which I have not encountered anywhere else.

Liberals are constant wanderers and changers. Steadily looking for more freedom and the new that comes with it, they move from the one to the other, showing little attachment to what is with them for the time being. They constantly emigrate from one situation to another, only to leave the latter for still another. Their emi- and immigration can be called liberal dialectics. Now if for the reasons stated Americans are more liberal than other people, they must be especially characterized by the hecticness of liberal dialectics. Their emigrant mentality makes Americans into people constantly out for more freedom. In tune with their liberal nature, they are not content with what they have achieved. They keep looking for ever new territorial, professional, and other places to go, which only serve as new starting points for further exploits, for further emigrations. The dialectics of liberalism is the dialectics of America, the dialectics of America is the dialectics of liberalism. The drive for more freedom, keeping liberals captive, demonstrates the human condition of American life.

This drive also exists in those parts of the population whose ancestors were imported as slaves or were more or less made captives, namely, blacks and Indians. They constitute part of the American condition that cannot be ignored. The drive for liberty exists in everybody, latent though it often may be. The liberal movement increasingly awakened it. Emigrants going to the New World of their own free will demonstrated that the drive for liberty was awake in them. That drive was kept awake by their descendents and by new immigrants coming as free men and women. This does not mean, however, that the drive for liberty was confined to these people.

Liberalism is contagious. It spreads. On December 26, 1820, Jefferson in a letter to Lafayette wrote: "The disease of liberty is catching." If a part of a population enjoys freedom and takes all kinds of liberties for more and more extravagant amusements, others not partaking of much liberty will be disgruntled and will strongly desire a greater share of freedom. Envy and comparison are powerful motivations of human behavior.

White immigrants proved their drive for liberty with their emigration. Those enslaved did not have to prove it that way. Throughout history, slave uprisings everywhere have done it amply. Their drive for liberty was built up over centuries. Lincoln's Emancipation Proclamation perhaps stalled an uprising of the slaves. Those emancipated and their descendants naturally retained a strong desire for more freedom. And just as Lincoln may have prevented an uprising of slaves, the civil rights legislation of 1964 probably slowed further black unrest of the kind that since World War II has increasingly disturbed America, although it actually lasted until the end of the 1960s. In 1950, blacks amounted to 9.9 percent of the population, in 1960, 10.5 percent, in 1970, 11.1 percent, and in 1980, 11.8 percent. They show a growing strength and are fully aware of it. Probably as a result of long discrimination, their drive for liberty often is more active than that of whites. They are to be reckoned with in politics and frequently decide who will be elected to public office on the local, state, and national levels.

By contrast, the Indians appear to be irrelevant and passive. Driven away by stronger ethnic groups, they seem to be dying out. The census of 1980 stated that out of a total population of 231 million there were only slightly over 1.5 million Indians, Eskimos, and inhabitants of the Aleutians. This does not mean, however, that the drive for freedom is absent in those who originally possessed the country.

Thus the quest for freedom can be found in all parts of the population, much as their actual freedom may differ. That quest probably is stronger in the land of the free than elsewhere, and the experience of emigration and immigration does not account for it alone. Liberalism also was aided by the fact that in America feudalism, with its inherent restrictions of freedom, hardly existed. Unlike the French and Russian Revolutions, the American Revolution was not really directed against an absolute regime characterized by oppression. It was primarily a fight for national independence from Britain: until the Declaration of Independence, Americans, obviously feeling that the English way of life was not too illiberal, had claimed their "rights of Englishmen." After all, the Glorious Revolution had left no doubt that the divine right of kings, maintained by the Stuarts, was not in tune with the English tradition. That tradition had been liberal even before the Magna Carta (1215), being based on a contractual relationship between the king and those under him, in contrast to continental feudalism with its Theistic kingship.

Thus emigrants coming to America not only entered a society composed of those looking for more freedom. They also became part of one that, being basically English, was freer than continental nations. America had, so to speak, greater liberal dimensions. In this freer New World, further freedom could well be expected. Emigrants seeking more liberty were followed by migrants doing the same.

8 Moving, Roving

Migrations, characteristic of Americans, are based on about the same considerations as emigrations. In the USA, a distinction is drawn between emigration and migration. The former is understood to mean moving from one country to another as, for instance, from Ireland to the United States. *Migration* means moving in a more general sense. The term is used for changes of places within the nation, from one region to another, one state to another, one city to another, and so on. *Outmigration* is distinguished from *inmigration*. Migration as well as emigration are thus concerned with moving from one place to another and have a certain identity. This is not surprising in view of the fact that in late Latin *emigratio* was used for *migratio*.

After the decline in emigration from other nations, migration moved into the foreground for most Americans, being so-to-speak closer to them. This closeness does not imply that migration could not be more comprehensive than emigration. While it means less in view of the fact that a merely migrating individual does not consider a change of citizenship, it must not be overlooked that the ordinary emigrant usually just wants to be free enough to no longer suffer from specific oppressions prevailing in the old country. He is not too demanding as far as freedom is concerned but is just looking for a kind of liberal minimum he is denied in the place he is leaving. Although his demands may well grow on account of the liberating experience of the sea voyage, this experience usually will not change the fact that most emigrants first will aspire to a mere minimum of liberal existence, just as refugees as a rule will be content with having a roof over their heads after escaping. The situation is different with those living in America. They enjoy the liberal minimum of which emigrants dream—and often considerably more. Nevertheless, they migrate in order to have still more freedom, perhaps even a maximum of freedom. This is not surprising, for men's desire for freedom is insatiable, especially in the case of liberals—and, a fortiori, of the liberals *par excellence,* the Americans. Therefore, as to the quality and quantity of liberty, migration goes further than emigration as usually understood in the United States.

This does not preclude broader concepts of emigration, as was, for instance, shown with respect to inner emigration. Also, the idea of a minimum liberal existence, characteristic of emigration, can be applied to migration: migrants will seldom ask whether or not, from an objective point of view, they already are enjoying that minimum. Rather, they will emphasize that, from a subjective standpoint, this is not the case and, through migration, try to attain a new liberal minimum more to their liking. Thus the attitude of the migrant remains similar to that of the emigrant. Nevertheless, for movements inside the United States I shall use the term *migration.* For I now shall be less concerned with the behavior of those emigrating to America or immigrating into America than with today's Americans, the large majority of whom are born or naturalized Americans. I plan to discuss the present rather than the past.

Americans—and this generalization does not apply to all of them—live for the present and for the ever more they expect from it. Such an attitude is nothing new. In the sixteenth ode of Horace we find the appeal to enjoy the present and not to worry over the future: "Laetus in praesens animus quod ultra est Oderit curare et amara lento Temperet risu." In his *Carmina* (1), there is the concise carpe diem (enjoy the present). In Samuel Johnson's *Irene* (3, 2) we read that "the present hour alone is man's." In *Tasso* we hear that the present is a mighty Goddess (4, 4). We know that its author, in his poem dedicated to the United States, urged Americans to make use of the present with luck. To Goethe, the present is something to be admired, something ruling, that is to be used with luck, probably in a utilitarian pursuit of happiness. In *Society and Solitude: Works and Days,* the transcendentalist Ralph Waldo Emerson wrote: "An everlasting Now reigns in nature, which hangs the same roses on our bushes which charmed the Roman and the Chaldean in their hanging gardens." A contemporary of Kierkegaard, Donald G. Mitchell, wrote in *Revelries of a Bachelor:* "The past belongs to God: the present only is ours. And short as it is, there is more in it, and of it, than we can well manage. That man who can grapple it, and measure it, and fill it with his purpose, is doing a man's work; none can do more; but there are thousands who do less" (4).

Certainly there are such thousands in the United States. But in spite of its great political strength, they to this day have not succeeded in destroying the traditional image of Americans as doers. Quite generally, Americans still follow the words in Longfellow's "A Psalm of Life":

> Trust no Future, howe'er pleasant!
> Let the dead past bury its dead!
> Act,—act in the living Present!
> Heart within, and God o'erhead!

These lines tell something different from those of Henry David Thoreau, the advocate of nature's idyll at Walden Pond, published in 1863 in *Excursions:* "He is blessed over all mortals who loses no moment of the passing life in remembering the past." Thoreau's words reflect the opinions of some of his countrymen. Those of the great majority are expressed by Longfellow.

"A Psalm of Life," with its emphasis upon the present, can be considered the psalm of the American way of life. Therefore, I shall deal with it at some length. The past is dead, one should let the dead past bury its dead. The opinion hardly can be expressed more clearly and with less piety. The other lines are less unequivocal and a veritable cornucopia of possibilities. The first one can mean one should not trust the future, however pleasant it may be. But it also can warn of lazily dreaming of the future whatever it may promise. At any rate, in the living present one should act and act with all one's heart and under God. Here again, different interpretations are possible. It may mean that acting in the present does not preclude a comfortable future, although one should not bet on it and lazily dream of it. But it may also mean that one should care about the future as little as about the past and only think of what one can get out of the present. The well-known words of Leibniz, "Le présent est gros d'avenir," are juxtaposed to the even better-known proverb, "Après nous le déluge," responsibility for the future to nonchalance. Both interpretations distinguish the promising future from mere present activity, which simply must be under God and carried out with one's heart. This reminds us of Calvinism, which is popular in America and according to which God's grace shines on work and its rewards. But what happens if the human heart does not recognize the God overhead as the ruler but only as a being presumably in the beyond; sees in God something that is spatially away from it, away from the present of this world, something that does not really prescribe anything for the individual acting heart within man, does not really mean anything to him? What happens if the heart separates itself from that God and totally lives for its present emotions and desires? Or, if it is willing to recognize a God, that God only is one that corresponds to its desires, one mirroring man in his own godliness, so that man may do whatever he likes, without any religious inhibitions, as long as he is just doing something, is a doer, perhaps driven on by a God whom he has reduced to a mere tool of his human activities? Finally, there is the possibility that the key line, "Act,—act in the living Present," will be cited and followed all by itself at a time more and more characterized by "shortcuts," as one says in America, where such cuts are especially popular. In that case, too, that line would urge one to be a doer, whatever is done, and with or without God's blessing, with or without *Erlösung*—redemption, salvation in the Faustian sense—which to the average American probably is as little known as, according to Goethe, Kant.

Perhaps Longfellow, when writing these lines, was not aware of their enormous potential, despite the fact that he lived at a time (from 1807 to 1882) in which he could have observed many a liberal variation in his country. Be this as it may: nobody is safe from interpretations of his words. Sooner or later, they become independent of their author and acquire their own wisdom. The words often are considered wiser than their creator, whose intentions in the end are little cared about, especially if they never have been too clear to the uninitiated from the beginning, for nobody can know the thoughts behind the creation of a work. Longfellow's psalm probably will share the fate of biblical psalms, which are not necessarily interpreted in the sense of their creators. Those learned in the Scriptures have shown over the years what they may result in. In the land of unlimited opportunities and possibilities, this will not be different for a psalm of life that urges people to use these opportunities and possibilities here and now, directed as it is primarily at the American public. The basically liberal inclinations of Americans will take care of that and aid in bringing about many interpretations.

In each society there are three groups of people tied to the times: those captivated by the past, often called conservatives; those living for the present; and those looking toward the future, the latter two both in the liberal camp. These groups cannot be separated sharply. Those cherishing the past also live in the present and look to the future. Those living in the present will not be able to totally separate their thoughts from the past and the future. Those planning for the future will take their lessons from the past and the present. The living are the present ones. However, since the present hardly is of any duration, they are always aware of the close proximity of the past and the future. Man is thrown into the times. He measures his being in relation to the present, the past, and the future. He can judge things from the viewpoint of all these tenses in spite of the fact that his activities occur in the present.

All this does not preclude emphasis on any one of these times, and I have never been so aware of emphases on the present as in America. Nowhere is the past as much ignored as in America. Only with Americans is the Golden Age not in the past. For a long time, it was seen as being in the future, although in our century more and more Americans have looked for it in the present, as in the Golden Twenties and the Golden Sixties. This is not surprising. Just as young people think primarily of the present and mainly live just for it because it appears to them more enormous and powerful than other times, this will be the case with a young nation like America. And just as to young people the present is made easy by the shelter offered by the family, so present life appears uncomplicated to Americans on account of the security their country enjoys in economic and military respects. America's enormous wealth probably makes it the most autarkic Western democracy. Protected by two oceans, its "splendid isolation" is considerably greater than that of Great Britain. Possession is something enjoyed in the present. One translates and quotes the words of Omar Khayyam's *Rubáiyát:* "Ah, take the cash, and let the credit go, nor heed the rumble of a distant drum."

However, the present is not without problems. Actually, it hardly exists. When I write, each written letter immediately belongs to the past even before the word is completed. Every thought, every act makes us conscious of the fleeting nature of the present. Yet if every act, as something done, immediately becomes part of the past, people will look for an extended concept of the present in order to tie that act to the present and even to the future. The present, restricted as it is by the past, is extended and changed into something with a future. Although a written letter belongs to the past before the completion of the word, it has its future in the completion of the word. Similarly, the written word has a future in the completed sentence, the sentence one in the paragraph, and so on. One has spoken of the book of life. Now when the person living for the present nonchalantly says, "after me, the deluge," he does not have in mind a deluge coming after each one of his actions. Only after his life's work, at the end of his life, does he not care any longer whether or not the world goes down, but not after each one of his activities throughout his life. Hobbes emphasized that men are primarily interested in staying alive. Those living for the present will be inclined to consider their whole life as their present composed of various periods and what was done in them. For them, each one of their actions, much as they may belong to the past, had a future in some period, in the whole life. Those living for the present add present to present and thus arrive at what Ortega y Gasset called "composite present." They can consider every past action one that enlarges the present and points to the future.

As a result, Longfellow's lines can mean that, while one should not bet on the future, one can work with a view to the future in order to create a life's work that makes life worth living. The Americans' orientation toward the present can therefore be related to future phases of their lives, to their whole life. They can act and act and act in order to buy the future with the present, thus following the words of Samuel Johnson in *The Rambler* (no. 18). In their commitment to the present they will run from one present to another, drifting and tumbling, out for presents that they present to themselves or to others as proof of their ability. In this rush, the present may well appear to them to be the worst of the three tenses, as it does in the first act of Shakespeare's *Henry VI*. In *Prometheus Unbound*, by the Romantic poet Percy Bysshe Shelley, whose late childhood and early youth fell into the time of Jefferson's administration—which saw an enormous extension of American territory—we read:

> And the future is dark, and the present is spread
> Like a pillow of thorns for thy slumberless head.
>
> (Act 1)

In spite of his far-reaching liberties, Homo Americanus finds himself on the treadmill of present activities that quickly succeed each other. He demonstrates the *furor Americanus*, a veritable cult of activity worship. In its obscurity, the future looks dark to him. He tries to clarify it through unceasing activity. Emerson, in his essay on character, indicated that Americans, taking pains to build their futures, appear egoistic to those not worrying over the future. It probably is similar the other way around: those caring for their future will accuse those who only live for the moment of egoism.

Naturally optimistic, Americans hope to progress by virtue of steady activity in order to lighten up the dark, unknown future through ever new presents. If they do not advance as desired or if they begin to doubt their country's progress, those encouraging them will soon enter the scene, for optimism constitutes an optimal political capital. During the Great Depression, Franklin D. Roosevelt fought the pessimism of the people by exclaiming that "the only thing we have to fear is fear itself." Later on, after John F. Kennedy had complained in his campaign for the presidency that under President Eisenhower there was too much stagnation in the United States, he said in his inaugural address "Let us begin" in order to end his listeners' worries. Finally, Ronald Reagan praised his campaign platform for being "a new beginning," for all too long had the hostages been kept in Teheran, hurting the feelings and the pride of his countrymen. Thus during the past fifty years, the three most popular presidents urged action, immediate action, for the sake of the present. However, generally speaking, Americans did not even have to be urged to become active. Therefore, what these presidents did was simply underline what in normal times has been the American credo all along; business and activity, activity and business are the maxims of the American people. They demonstrate a persistent migration for the sake of more freedom and show the dynamics of the American way of life. The pursuit of happiness gains in perfection if it is accompanied by fun, like that at Maxim's in the *Merry Widow,* Franz Lehár's amusing, good-time, light operetta, which in the United States is still running from success to success, omitting its last words, "Hanna, you have no money? I love you!" Obviously, in a materialistic country in which moneymaking ranks highly, such an ending is not thought to go over too well with the audience.

In the overwhelming presence of acting and doing, changing and trading, those stars of the ever migrating American people living in and for the present, we must not forget that all these stars are aspects of the pursuit of happiness, that overriding principle determining Americans, a principle to a large extent designed to serve hedonistic inclinations. In his famous chapter,"Why the Americans Are so Restless in the Midst of Their Prosperity," Tocqueville stated that they are that way until they have done their best to eventually enjoy the rest of their lives at a place to their liking in pleasant social surroundings. Perhaps the idea of settlement, of remaining on a homestead, was acceptable at a time when there still existed a westward movement, when there was free land for everybody. Perhaps it was even applicable in other respects, in the sense of settling down and being content with a certain job, a certain social standing, and so on. On the other hand, the French observer wrote prior to the great waves of immigration and the spirit of migration they brought to the land of unlimited opportunities. Actually, Americans, especially after the end of the moving frontier in 1890, were less and less willing to settle down and be content with what they had accomplished. They rather desired to move on and on. The moving American continued to move from place to place. To that kind of moving there was a corresponding moving from standpoint to standpoint, from point of view to point of view. Down to our time Americans have moved in many respects, in a moving economy, a moving technology, a moving democracy, and so on. In cinema houses, they relish movies, with their happy endings. Men of action, they expect from the movies that one action will follow the other, one scene the other, in quick succession. More than in other countries, actors become popular demigods. The temptations of better living conditions, more lucrative businesses with their profits, securer positions and higher wages, as well as other things were intensified by a far-reaching social mobility. And behind everything there was the thought of making one's life as pleasant as possible, the drive for the joy and lust of life. We turn to the lust principle of Sigmund Freud.

America is Freud's house. The doctor from Vienna is better known there than Franz Lehár. He enjoys authority and probably is the most publicized European. His relevance is obvious in many respects, all of which basically derive from the drive for liberty. Freud is a great apostle of American liberalism.

To the man in the street he is best known as the discoverer of the importance of sex and the apologist for intercourse. For he who stresses the importance of something will often be made its apologist. Although for Americans sex is not tantamount to all happiness, its emphasis upon it has grown enormously in our time. In 1957, Max Lerner explained the American absorption with sex as a reaction to the Puritan tradition, with its inhibitions (*America as a Civilization*, p. 679). He without much doubt has a point there. However, his statement hardly explains why the obsession of Americans with sex is so much greater than that of the English, whose Puritan tradition was quite strong up to the Victorian age. This obsession, which probably is unique and is found mostly in Americanized nations, has been under attack—from the Left as evidence of capitalist decadence, from the Right as proof of the horrendous results of atheistic materialism. Pitirim A. Sorokin saw in it the climactic expression of the widespread disease of the "sensate culture" of the Western world, considering American sexual freedom as leading directly to the inner collapse of Western society and to the conquest of the American imperium by barbarians, as in the case of the Roman Empire (*The American Sex Revolution*, 1956).

The role of sex strikes the observer in many places. For instance, it is telling that the monthly magazine for men with the neutral title *Esquire*, published in a modest edition, has increasingly been replaced by *Playboy*, coming out in considerably greater numbers. The former generally refrained from publishing pictures of nudes. Still, decades ago it had difficulties with the postal authorities, which considered it too daring. *Playboy*, full of pictures of full-bosomed naked women, later on did not encounter such difficulties. After it had become established and was followed by the establishment of Playboy Clubs all over the nation, it was complemented by the magazine *Playgirl*, so that people could take delight in looking at photos of naked men. Other magazines followed with even more blatant orientations toward sex. This may have motivated a man like William F. Buckley, the editor of *National Review*, one of the intellectual fathers of American conservatism and a friend and adviser of Reagan, to contribute to *Playboy*. Perhaps he was induced to do so by the big honorarium that that magazine pays, for millionaires also are interested in making money. On the other hand, Julie Nixon, the daughter of the former president, did not accept an offer of a million dollars to pose in the nude.

Parallel to the publication of these journals was the publication of more or less scholarly reports. Like newspaper articles, they are tinged with journalism and find a wide distribution. In 1948, Alfred C. Kinsey, a zoologist, and two collaborators published the first Kinsey Report, *Sexual Behavior in the Human Male.* Between January 5 and February 2, it ran to five printings, and further printings followed. It was similar with the second Kinsey Report, published in 1953, *Sexual Behavior in the Human Female.* Both reports were widely discussed, not just in the book by Jerome Himmelhoch and Sylvia Fleis Fava, *Sexual Behavior in American Society: An Appraisal of the First Two Kinsey Reports* (1955). Similar reports followed and became more or less the fashion of the day. William H. Masters and Virginia E. Johnson, employees of a scholarly institute, published *Human Sexual Response* (1966), *Human Sexual Inadequacy* (1970), and *Homosexuality in Perspective* (1979). Shere Hite's *The Hite Report: A Nationwide Study of Female Sexuality* (1976) also received wide attention. Aside from these reports there came about a growing literature by reknowned authors, to say nothing of smut literature. Vance Packard's title, *The Sexual Wilderness: The Contemporary Upheaval in the Male-Female Relationships* (1968), is as telling as Morton Hunt's *Sexual Behavior in the 1970s* (1974), with its title of the first chapter and the latter's subtitles: "Sexual Liberation: A Generation of Change," "The Sweep of Change," "A Typology of Contemporary Sexual Styles: Uptights, Swingers and Liberals." On page 678 Lerner wrote: "Since freedom generates its own tensions, which grow more assertive with every new gain by freedom, every gain in sexual freedom in America has generated the appetite for further gains. . . . America has become in many ways a sensual and sexual society, but with a curious blend of blatancy and deviousness." It seems to me that during the past decades the former has increasingly pushed the latter aside.

There can be little doubt that in our time there has taken place in the United States such a far-reaching liberation of the libido that one can speak of a sexual jungle. It calls to mind the state of nature mentioned by liberal philosophers of all shades in the age of absolutism. In that jungle, everybody can practice practically whatever he likes in hetero- or homo- or any other sexual fashion. What for a long time had been branded immoral has become acceptable, the perverse appears natural. Rousseau complained that man was born free and yet was in chains everywhere. The sexual jungle in the United States no longer is just an upheaval in male-female relationships, as it was seen by Packard in 1968. It goes much further today. Indications are that Americans, certainly with respect to sex, have become liberated to a large degree. One can speak of all kinds of sex for all kinds of people. Whether or not this state of affairs will prevent the war of all against all, described by Hobbes, is another question. If one takes into account how many animosities have come about because men desired the same woman, and women the same man, the tensions in society may, in spite of all tolerance toward homosexual and lesbian relationships, grow because of jealousies among men over the same man and among women over the same woman. In his "house divided" speeches, Lincoln compared his country to a house that had to be kept intact and undivided. In today's America, Freud's house, there can be observed many features of disintegration as a result of sexual liberations and wildernesses.

Is, then, America, Freud's house, a *Freudenhaus,* a house of joy? Not necessarily. Be it first said that nearly all states prohibit brothels, Nevada being the best-known exception. However, the absence of such public houses does not mean the absence of public prostitution. B-girls can be picked up in bars, call girls can be called to hotels and living quarters, and V-girls are ready to entertain businessmen and participants in conferences coming from other places. There are health and massage salons, bathing houses and similar establishments. To female prostitutes there have been added, especially since the abolition of punishment for homosexuality, male ones. For the time being there is a tendency to close their meeting places on account of AIDS. As a matter of fact, there can be observed during the past years a certain reaction to sexual permissiveness, aided, but not brought about by, AIDS. President Carter recommended to young people that they get married instead of living together. Under President Reagan the "moral majority" was emphasized. Nevertheless, the number of those living together increased. I saw car stickers with the words "The moral majority is neither." To me, this reaction appears to be some kind of a breathing spell, which is not going to stop further sexual emancipation. Although marriage for many people still is the kind of lifelong commitment it used to be, in the opinion of observers it has increasingly degenerated to a mere arrangement for the satisfaction of sexual desires, being conceived from the beginning as a mere orgasm contract. No longer do partners intend to stay together until death does part them, but only as long as they have an appetite for one another. The growing number of divorces seems to be proof of this. For again and again one hears that the marriage came into existence only on account of sexual attraction.

It may go too far to assert that Freud's house is a house of joy in the customary sense of the term, but it cannot be denied that Americans live for the joys of the present and that sex plays an essential part in these joys. Its connection with present happiness on this earth was demonstrated by Jefferson, who coined the concept of the pursuit of happiness. His plan for the University of Virginia provided for a brothel for students. He himself had relationships with his female slaves. After his death, two of his daughters were sold on a slave market in New Orleans despite his request to the authorities in his home state that this should not happen. Perhaps it is, of all things, the emphasis on sex that makes Americans realize the importance of the present. It is dubious whether or not the sex drive is man's strongest drive, yet without doubt there can be no life without it and, therefore, no affirmation of life. The latter is something belonging to the present. Without it, men would not care about life and might even want to terminate it. As the joy and lust of life, that affirmation to a large extent is brought about by sexual satisfaction, be it one for procreation or not. Similarly, it probably admits of no doubt that the sex drive—the problems of its "naturalness" or "perversity" shall not be dealt with here—is a present one natural to human beings and that life in the present can be measured by it. Therefore, it hardly is open to question that the present hedonism of the American people, tied as it is to the present, in a large measure shows their preoccupation with sex.

Thirty years ago Lerner could point to the strict self-censorship of the American film industry with respect to sex. Ever since, this has changed a great deal. All over the nation there are pornographic films. People look for, and see, sexuality in things. Often, this takes quite strange forms. Once I was looking at Murillo's *Little Girl with Her Dueña*. I always had considered the face of the girl, about sixteen, with its childlike and naive smile, a wonderful expression of innocence. Then I heard a guide of a group, a member of a distinguished educational institution, tell her audience that this girl was a prostitute waiting for customers. The group listened attentively. I gained the impression that it was this comment that made the painting interesting for them. I experienced similar trends toward the sexual in other American museums. The sex drive in many places has developed into a flourishing sex industry, which probably can be attributed mainly to Freud's influence. The discoverer of the unconscious through his emphasis upon the lust principle prepared the way for the sex revolution, which after World War II greatly influenced and determined the lives of the American people. Americans obviously were ready for that revolution, and the doctor from Vienna and his school did their best to get them ready. The Kinsey Reports and the literature in their wake, complemented by film and television, peep shows and their ilk, probably met public desires. In spite of his devotion to scholarship, which let his reports transgress everything previously published in that field, Kinsey was prompted by a desire to liberate man. He attributed existing sexual inhibitions to social conditions and ruling moral traditions and hoped emancipation from these taboos would result in healthier and more natural conditions. He was considered a guilt killer and a liberator.

While Kinsey confined himself to sexual matters, the liberation desired by Freud and his school of psychoanalysts, psychiatrists, and psychologists went further. It looked for a more general, pure liberty. In 1946 G. B. Chisholm wrote in the journal *Psychiatry* on the reconstruction of society in peacetime, saying that it was the task of psychiatrists to free the human race from "the crippling burden of good and evil" and the "perverse concepts of right and wrong" and, thereby, to decide its immediate future. He proposed "the eradication of the concept of right and wrong which has been the basis of child training, the substitution of intelligent and rational thinking for the faith in the certainties of old people." The future high functionary of the World Health Organization praised the fact that "most psychiatrists and psychologists and many other respectable people have escaped from these moral chains and are able to observe and think freely." He planned to build up the immediate future by disregarding traditional concepts like good and evil, right and wrong. Thus for him the importance of the present for human activity was also obvious, as was a succumbing to the wishes of the moment by letting loose uninhibited desires. Chisholm and, with him, many Americans showed themselves to be followers of Freud.

Their teacher had described the source of such desires as the soul's empire of the unconscious, the It, the dark, secret part of the personality, the empire of drives, a chaos, and a kettle of bubbling excitements, something purely dynamic, which does not care about good and evil and other values. It absorbs the desires of the flesh and gives them psychical expression. Its energy is derived from the drives. It has no general will. It is not organized and is interested only in satisfying drives in tune with lust principles, which are free of ethical, moral, legal, and other inhibitions. The laws of logic don't matter. In its hodgepodge of substrata and fostering soils, opposite trends exist side by side without neutralizing each other, without subtracting one from the other. At the utmost, they might form compromises due to existing economic pressures in order to spend their energy.

The I, which Freud joined to the It as "some kind of façade of the It, a foreground, so-to-speak an external crust of it" (*Die Frage der Laienanalyse,* 2. Abschnitt), aids in bringing about such compromises. It is that part of the It that, on account of the proximity and influence of the external world, modifies and is there for the sake of "receiving and protecting enticements" ("zur Reizaufnahme und . . . zum Reizschutz," *Abriß der Psychoanalyse,* chap. 1). The I makes the It aware of the realities of the environment. It tries to moderate the latter's pure urge for satisfying its drives in order to prevent it from perishing. It is thinking and directing in the empire full of drives, is some kind of rational outpost of the unconscious. Taking into consideration experience, it is supposed to check the insatiable lust principle dominating the It and to control the latter's actions and movements. However, great thinkers know about the precarious nature of thinking, demonstrated for thousands of years when it was pushed aside and oppressed by irrational drives. Freud did not doubt that the I only acts and only can act on orders from the It. And just as the I represents the exterior world to the unconscious world of drives, it also represents the latter to the former. It is nothing but a kind of ambassador of the empire of the drives, diplomatically attempting accommodation and adjustment. It at any time can be recalled by its master and put in its place. The authority of the I to correct the lust principle ruling the unconscious basically is merely of a consulting nature, for the It is the sovereign of the I. Celebrating Freud's eightieth birthday, Thomas Mann said that the I derives its energy from the It and had to carry out the latter's intentions. Although the I would like to see itself as horseman and the unconscious as horse, it actually is many times, being ridden by the unconscious, often getting farthest that way.

Freud's thoughts remind one of the liberation theories of liberalism. In view of the fact that Freud's unconscious seeks the satisfaction of drives, that is, liberation from drives—a drive for serfdom makes little sense—then Freud's unconscious, with its drives rejecting all values, turns out to be pure liberalism, which also does not ask whether or not it produces good or evil. Freud's I can be compared to a specific liberal variant. Although this variant is nourished by the idea of pure liberalism, it adjusts that idea to existing circumstances by sacrificing its purity. As a result, pure liberalism cannot completely appear and take effect.

All this can be applied to liberals. Unconsciously, liberals desire to realize their dark drives for more freedom. However, they are constrained by their I to stay within certain boundaries, which respect values such as ethics, morals, and law, because these values are respected by the environment. However, pure liberalism, full of emotions and strong willed as it is, does not permit liberals to be content and requires them to demand ever more liberties. The same can be said of liberal parties and societies. *Par excellence,* it is applicable to Americans.

At a UNESCO conference on the New World and Europe, André Maurois remarked in 1954 that what to Europeans appears as a *manie itinérante* of the Americans, was something quite normal, prompted by considerations of change and improvement: "l'état normal de l'Américain c'est le mouvement." He had in mind migrations from one place to the other. So does Pierson's book, *The Moving American.* On its cover are the following words, which the author obviously wanted to emphasize: "The causes of our New World fever must have varied—but the fever has been with us from the beginning. Here today and gone tomorrow. Planters by destiny, we refused to stay planted: settlers forever, we have never settled down. Was it hope? Was it just curiosity? Was it rather some nameless anxiety? Whatever lay behind this mysterious, pervasive uneasiness, the spectacular mobility of the pioneers has only intensified with the years. Willing and unwilling, aimless or purposeful, feverish or out of habit, we Americans have moved and moved and kept moving. But how is one to glimpse the deeper meanings—how grasp this quicksilver *mobility,* and squeeze out its psychic implications?"

After the aforesaid, I think this question can be answered by saying that the basic motive for the migration of Americans is their innate drive for freedom with all its implications in the land of unlimited opportunity, especially with respect to the pursuit of happiness and its hedonistic aspects. And it must be added that this migration has not been confined to territory. It comprised, as noted above, much more. This was indicated at the beginning of the fifties by Thornton Wilder in his Norton Lectures at Harvard University. In the opinion of Europeans, he remarked, "An American is nomad in relation to place, disattached in relation to time, lonely in relation to society, and insubmissive to circumstances, destiny or God." In all probability Wilder himself saw his compatriots more or less unbound and unconnected in their quest for ever more freedom. He spoke of a "disequilibrium of the psyche which follows on the American condition." In the New World of unlimited opportunities, a people of emigrants and immigrants and their descendents moves in the enjoyment of far-reaching liberties toward an ever greater freedom. In God's own country, it strives through continuous migration toward salvation on earth. Here and now.

Nietzsche, the great liberator, perhaps would have liked that. On the other hand, as a man who excelled in the art of self-denial, the author of *The Birth of Tragedy from the Spirit of Music* probably would have entertained doubts. He was looking for the land of the Greeks, as Winckelmann had done with the soul. That meant something different from today's visits to the Greek islands by tourists from the United States who, in tune with the hedonistic philosophy of the land of the musical and its happy ending, usually come for physical relaxation, often with a "go now, pay later" arrangement. F. A. Hayek, considered a liberal, the advocate of the free market, accused his fellow Austrian Freud, also considered a liberal, who deemed his teachings on dreams a scientific new territory wrested from popular beliefs and from mysticism, of undoing culturally acquired repressions and freeing man's natural drives. Such undoing and liberation could be increasingly observed in Americans during the last decades. Freud's seed has blossomed. Obviously, the American soil had become fertile for it after Jefferson replaced Locke's term *property,* with its inherent meaning of propriety, by the words *pursuit of happiness* and thus supplied an interpretation favoring convenience here and now. The drives Freud mentioned could now quite easily be considered legitimate and could prosper easily. Freud's desire, "where there was It, there shall be I," was fulfilled in the land driven by individualism: the environment ruled by the It made it rather easy for the I to become an independent force by recognizing and sanctioning the unconscious with all its drives. That force, however, is nothing but the alter ego of the It: the It is, so-to-speak, absorbed by the I. This is not surprising. In the United States, especially, it could hardly be expected that the I would impede the It for very long. It rather could be assumed that, by giving up its impeding function, the I would constitute itself from the It. Freud's ideas, as they were seen and accepted by Americans, continued those of Jefferson as these were interpreted by them in the course of time, complementing these ideas in a way that broadened American liberal thought, making it increasingly more pure and value-free.

The development toward pure liberalism was facilitated by the factors mentioned. To repeat them: There was the New World America, for most people a blank sheet. The *mundus novus* as *terra pura* was a tabula rasa. The first immigrants came predominantly from Great Britain, a nation in which feudalism favored subjects more than it did on the continent. Nevertheless, it was found oppressive by those who decided to emigrate in order to become more free. The American Revolution brought about further freedom from England. It was justified with the kind of argument used in 1215 by the barons to win the Magna Carta and in the seventeenth century by the Whigs and Parliament in their fight against the Stuarts—that is, the liberal argument. Similar thoughts brought about the quest for the Constitution, framed in 1787 and adopted in the year of the outbreak of the French Revolution, under assertions that the United States with its free government was the hope of mankind and the refuge of the poor, oppressed, and persecuted. An announcement to that effect can be found at the "golden door" in the East, just as the Golden Gate near San Francisco in the West admitted emigrants into the land of unlimited opportunity. They numbered in the millions and made the American people one of immigrants and their descendents. Their constant drive for more freedom through further migrations was not confined to moving from one locality to another. It comprised other types of changes. The liberalism of Americans was tied to this world and to the present. Jefferson's idea of the pursuit of happiness and its interpretations resulted in hedonism and materialism. Freud's teaching and its setting free of drives further paved the way for value-free liberalist inclinations.

Liberalism, or the drive for more freedom, from the beginning included the desire for greater equality, which was another motive for liberalism. Rousseau's assertion that man was free yet in chains everywhere probably meant to the author of a treatise on inequality that the chains were due to the unequal treatment and positions of men. Following the statement that all men are created equal, there comes in the Declaration of Independence a long enumeration of how the colonists had been discriminated against by the English. Jefferson left no doubt that it was these discriminations that led to the Declaration of Independence, a declaration of freedom from Great Britain. Rousseau and Jefferson thus agreed that the absence of equality amounted to an absence of liberty. Those who felt they were not free often emphasized freedom through equality!

The American quest for more freedom thus demonstrates that it was also motivated by the desire for greater equality. The first immigrants left Great Britain to a large extent because they felt discriminated against. The thirteen colonies fought for their independence because they were denied their rights as Englishmen, were not given the same rights that those in the mother country enjoyed. Most emigrants coming to the United States felt they were not free in their home countries because they were not the equals of others. This was not just the case with the Jews, probably the best-known example, who on account of pogroms left eastern Europe—states on the Baltic, Poland, Russia, and later on, Austria and Germany. Finally, the drive for more freedom for those resident in America was motivated by the desire for greater equality. We think of the blacks who retained that desire after their emancipation and were not content with the decision in *Plessy v. Ferguson* (1896), providing for equal, but separate, treatment. Even after *Brown v. Board of Education* (1954) abolished segregation in schools, black demonstrations made evident that the quest for equal treatment and equal opportunities did not subside. Today Hispanics also request greater equality in order to enjoy more liberty. The drive of many Americans for equality is not confined to certain races. It also exists in economic respects, although often the color of the skin implies economic disadvantages. Social laws, which in our century have enormously increased, derived from the quest for greater equality for the sake of more freedom. They are supposed to make more equal people more free.

Aside from the drive for equality, liberalism includes a drive for participation in government, for democracy as a means for the protection of freedom. From the beginning, direct popular government was known in America, as was representative democracy. There were elected legislatures in the colonies. Under the Articles of Confederation the elected Congress was the government of the United States. The Constitution deals with the elected Congress in its first article. In tune with the philosophy of John Locke, there was majority rule. It must not be overlooked now that the acceptance of majority rule by liberal Americans rather demonstrates their interest in protecting themselves by means of society than their often-praised community consciousness, a feeling of obligation toward society. The liberal looking for more freedom primarily thinks of how he can increase his own liberty even at a cost to others. His drive for freedom being egoistic, he will consider every type of government, including majority rule, a means for the promotion of his own interests, the protection of his ego. As long as the ruling majority will leave him alone, he will not particularly care to belong to it. If that changes, he will join it. The liberal's concept of freedom will be formed by his interest, by his idea of free government that most corresponds to his present desires, irrespective of whether under it individuals are free or the government is free to oppress those not represented by it. In his drive for his own individual freedom, the liberal will choose and support that version of free government that he likes the best for the time being.

Concluding our characterization of the American people, we must go beyond their desire for liberty. They are composed of more ethnic groups and races than any other nation. Their least disputable common denominator is liberalism. Emigrants seeking freedom became immigrants doing the same. Their descendents became migrants looking for liberty. Programs of Americanization, planned to integrate the immigrants into American society, changed little, for the immigrants were integrated into a society oriented toward liberalism, a society in which groups and individuals are out for more freedom and do so with official sanction. Among Americans the drive for liberty has been maximized, although it has not yet reached the complete realization of pure freedom. It comes close to the thoughts of William Blackstone, an English jurist often quoted by the colonists to justify their independence from the mother country. At the beginning of the first volume of his *Commentaries on the Laws of England,* he spoke of "wild and savage liberty," saying that "natural liberty consists properly in a power of acting as one thinks fit, without any restraint or control, unless by the laws of nature." A century later this idea was expressed by John Stuart Mill, a liberal popular in the United States. In his *Essay on Liberty*—toward the end, as if this finding could not be escaped—Mill wrote that "liberty consists in doing what one desires." Blackstone and Mill thus stated what unlimited or pure freedom is, a freedom approached in America to a greater extent than elsewhere. In view of Hegel's fear that man could see in the liberty to do what he desires a direct invitation to theft, murder, sedition, and so on (*Philosophie des Rechts,* sec. 319), this is is not without problems.

One need not know Dostoevski in order to sense human passions, the setting free of which can hurt other people. One need not know Nietzsche, who often mentioned the Russian and considered him his great teacher, in order to know how individuals reevaluate values in their own interest, how they make valuable things into valueless ones, and vice versa. Our century has demonstrated that the joys of some are the sorrows of others. Perhaps we had to suffer so much, to learn how to suffer through the healing methods (*Heilmethoden*) of Freud. For their liberations of drives did not apply just to individuals. As the "Heil" shouted by the masses hoping for their *Heil* has amply demonstrated, they also had their impact on groups and parties. According to Hayek the attempts of psychiatrists "to heal men by undoing the culturally acquired repressions and freeing the natural drives" have had disastrous consequences on culture, with Freud probably being the greatest destroyer of culture (*Law, Legislation and Liberty*, 3, 174). However this may be, Freud in all probability promoted the outbreaks of passion described by Dostoevski and Nietzsche. The Russian lived at a time when the motivations and abysses of the human beings he described were looked upon as criminal and made people shudder. Nietzsche also shocked his fellow men who were moving in regular moral and legal ways. He criticized what was generally accepted and praised. It was only after his death that he found a larger audience, when more and more of his followers attacked existing values. The Austrian Freud lived to see the victorious march of his ideas, most obviously in the New World. He helped to bring about understanding in the most Western of Western nations for the emotions of Dostoevski and the ambitions of Nietzsche. He made scientifically respectable the passionateness of the author of *The Brothers Karamasov* and the inspiration of the author of *Ecce Homo*. Both could complement the present-oriented practical thinking of the inhabitants of a nation that in the age of rationalism had developed from sober, businesslike, calculating Englishmen. They could make their calculations, in a more or less unlimited way, their passion, a passion less and less reproachable in view of the fact that newly arriving immigrants with the intellect inherent in them in the Golden Twenties and thereafter went out of their way to convince the Americans, inclined as they were toward the pursuit of happiness and toward taking it easy, of the correctness of Freudian ideas.

Since the USA has become Freud's house, the migration of its inhabitants can be said to have been influenced mainly by three factors. Paralleling Freud's It, I, and Over-I, I want to call them drive, common sense, and conscience. Accordingly, there also is possible a drive for emancipation leading to something good. While Hegel was afraid of pure freedom, freedom exercised according to moral imperatives was considered by him something good. Perhaps he thought as highly of Schelling's remarks on liberty as he did because his former roommate saw in liberty an ability to do good and evil. This ability Americans possess, be it as individuals, as a majority, or as a nation, irrespective of whether or not they are ruled by drives, common sense, or conscience, or as in most cases, by their combination. Drive, common sense, and conscience together determine human action, the machine of human cooperation.

People have been presented as types, as Americans, Germans, and so on. This is not without risk. Rousseau resented representation as an adulteration of the will of those represented. Madison's argument in essay 10 of the *Federalist* that representations constitute a refinement of public views hardly contradicts the opinion of the man from Geneva. Even the best representation does not totally reflect the will of those represented. Furthermore, it must never be forgotten that representatives may intentionally or unintentionally make mistakes in whatever they are doing. The risk of an adulteration of the will of the represented grows with their number. That risk appears to be especially great in a nation of nearly a quarter of a billion, living in a great many climatic zones, and being ethnically more diverse than any other nation.

Nevertheless, one often has spoken of "the American." This seems to be justified because it is difficult to characterize the American people as a whole with all its particular features. If one speaks of "the American," the reader knows that this is a generalization, a fiction, and treats it with caution. Besides, such an artificial construction seems to be advisable in the case of a nation that did not grow organically during a long history but came about in a rather artificial way by virtue of different processes of naturalization. Be this as it may, in the following I should like to describe my own opinion on the Americans' way of realizing their drives for liberty, speaking either of "the American" or "the Americans," as they can be found in smaller and larger groups and associations, in the whole nation. Americans are Promethean in the most Promethean sense because, in tune with their Declaration of Independence, they all are created equal and always have tried to get rid of the chains of which Rousseau spoke. Activity in today's America, "doing things," means perpetual migration to more freedom. Liberals, Americans possess an unusually great ability to do good and evil.

Their willingness to do voluntary, unpaid work is especially impressive. In 1965, Richard C. Cornuelle published *Reclaiming the American Dream*. He regretted that an ever increasing number of his compatriots rely on support by the state, whereas previously it used to be customary to expect help from friends and neighbors—without becoming humbled, since such help was gladly given. However, this opinion of the American Dream—one of many—has never disappeared altogether. Good neighborliness still exists today in many places. The neighbor is aided not only when in need but also for the sake of his advancement. Those helping are prompted by the consideration that they themselves find satisfaction in their good deed, liberation from their desires to help, so that the neighbor may be happier and freer and be without sorrows. There is volunteer work all over, not only in the case of natural catastrophes such as hurricanes and floods, but in everyday life. People help out in hospitals, churches, museums, and in many other respects, providing good examples of altruism. Members of all races help that way, young and old. They usually come from the well-to-do strata of society, women predominating. And they all give blood in bloodmobiles, which go from work place to work place, from institution to institution, university to university, and so on.

Aside from these good uses of liberty, there are bad ones. I have often asked myself whether or not the latter remain longer in the memory, as Anthony's funeral oration for Caesar indicates. Aside from donating blood for others, there is the shedding of blood of others. Far-reaching altruism has been contrasted by extreme egoism, a community consciousness going beyond legal obligations, by illegal, highly egoistic actions. Americans have used their liberty in a way that Hegel feared, for theft, murder, sedition, and so on. "And so on," wrote the representative of the idealistic philosophy. But he probably did not think of new kinds of crimes invented in the New World. He had not been dead for ten years when in 1838 the young Lincoln, in the Young Men's Lyceum at Springfield, denounced lynch justice and its "wild and furious passions." After World War I many criminals organized themselves in gangs and mobs. America hasn't gotten rid of organized crime ever since. Kidnaping came about. In his *Rechtslehre,* Kant wrote that the worst crime was to hurt a ruling tyrant or to threaten his life. Ever since the assassination of Lincoln there have been murdered in America a great many more regularly elected presidents (who had nothing in common with the tyrants Kant had in mind) than in other countries. With the assassination of Kennedy, 11 percent of all presidents were murdered. This high percentage is even more disturbing if one considers the fact that from 1865 to 1963, four out of twenty presidents were killed: 20 percent.

In between the extremes of volunteers and criminals, of altruists going beyond their legal obligations and egoists not obeying these obligations, there is the bulk of the people. From day to day, they go about their legal pursuit of happiness by virtue of trade or other business without thinking much of the ethic or moral aspects of their various activities. This is the good old middle class, for America is a middle-class country and its inhabitants are proud of it. Yet this middle class is not necessarily what in antiquity Euripides said of it, namely, a class that supports and maintains the state. True, it has been said that a liberal society, engaging in trade and other lucrative pursuits, could be both stable and stabilizing because it is based upon a healthy middle class. In many cases this is correct. Nevertheless, it shows a captivity by historical liberalisms that considers the state necessary for the maintenance of such things as law and order, or a society under private law in the sense of Franz Böhm. It ignores the enormous possibilities of pure liberalism, under which human behavior can be detrimental to society and the state. For that reason, liberals like Hayek and Röpke, in spite of their differences, distanced themselves from unlimited laissez-faire and laissez-aller, following Adam Smith. They saw that taking these concepts literally, as has been done by many liberals, could, as *laissez-passer,* have disastrous consequences. Therefore, they made the rule of law an ingredient of their thus limited concepts of liberalism.

Acting legally, the American can use his freedom for good and evil, for the beautiful, the ugly, and so on. He can develop from the Homo sapiens to the Homo faber, from a wise man to a manufacturing one, to that "smart man" who more or less puts up with the laws while smarting under rules and regulations, who under the laws acts and is disturbed just as he sees fit. He can consider law an ethical minimum or maximum, can apply it, have it applied ethically or unethically, morally or immorally; he can interpret the ethics and morals of a law widely or narrowly. He may refrain from making use of, and from abusing, the legalities of legal provisions in an unfair manner. But he may do the very opposite and, to his own advantage, look for gaps in the law, for angles to twist it, and for skulking places to hide in order to circumvent the law. He may seek the advice of lawyers with good reputations, but also that of those with dubious ones and that of shysters—or be his own ethical or unethical lawyer. He may use and abuse mere legality to pursue dubious businesses and manipulations, hoping to get away with lies in legal proceedings, counting on the naïveté or the sentimentality of a jury. He may interpret Longfellow's "Psalm of Life" his own way and in a God-fearing or God-despising manner live in, and for, the present with all its temptations. If he does not like the laws in one state, he may leave it and move to another one. He may emigrate, immigrate in order to further migrate. His choice is big. There are forty-nine other states where he may try his luck. His movement is enhanced by the fact that the laws on the national and state levels are on the whole quite liberal and friendly to the individual. In the course of time they have done their best to encourage the individualistic American to steadily migrate to new opportunities—to produce a certain opportunism. Laws are formative forms and substances.

In the course of time Americans also have done their best to discover the many opportunities opened by liberal laws, taking advantage of them in a way that, on account of the diverse legal systems of their country, probably are unique. In order to see what the activities of Americans have brought about, one need not read the voluminous decisions of the courts, lengthy legal commentaries, or other literature. A look at newspapers provides ample information. Americans have not been content with using, and taking advantage of, the enormous potential of liberal laws. In their desire for ever more, they have, while generally shying away from crime, legally changed the laws, dubious as that may have been. Warnings like those voiced in the sixteenth century by Richard Hooker's *Of the Laws of Ecclesiastical Polity,* in Madison's essay 62 of the *Federalist,* or in Savigny's *Vom Beruf unserer Zeit für Gesetzgebung und Rechtswissenschaft* (1814), do not seem to have been heeded and probably were not known to many.

While Americans have individually exploited existing law, they have preferred, for reasons of comfort and security, not to fight against old, and for new, laws, single-handed. Aside from more freedom, liberals care for comfort and security. Furthermore, the chances for changes in the law through common action are better than through individual action, and Americans are practical and realistic. Progressing according to the law is done, above all, by the individual. Moving toward changes in the law is done by the majority—certainly in a democracy. Therefore, the individual wants to belong to the majority or at least to a group that shares his desires. Americans pass petitions and like to collect signatures. I again and again have been struck by how they try to secure the support of others for their ideas, to operate while being protected by a group, preferably the majority. Loners favoring new laws are rare. It is as a member of a professional organization or of a political party that the individual seeks to gain influence, often behind the scenes with the help of pressure groups or lobbyists. Although the voting record of delegates is known, it is difficult to find out why they voted the way they did and who influenced them. Given the activities of voters, pressure groups, logrolling, and so on, the legislative process is a jungle in which the activities and influences of individuals to a large extent are beyond scrutiny, however much may leak out and become known to the public. This enables legislators to change their attitude at will without having to fear that they will lose face—if they even care about that at all. For according to liberalism, losing face is not really possible, just as being a turncoat isn't: the liberal always is free to change sides, to reorient himself, to turn at his pleasure, and the migrating American basically is a liberal. This explains why politicians who switch from one party to another are not looked down upon by the voters and do not commit political suicide.

In liberal drives, many laws have been made in the United States. Customary law, cherished for a long time, has increasingly been replaced and pushed aside by codifications. It may be said that the age of legislation began in the New World with the American Declaration of Independence, the written constitutions of the various states and the United States, and the laws passed later on by legislative bodies all over the country. They reflect present popular desires, transmuted into law by the majorities of the day, be it through direct or representative democracy, initiative, referendum, or delegates of the people. The enormous number of laws demonstrates the American inclination toward change and laws conducive to the pursuit of happiness. These laws usually were compromises and were not due just to economic considerations, as Marx indicated they would be, although many were. Formations of compromises bring to mind malformations. As a matter of fact, the perpetual replacement of some laws by others shows that laws, being compromises, were soon seen as compromising and for that reason were replaced by others, which again came to be regarded as compromising compromises, which had to be replaced by new laws, which sooner or later suffered the same fate. Liberal progression thus consists in abolishing formed compromises that turn out to be compromising malformations and replacing them with new compromises, which end up the same way. The individual is continually tempted to look for new laws in order to improve his condition under them.

Since in the competitive climate prevailing in a liberal society what is good for one often is bad for the other, everybody will try to shield himself from disaster and seek the support of the majority. For that purpose, he will try to belong to it. These accesses to the majority are likely to change its composition, making it a compromise formation, which sooner or later will be considered a compromising one and be replaced by a new compromise formation. Such majorities will favor the voters' present concept of the pursuit of happiness. This explains why people took the liberty of moving from one concept of free government to a contrary one, from free enterprise to regulation of the economy, from the abolition of the death penalty to its restoration, and so on and vice versa. Since in the United States there are basically just two parties, there are one-party governments. Unlike countries on the European continent, there are no coalition governments. Nevertheless, laws often are the work of coalitions because the absence of the imperative mandate permits members of both parties to unite in voting. Therefore, laws are compromises made by compromising legislators.

The situation is similar with respect to foreign policy. Treaties concluded by the president require the approval of the Senate. But in many other cases, the president follows the wishes of the majority or those of loud minorities, which could be in a position to influence the majority. Even a popular president like Reagan, elected in forty-nine states and known for his consistent behavior, under the pressure of public opinion in a to-and-fro of planning took the liberty of altering the program of a visit to Germany that originally had been agreed upon with his hosts. President Nixon took the liberty to dump Nationalist China, for decades the ally of his country, for the sake of Communist China, which for as long a time had severely denounced the United States. Among other things, the market of Communist China beckoned, with its great sales potential. After a long engagement, it was finally decided to give up Vietnam. In all these cases it was emphasized that one did not lose face on account of these changing attitudes. From a liberal orientation, this is correct.

The described changes by individuals, legislative majorities, and presidents are examples of migrations customary in a nation composed of emigrants, immigrants, and their descendents. These migrations are characterized by unsteady vagaries, by going here and there in many respects, be it in aimless passions or with purposeful calculations, in search of ever more freedom, for which the migrants demonstrate and agitate. The latter takes place in a manner that prompts the question whether or not these vagaries amount to vagabondage, to a veritable dependence upon moving around, and to a corresponding promotion of the freedom of agitation.

9 Demonstrating, Agitating

While roving around, American migrants demonstrate and agitate. This is not surprising. Migration is related to demonstration, and the latter, to agitation. If I want to go from one position to another, I demonstrate my will to migrate. Thus every migration is a demonstration, and every demonstration, whether or not it amounts to agitation, is a migration.

Demonstrating and agitating is natural to Americans not only because as a people they derive from emigrants but because their political philosophy, more than that of another nation, is based upon the idea of changing to a better present, even if such a change has to be brought about by violence, by revolution. And just as revolution follows demonstration and agitation, it often is the source of demonstrations and agitations. Certainly this can be said of the American Revolution.

The American Revolution went further than Locke, who usually is considered its spiritual father. He had spoken only of a right of rebellion. The Declaration of Independence speaks in addition of the "Duty, to throw off" an oppressive government. It will be argued that this is just theory and legally irrelevant because the Declaration is not a law. However, theory is an important force and should not be underestimated. Theories destroyed laws and brought about new ones. Furthermore, the Declaration is legally relevant insofar as it broke the legal bonds to the mother country and justified a revolution, a fact that according to Georg Jellinek created new law. There also have been, under the Constitution, judicial decisions based upon the Declaration of Independence.

Aside from a right of revolution, the duty to rebel was also mentioned in various state constitutions then made. The constitution of Virginia of June 1776, while enumerating purposes of the government useful to individuals and the people, states in its bill of rights, "when any government shall be found inadequate or contrary to these purposes, a majority of the community hath an indubitable, inalienable, and indefeasible right to reform, alter, or abolish it, in such manner as shall be judged most conducive to the public weal." Similar provisions can be found in the constitutions of Pennsylvania (1776), Vermont (1777), and Massachusetts (1780). Such constitutions themselves provide for a right of rebellion against the very governments they establish: a *novum* in constitutional history brought about in the New World. But this is not all. The constitution of Maryland (1776) even speaks of a duty of revolution, stating that "whenever the ends of government are perverted, and public liberty manifestly endangered, and all other means of redress are ineffectual, the people may, and of right ought, to reform the old or establish a new government. The doctrine of non-resistance, against arbitrary power and oppression, is absurd, slavish, and destructive of the good and happiness of mankind." The constitution of New Hampshire (1784) has the same provision, and that of New York (1777) quotes the corresponding words from the Declaration of Independence. Something additional and new was thus legalized in the New World!

Assertion of a right, even a duty, to rebellion thus can be found at the very beginning of the American nation. It is an essential aspect of American thought at the time of the Revolution. Revolution was seen as a concrete historical event, lasting throughout the War of Independence or for the thirteen years from the Declaration of Independence to the ratification of the Constitution. It has been argued that a right or a duty to revolution was confined to these specific, limited periods of time, due to the enthusiasm then existing, and was invalid thereafter. However, revolutionary ideas do not come to an end with the end of a revolution. A revolution taking place at a certain time keeps alive these ideas for later generations. Without doubt, the revolutionary thoughts mentioned were prominent during the American Revolution. Yet much as they may have been conceived as limited in time, they were likely to become a firm ingredient of the American way of life and its characteristic drive for freedom, or liberalism.

They had to come into the foreground even more once the American Revolution was seen as unlimited by time. Such interpretations have existed to our day. They go back to the formative period. Their best-known exponents at that time were two signers of the Declaration of Independence, John Adams, a jurist from Massachusetts, and Dr. Benjamin Rush, from Pennsylvania. Both actively participated in the development of their respective states as well as in that of the United States. Their comments were made at the beginning of the year in which the Constitution was formulated, namely, in January 1787. In that month Adams wrote his answer to Turgot, *Defence of the Constitutions of Government of the United States of America,* and Rush made an often quoted speech on the Revolution. Both dealt with problems of democracy and free government, problems the Constitutional Convention in Philadelphia tried to solve.

Rush said: "There is nothing more common than to confound the terms of the American Revolution with those of the late American War. The American War is over: but this is far from being the case with the American Revolution. On the contrary, nothing but the first act of the great drama is closed. It remains yet to establish and perfect our new forms of government; and to prepare the principles, morals, and manners of our citizens, for these forms of government, after they are established and brought to perfection. . . . THE REVOLUTION IS NOT OVER."

A generation later, after the government of the new nation had become established and the United States had won its second war against England, the old John Adams on February 13, 1818, wrote to Hezekiah Niles, who in 1822 edited a volume on the principles and acts of the Revolution. Adams's letter showed the many aspects of American liberalism: "The American Revolution was not a common event. Its effects and consequences have already been awful over a great part of the globe. And when and where are they to cease? But what do we mean by the American Revolution? Do we mean the American war? The Revolution was effected before the war commenced. The Revolution was in the minds and hearts of the people; a change in their religious sentiments of their duties and obligations. While the king, and all in authority under him, were believed to govern in justice and mercy, according to the laws and constitution derived to them from the God of nature and transmitted to them by their ancestors, they thought themselves bound to pray for the king and queen and all the royal family, and all in authority under them, as ministers ordained of God for their good; but when they saw those powers renouncing all the principles of authority, and bent upon the destruction of all the securities of their lives, liberties, and properties, they thought it their duty to pray for the continental congress and all the thirteen State congresses, &c. There might be, and there were others who thought less about religion and conscience, but had certain habitual sentiments of allegiance and loyalty derived from their education; but believing allegiance and protection to be reciprocal, when protection was withdrawn, they thought allegiance was dissolved. Another alteration was common to all. The people of America had been educated in an habitual affection for England, as their mother country; and while they thought her a kind and tender parent, (erroneously enough, however, for she never was such a mother,) no affection could be more sincere. But when they found her a cruel beldam, willing like Lady Macbeth, to 'dash their brains out,' it is no wonder if their filial affections ceased, and were changed into indignation and horror. *This radical change in the principles, opinions, sentiments, and affections of the people, was the real American Revolution.*"

Adams and Rush thus extended the period of the Revolution considerably. Adams did not just maintain that the Revolution began prior to 1776 with a certain event such as the Boston Tea Party at the end of 1773 or the resistance to the Stamp Act in the preceding decade. He said quite generally that the Revolution was in the minds and hearts of the people, leaving its actual beginning shrouded in mystery. Rush supplemented the uncertainty as to the Revolution's beginning by an uncertainty concerning its ending. Saying nearly four years after the Peace of Paris, which brought to an end the Revolutionary War, that the Revolution was not over; speaking of the necessity of establishing and perfecting the new forms of government and to prepare the citizens for these forms of government after they were established and brought to perfection; leaving it open when this process will be concluded: he implies a never-ending, permanent Revolution. This idea has remained alive in large parts of the American population to this day. It was not just entertained by the editors of *Fortune* magazine, who in 1951 published a book *U.S.A.: The Permanent Revolution*.

In conclusion it may be said that the American Revolution, often considered a continuation, under a formal republican banner, of the English Revolution made by the Whigs, was motivated by the quest for more liberty. Its liberal ideas, including the right, even the duty, to revolution, did not disappear with the American Revolution in the narrower sense of it being a specific historic event, limited to a certain period in the past. Quite the contrary was the case: these ideas were likely to suggest and promote further drives for freedom, be they in the form of demonstrations, agitations, or revolutions. This probably grew even further on account of the fact that the American Revolution was seen as something permanent. It is significant that Adams and Rush spoke of the "principles" of the Revolution, thus using a concept permitting exceptions, even when used in the singular. However, they used it in the plural. This can mean that individuals believed in different principles or that there were certain principles enjoying general acceptance. At any rate, the fact that during the American Revolution there existed many opinions hardly is open to doubt. Alpheus T. Mason was right when, in the dedication of *The States Rights Debate: Antifederalism and the Constitution* (1964), he spoke of the "labyrinth of eighteenth-century American political thought." The latter was, above all, a labyrinth of liberalisms. It has remained that to this day.

The book is dedicated to Julian Boyd, an outstanding expert on Jefferson and the editor of the last edition of his *Papers*. Therefore, a few remarks concerning the general juxtaposition of Adams to Jefferson are perhaps appropriate. That juxtaposition is not just due to the fact that in 1801 Jefferson succeeded Adams to the presidency, in what has been considered a revolutionary victory of the Republicans over the Federalists. It also derives from the different political outlooks of these men, Adams being regarded as the spiritual father of modern American conservatism, and Jefferson, as that of today's liberalism. His remarks on the American Revolution make Adams appear very much like Jefferson. This is not surprising. After all, both signed the Declaration of Independence, which Adams helped to draft. In the Declaration, Jefferson spoke of "Nature's God"; Adams, later on, of "the God of nature." Both thus did not mention the Theistic concept of God. They preferred the Deistic one of the Enlightenment, one better corresponding to liberal tolerance and permitting more liberalism. Adams emphasized education, something conducive to free thinking. Jefferson, the founder of the University of Virginia, did the same. Adams's justification of the Revolution reminds one of that of the Declaration. Both the letter of Adams to Niles and the Declaration of Independence are confessions to freedom according to traditional law, as interpreted by both authors in favor of liberty. And when in the end Adams even stressed the "*radical change in the principles, opinions, sentiments, and affections of the people,*" he appears to be a liberal rather than a conservative. His conservatism reveals itself as a facet of liberalism. Perhaps the fact that these ardent opponents in the election campaign of 1800 corresponded until their deaths is an indication of liberal discussion and of the wide range of American liberalism, so very obvious in Jefferson's Inaugural Address. "We are all republicans, we are federalists," he said, indicating that despite different party affiliations Americans were bound together by their belief in free government. Both Adams and Jefferson, in many respects antipodes in political thought, were liberal. Their death on the same day, July 4, 1826, fifty years after the Declaration of Independence, can be considered a symbol of sealing American ideology, of the great variety of its liberalisms. Following Friedrich Gentz's comparison of the principles of the American and French Revolutions, published in 1800 in the *Historisches Journal,* that liberalism came to follow mainly the English Whigs.

A few years after the deaths of Adams and Jefferson, the nobleman Tocqueville, whose family had suffered under the Jacobins, visited the United States. In chapter 21 of the second volume of *Democracy in America* he explained why great revolutions will become more rare. He doubted that equality of social condition, furthered by nearly all revolutions, would habitually and permanently lead men to revolution and dispose citizens to incessantly alter their laws, their principles, and their manners. Not only are men of democracies not naturally desirous of revolutions, but they are afraid of them. The majority of the people do not clearly see what they have to gain by a revolution, but they continually and in a thousand ways feel that they might lose by one. Commercial considerations are especially opposed to revolutionary attitudes. Commerce is naturally averse to violent passions; it loves to temporize, takes delight in compromise, and avoids irritation. It is patient, insinuating, flexible, and never has recourse to extreme measures until obliged by the most absolute necessity. Commerce renders men independent of one another, gives them a notion of their personal importance, leads them to seek to conduct their own affairs, and teaches them how to do so successfully. It prepares men for freedom but preserves them from revolutions. Since the principle of equality in a large measure is realized in democracies, their inhabitants usually are property owners who have more to lose than to gain by revolution. Once equality of conditions has become undisputed, people will shy away from dangerous experiments such as revolutions. If ever America undergoes another great revolution, it will be brought about by the presence of the black race. It will owe its origin not to the equality, but to the inequality, of conditions.

Tocqueville usually spoke of revolution in general, sometimes of great revolutions. Yet in view of the topic of the chapter as well as the context in which he mentioned revolutions in general, he seemed to see the latter as great revolutions, also. Therefore, his assertion that great revolutions would become more rare does not necessarily imply that revolutions on a smaller scale would not also become more rare. Nevertheless, Tocqueville, much as he doubted the probability of revolutions in democracies like the United States, did not preclude the drive for change in that country. On the contrary, the reluctance to make revolutions seemed to him to whet the appetite for demonstrations and agitations in favor of less radical change.

Although people in democracies are afraid of revolution, he wrote, they desire plenty of change. They are not stationary. A perpetual stir prevails in them. Rest is unknown. They are forever varying, altering, and restoring secondary matters, even though they carefully abstain from touching what is fundamental. Although Americans are constantly modifying or abrogating their laws, they do not display revolutionary passion. Public excitement can grow alarming, passions be roused to a high pitch. In spite of the difficulty in getting rid of people's prejudices, to change their beliefs, and to replace established principles of religion, politics, and morality by new ones, Tocqueville, while impressed by the stability of certain principles, emphasized the mutability of the greater part of human actions. The human mind is in constant agitation. Few men are idle in democratic nations. Life is passed in the midst of noise and excitement. Men are so engaged in acting that little time remains to them for thinking. They are always in action, and each of their actions absorbs their faculties. The zeal they display in business subsumes the enthusiasm they might otherwise entertain for ideas. It is difficult to excite the enthusiasm of citizens for great revolutions or for theories leading to them. However, this can be done with respect to matters that have a palpable, direct, and immediate connection with the daily occupations of life.

At the beginning of chapter 21, Tocqueville emphasized that among people whose ranks are nearly equal, no ostensible bond connects men or keeps them settled in their station. None of them have either a permanent right or power to command; none are forced by their condition to obey. But every man, finding himself possessed by some education and some resources, may choose his own path and proceed apart from all his fellow men. The same causes that make the members of the community independent of each other continually impel them to new and restless desires and constantly spur them onward. It therefore seems natural that in a democratic community many things and opinions are forever changing and that democratic ages should be times of rapid and incessant transformation.

At the end of the paragraph Tocqueville spoke of transformation. He did not mention the word *revolution*. This is in tune with his opinion, expressed in the following paragraphs, that Americans desire all kind of change but not in revolutionary ways. Nevertheless, one gains the impression that he was describing an expected revolutionary behavior while immediately explaining why in practice Americans shy away from revolution and desire only nonrevolutionary changes. He seemed to contradict himself or, at least, not to express himself clearly. It looks as if he was in a hurry when writing. On the other hand, we know that he wrote the second volume more slowly than the first one. Perhaps he was not sure where to draw the line between revolutionary and nonrevolutionary change. This is indeed hard to do, as is proven, for instance, by the fact that to this day both the beginning and the nature of the American Revolution have been disputed. It also is possible that the Frenchman, being a good liberal, planned to draw that line in a fuzzy way, trying to shirk precision. His distinction between theory and practice was more precise. It also is clear that he described practice rather than theory. He thus resembles the Americans he described, those doers who care little about theoretical considerations. However, this does not mean that theory could not overshadow practice and in the end catch up with it or even determine it.

Tocqueville observed America after the Jacksonian revolution of 1829 had taken place about as peacefully as the Jeffersonian revolution of 1801. He wrote, then, at a time when Americans could speak of two "revolutions" that actually had not been real revolutions. When he began his visit it had been demonstrated that the transfer of power from presidents hailing from Virginia to those coming from Massachusetts (from George Washington to John Adams in 1797 and from James Monroe to John Quincy Adams in 1825) took place without friction, as did the transfer to General Jackson, a representative of the West. It had been shown that under the Constitution a nonaristocratic president could succeed aristocratic ones, a military man, civilians. The first great foreign observer of the United States, a contemporary of Joseph Story, the first great commentator on the Constitution, could well gain the impression that the hope the Founding Fathers had put in their work was justified, that the government they established had become consolidated, that the citizens living under it no longer desired revolution and were content with demonstrating and agitating for change in less radical ways.

More than half a century earlier, Rush had spoken on his concept of the American Revolution. Tocqueville confirmed that concept. Just as Rush had not precluded the "Revolution of 1787" leading to the adoption of the Constitution, Tocqueville did not preclude a great revolution on account of the inequality of the black population. Such a revolution came about with the secession of the South in 1861. It nearly occurred a hundred years thereafter, when blacks complained of discrimination. And just as Rush had indicated an evolutionary continuation of the American Revolution following ratification of the Constitution, Tocqueville expressed similar thoughts: "I do not assert that democratic nations are secure from revolutions; I merely say that the state of society in those nations does not lead to revolutions, but rather wards them off. A democratic people left to itself will not easily embark in great hazards; it is only led to revolutions unawares; it may sometimes undergo them, but it does not make them: and I will add that when such a people has been allowed to acquire sufficient knowledge and experience, it will not allow them to be made." Shortly thereafter he wrote: "Two things are surprising in the United States: the mutability of the greater part of human actions, and the singular stability of certain principles. Men are in constant motion; the mind of man appears almost unmoved."

These words remind one of Rush, who said that after the War of Independence it remained yet to establish and perfect the new forms of government and to prepare the principles, morals, and manners of the citizens for these forms of government. Thus both authors emphasized generally accepted principles credited with a certain stability. However, these principles are by their nature not rigid. They permit exceptions. Furthermore, they are, according to Rush, to be perfected, improved and, in the opinion of Tocqueville, accompanied by continuous desires and changes. The writings of Rush show that he favored a constitution under which the ruling majority had to respect the rights of individuals, including their property rights. Tocqueville also preferred this kind of constitutional popular government. And both made plain that they were concerned with principles that, in tune with the democratic-liberal principle, are flexible and thus subject to democratic and liberal whims of legislation. Rush complained in his speech that in their struggle against England Americans bolted the door to monarchical despotism but left the door to democratic tyranny wide open, a door that now had to be closed. Believing in the measured liberalism current in the eighteenth century, characterized by a balance between the freedom of the individual and the order of the state, Rush saw the many doors and back doors of pure liberalism. Through them, all possible and, in the opinion of some, impossible liberalisms could arrive and alter American institutions—liberalisms such as those that protect individuals from the ruling majority or let them be oppressed by the majority, as well as different types of perfections and "perfections." Tocqueville's opinion was similar. He spoke of principles that, in an egalitarian society like America, are safe from revolutions. On the other hand, he did not consider American society egalitarian enough to preclude a revolution made by blacks. He also made plain that these principles could not prevent resolute requests for reform in a liberal, democratic nation. After all, they did not appear to him absolutely stable. Thus both authors presented a mishmash of probabilities, improbabilities, and possibilities of change, to which there seemed to be no end. The American people have unlimited alternatives at their disposal, an enormous variety of possibilities beckoning to bolster opinions that may appear off and on, here and there.

As to these opinions, Tocqueville wrote that, once they took root, it would seem that no power on earth would be strong enough to eradicate them. According to him, in the United States general principles of religion, philosophy, morality, and even politics do not vary or, at least, are only modified by a hidden and often imperceptible process; even the grossest prejudices are obliterated with incredible slowness. He had doubts about the opinion that it is in the nature and the habit of democracies to be constantly changing their opinions and feelings. This may be true of small democratic nations, like those of the ancient world, in which the whole community could be assembled in a public place and then excited at will by an orator. But he saw nothing of the kind among the great democratic people that dwelled upon the opposite shore of the Atlantic. What struck him there was the difficulty of shaking the majority in an opinion once conceived. Neither speaking nor writing could accomplish it.

These remarks were made when the American people were relatively homogeneous. They were basically of English descent, used to English institutions, which had become transmuted into laws and constitutions. The federal Constitution was not yet fifty years old. The people were, generally speaking, proud that it had proved and consolidated itself. They did not think of far-reaching changes and of new ideologies, which prior to the immigrants of 1848 hardly existed anyway. One was satisfied with discussions concerning the interpretation of the Constitution. The period became known as that of the Great Debates, which mainly occurred in the Senate. It took some time for news to get to the people throughout the nation, for travel was slow. People lived more or less isolated from one another and cared more for local than for national events, of which on account of the distance from Washington they were not well informed. A trip from Boston to New York was strenuous and lasted for days. It was similar with connections between other major places. Yet the route along the Atlantic coast was relatively short and comfortable compared to the roads leading into the interior of the original thirteen states. The situation was still worse farther west, at that time a truly Wild West. In view of this, a national public opinion could not easily be formed. Tocqueville was impressed by the strength of public opinion in the various places he visited and, since he found them to be similar, concluded that there was a corresponding public opinion on the national level. In his time, public opinion in the United States was nothing but the sum of local opinion. It was not summarily imposed upon the different localities, for there were no national media, only local newspapers.

This changed with the further opening up of the country, aided by the march of modern technology, which increasingly brought about mass culture. In 1924, Friedrich Schönemann could publish a study on the art of mass suggestion in the United States, reprinted two years later. In 1922 Walter Lippmann published *Public Opinion* and, in 1925, *Phantom Public*. After the arrival of the great national dailies and the radio, American public opinion was seen quite similarly in Germany and in the United States. The power of the art of mass suggestion and of the phantom public was brought home to me at a time when television began to push aside the press, the radio, and film. In 1950, I declined a scholarship to the University of California at Berkeley—where I would have liked to have gone in order to study with Hans Kelsen—because it paid only $650. I went to UCLA, which offered me $150 more—for I had no other means available. Near Hollywood I shared a furnished room with an American student in the house of a high school teacher in the state of California, then known for its high level of public education. One day, when my roommate was gone, the teacher entered my room, having something on her mind. She was a pretty thing, and I would not have minded an occasional free meal or even a reduction in my rent. But her coming proved to be pedantic rather than romantic. After a few trivial remarks, she came to the point. "What kind of a man was Hitler?" she asked. "Was he a communist?" I soon became aware of the logic of her question: until the end of World War II and in the years thereafter the media had depicted Hitler as a devil. Now it was the communists' turn, following the arguments of Senator Joseph McCarthy and the sentencing of American communists to prison. When for years Hitler and his followers had been considered the bad guys by the powerful media, and now it was the communists, wasn't it natural that she would conclude that Hitler was a communist? I became aware of the enormous power of the media to form American public opinion and to reform it at their pleasure. That was more than the art Schönemann described. It was magic.

Today I consider the media's manipulation of public opinion neither magic nor art. I see in it a natural consequence of liberal development. New orientations are a feature of liberalism and so are reorientations. They all are aspects of liberalism's inherent trend toward changes and turns and turnabouts, however its liberties may be conceived. Especially in a nation where pure liberalism is approached more than anywhere else, no changes of opinion, not even the most unbelievable ones, can surprise. They result from the free development of the media, from the newspaper to television, from small to large editions and the corresponding consumption of news, from the freedom of the press to that of all the media. Liberalism includes the freedom to give and take. It implies not only to be free to make someone believe something. It also implies the freedom to believe somebody. Freedom exists in the passive and active senses, in the receptive as well as the aggressive. Just as the liberal can put over all kinds of stories and things on others, he also can fall prey to the acts and stories of others.

Aggressiveness and receptiveness are usually kept within limits in liberals of moderation. When faced with the opportunity to form and manipulate opinions, they will think of how much those whom they want to influence will take from them, being aware of their skepticism. To a large extent, that certainly was the case as long as only the written word influenced public opinion. Writing takes time. With it, there comes reflection, which gives to the written word a certain prestige. This is the most obvious in the case of longhand. The ink flows gradually into each letter. Typewriting is already different. The whole letter is thrown on the paper at once; the mechanics of it shorten thinking. I can understand Heidegger's resentment of typewriters. Reading longhand, the reader is forced to go over the thoughts expressed more slowly—and more carefully. What has been written by typewriters can be read faster, can more easily just be scanned, looked over hastily. The same is true of what one reads in newspapers. Still, one must read. Mere listening, as in the case of radio, connected with mere looking, as in that of film and television, is not possible.

Thus a fleeting and superficial reception of what is being communicated is less likely if one has to read it.

As long as newspapers were of a local nature, authors and editors, usually living in the place of publication, had to give thought to what they could offer their readers. Theirs was a personal fear of being caught in a lie. They knew their fellow citizens and knew about what they could dish out to them without jeopardizing their own standing in the community. The desire for quality was supported by the fact that the paper did not appear daily. The reader was not plagued by too much reading. He had the time and leisure to read his paper slowly, even to study it. The daily changed this. It is produced and read in a greater hurry and hardly ever studied carefully. Still, local dailies were unlikely to unduly influence their readers, for the latter knew that these papers published the opinions of people they often knew, not opinion in general.

This assuring feeling got lost with the coming of mass editions designed for big audiences, often the whole nation. What widely distributed newspapers brought was increasingly considered authoritative. The reader was impressed by the big format, by the number of editors and correspondents, by their general education and expertise in different fields, as well as by the fast transmission of news. The broad reading public as well as many informed readers came to rely upon the news thus brought and upon its truth. It soon could be said that the global character of the newspaper, as emphasized by some titles, not only referred to the scope of what was printed (as reflected in the motto of the New York Times: "All the news that's fit to print"), but also to the size of the edition and distribution and to the belief of many readers that the paper mirrored public opinion. The emergence of newspaper tsars and their empires, comprising whole chains of newspapers, journals, and other publications, increased this impression. Mass editions brought mass capitulations insofar as the masses subjugated themselves to the papers. Rotation engines became agitation machines. They daily mixed new and newest news with new and newest opinions and thus dished out stories that people could hardly digest or critically evaluate.

Readers became used to changes in opinion and news. They were conditioned to them and in the process often lost their coordination and independence. Originally a mere tool for pressing letters on paper, the press now pressed its opinions upon people. The term *popular press* became ambiguous. Newspapers became powerful manipulators of the public. There came into existence a power that could lead to worse things than those described by Heinrich Böll as the lost honor of Katharina Blum. It could lead to war, total destruction, and annihilation. I do not want to dwell on these enormous possibilities, which have become all too obvious. For I am interested, above all, in showing how the press gained a position enabling it to rapidly form and change public opinion in the most liberal fashion. The old freedom of the press, a freedom from government censorship, increasingly has become a new freedom of the press, a freedom to censor governments, groups, and individuals, to denounce and maltreat them in a manner detrimental to them, at the whim of those using and taking advantage of the freedom of the press. This is true of all nations with a free press. For me it is the most obvious in the United States, the most liberal of all countries.

I do not dispute the fact that many a daily contains contributions of such high literary and scientific caliber that they will be valuable for quite some time and not put aside right away after publication. However, such contributions usually do not affect the general formation of public opinion and hardly balance what is called the general orientation of a paper. It will be argued that the different orientations of newspapers will prevent one particular and specific opinion from overwhelming public opinion because they will neutralize one another. In many respects, this argument is correct. However, it hardly is valid when specific themes come to the fore. They are treated in most cases with unanimity. This could be seen, during the war, in the antagonism against Hitler, thereafter in that against communism, more recently in that against apartheid or Reagan's visit to the Bitburg cemetery. Two things are striking in cases like that. One agrees to fight against something, and that something is found abroad. The formula *Zeitungsleute* = *Zeitungsmeute* (*reporters* = *rapporters,* in the sense of hunting dogs) does not only point to a nose for news but also what will capture the interest of the public. It seems to me that public opinion in the United States can be influenced more easily against, than for, something—and in tune with national pride, against something foreign rather than something American. Americans do not spare themselves self-criticism. However, public opinion in that respect is more divided than with respect to what happens abroad. In the latter case, nearly all press organs are in agreement on what public opinion they will create.

It probably is telling that concepts like newspaper orientation, boulevard press, and yellow press came about with the mass editions of dailies. But not only the yellow press is hasty. Basically, every daily is hasty, even if it does not appear in morning and evening editions and carries more or less timeless contributions. It is produced and consumed in a hurry. Headlines are not only thrown on the title page, they literally throw the readers. The latter cannot help noticing them, but read them fleetingly, in order to hasten through the rest of the paper, to push the paper aside or to throw it away, in order to hastily turn to another one that suffers the same fate, and to wait for the next day's edition. And so it goes on and on. Under these circumstances it is hardly surprising that the reader keeps in mind just what the papers agree to, namely, that against which they are agitating and demonstrating at the moment. In the land of the Rotary Club, rotation machines do what they can to influence people as desired by editors, who in editorials emphasize that, just as they serve their readers, they serve the community; they thus stimulate people to agitate and demonstrate for certain things, indefensible as these may appear to others.

However much newspapers might influence public opinion, they still do so as they have for generations, by means of writing and reading. With the coming of radio, film, and television, this changed. Just as the paper with a big circulation was a new dimension of the local paper, and was not read as carefully and as critically, the new media became a new dimension of the mass consumption of news and opinions, because they were only heard and seen. In the end, the screen of the television set became as ambivalent as the pages of the press. It is not merely a technical means of transmission. The *Mattscheibe* (TV screen) is a symbol of the *Mattscheibe* (stupidity) of men, of their poor mental condition in the midst of conspicuous progress, for this word carries both meanings. It shows that not everything that shines is light.

With a few excellent exceptions, the offerings of American television in spite of their costly and shiny settings show a mental flatness, which is camouflaged by the unusually bright colors used. For the most part, the programming is entertainment. It is of a childish naïveté, meant for a not very demanding audience. This lowering of the ability to critically think and judge conditions people toward accepting whatever is offered from childhood on, resulting in an even greater submission of the public to opinion-forming programs than in the case of the press. Television is meant for those who are satisfied with merely looking and hearing, those who do not care to take the trouble to read. They not only save themselves the exertion of reading but, furthermore, that of holding the newspaper and turning its pages. They know about agitations and demonstrations not just from reading and looking at lifeless, printed pictures. Television brings these events "live," simulating, imitating. All this has occurred in an increasingly intensive way, for TV marches on, both relatively and absolutely. According to the *Statistical Abstract of the United States of 1984* (pp. 562, 564), the number of newspapers decreased between 1960 and 1983 from 11,315 to 9,205, while that of television stations between 1961 and 1982 grew from 56 to 291 and the total time of transmission per week from 2,186 to 30,337 hours.

This enormous growth of transmission time reflects that of viewing hours. It shows the immense potential of television to influence public opinion. Obviously those in charge also know what people like and how best to influence them. Just as in the press, there is in television, irrespective of the great variety of programs, a certain unanimity as to the value of agitation against things foreign. This is in tune with the American liberal tradition. For the sake of freedom, Americans demonstrated against England and Germany in two wars, against Japan in one, against the Soviet Union in the Cold War. Immigrants protested against conditions in their home country, whether called Great Britain, Italy, Prussia, Russia, or otherwise.

These protests in due time were directed against what happened inside the United States. If one can agitate against foreign things, why not against American ones? Criticism of the absence of liberty, or liberalism, is extraterritorial. When the first immigrants in Massachusetts out of protest against the state church in England established a Puritan theocracy, couldn't one then demonstrate against that theocracy? That exactly was what Roger Williams did, and others followed him. And if the colonists agreed with respect to their agitation against England, couldn't they also demonstrate against the internal conditions in the colonies? Aside from his book on the Declaration of Independence, Carl L. Becker wrote a history of political parties in New York from 1760 to 1776. It points out that Americans then were not just interested in "home rule," or independence, from England, but also in the question of what this home rule should be like. That means they agitated against their rulers in Great Britain as well as against those at home. This fact is underlined in Philip Davidson, *Propaganda and the American Revolution* (1941). Benjamin Rush's call for unceasing improvements in the new American institutions was really a call for continuing agitations and demonstrations, in the name of freedom and its progress, against limiting establishments. His compatriots have constantly heeded that call. I don't think there is another country in which there are as many demonstrations and agitations by individuals and groups as in the United States. It seems that in the nation founded in a century known for its moralistic warnings, people, in a growing turbulence of changing attitudes toward moral inhibitions obvious in the writings of liberals like Montesquieu, Adam Smith, and Kant, increasingly have disregarded such inhibitions. Consciences more and more have become free of qualms of conscience and thus themselves have become eliminated, presumably to the individual's advantage.

For better or worse, there is something in the American people that does not permit them to come to rest, to be content and satisfied. It probably is the drive for freedom. This drive is sometimes open, sometimes clandestine. Yet in most cases it leads to uneasy agitating. Many people are faced by its great power, seem to be its defenseless, awed victims. This is not surprising in a nation of immigrants and their descendants, inoculated from the beginning of national independence with the idea that it is their duty to radically agitate and demonstrate against what they consider oppressive.

Thus the media, which for some time have played an important role in stimulating the lust for demonstrations, probably did not create that lust but rather awakened it. It is inherent in Americans and sooner or later would have been awaked from its occasional slumber anyway. There is here, I think, a collaboration between the people's inclination to protest and their stimulation by the media, intensifying the desire to agitate and demonstrate, for better or worse. If the number of customers increases with that of the media, supply probably fills the demand—a rule familiar especially in liberal societies, whose business is business. And if the media stimulate agitation and demonstration, it is because this is what their customers desire or at least are receptive to. Public opinion is formed by the people and by those who influence, lead, mislead, and seduce them, by those who as demagogues tell the *demos* things—although they really do not have to say anything. Whether public opinion acts to the advantage or disadvantage of the public weal is a question that has been asked again and again and has remained just as unanswered as that on the nature of freedom. There can be no doubt, however, that in democracies public opinion has a great impact. Its impact in the United States will now be examined in the following pages on American democracy.

III

American Democracy

10 The Constitution Newly Constituted

Democracy is influenced in liberal measure by the opinion of the masses, but the two are not identical. Powerful as public opinion may appear, it is not omnipotent. Much as it would like to rule, it does not always succeed in doing so. The drive for ruling is not identical to ruling. Public opinion is not legally binding. It is a mere indication of the will to rule, more or less taken into consideration by democracy as a form of government. It often, but not always, sanctions democratic law. It tries to influence legislation and usually succeeds. It can be compared to loud shouting, which can have an enormous effect but also might not be effective at all. By contrast, democracy as a real rule always can enforce its will through laws. The latter frequently give teeth to public opinion.

Democracy means popular government. There is no getting around the fact that the word does not indicate any restrictions. To a large extent, this accounts for its appeal. All the people are supposed to rule, not just some of them. A person proposing the latter is not considered a good democrat. A shrewd democratic politician like Lincoln saw that clearly when drafting his Gettysburg Address. "Government of the people, by the people, for the people," he said on a battlefield full of emotions. These words had no difficulty in becoming one of the best-known definitions of democracy, showing, as they do, democracy as all people ruling in their numerical totality. Lincoln knew that even after the emancipation of the slaves the better part of American citizens could not vote. Therefore, he refrained from describing popular government in America realistically but preferred idealizing it and showing it in its purity. He did not advocate democracy as it actually was but commented upon it in an appealing way, by classifying it most comprehensively. Government of the people, by the people, for the people: these words corresponded to the justification of the great democratic liberal revolutions in England, America, and France, according to which a government by the people automatically is one for the people. They are in tune with the opinions of the advocates of these revolutions, who also had refrained from saying that only part of the people was to be emancipated and to rule. Generally speaking, leaders and seducers of people have left little doubt about the totality of the concept *people*.

Yet we know that there never has existed total democracy, not even in the land of unlimited opportunity, even though Western democracy has been realized there more completely than in other nations. Whenever in the preceding parts of this study I spoke of the American people, I had in mind the people as a whole. On the other hand, I confined myself to emphasizing features that to me appeared especially characteristic, speaking of the people of emigrants, immigrants, and their descendants, of a people of migrants, vagrants, agitators, and demonstrators. I added that this people is, above all, ruled by the drive for liberty, that it approaches pure liberalism more closely than any other nation. I also said what in my opinion Americans are and what determines them. I was not concerned with the question who governs them and how governing is done. I shall now try to answer that question, giving due consideration to historical developments. These developments show how, as a result of the broadening of the suffrage under the aegis of pure liberalism, an ever greater part of the American people adjusted the Constitution to present desires by means of new interpretations.

When in 1949 I came to America for the first time, a fellow traveller told me that when he was naturalized the expected answer to the question who was ruling America was "the Constitution." Today the authorities also accept "the people" for an answer. This shows the growing recognition of the idea that the people are more decisive than the Constitution. It shows the removal of constitutionalism (subordination of the government, including democratic government, to the Constitution) by democratism (elevation of the people over the Constitution). It demonstrates the transition from conceiving of the Constitution as a law restricting democratic government to considering it a means justifying the existing government to have its way any way it wants. "Under the Constitution" is replaced by "through the Constitution." The Constitution as a respected and admired work is reduced to a mere tool in the hands of people who respect and admire themselves. This shows how older concepts of liberalism were replaced by newer ones. It indicates the flexibility and variability characteristic of liberalism, the wide range of free government. Commentaries on the Constitution, pointing out the historical and present meaning of that document, leave little doubt about that.

In America the historical is relevant to the present in a peculiar way. It will be remembered that in the very first chapter of his *Reflections on World History,* Jacob Burckhardt mentioned unhistorical people, barbarians, and Americans side by side. He added that Americans as a result of their basic renunciation of history cling to certain aspects of history parasitically, giving as examples the crests of the New York plutocracy, absurd forms of Calvinism, spiritualism, and so on. Most of all, it seems to me, do they emphasize the short period of their becoming a nation, the so-called formative period, from the Declaration of Independence to the adoption of the Constitution. Obviously, they do not want to ignore or pass over lightly the origin of the basic orientation of the country to the here and now. This is not only due to the fact that people who do not care about history as a matter of principle in the end shy away from being separated from their heritage altogether. It also results from the specifically American condition in which advancement comes first. Their consciousness of their formative period, with its various types of advancement, especially seems to give Americans the backing for moving forward and for not stopping. Just as the athlete carefully digs his starting holes in order to have a good start in a sports competition, in a like manner Americans seem to find encouragement in their emphasis upon the beginning of their nation for ever new beginnings of present activities. This emphasis is not incompatible with their orientation toward the present. On the contrary, it appears to energize present behavior, especially in view of the fact that during the formative period activity in the name of freedom was cherished.

July 4, the day the Declaration of Independence was signed, is a national holiday. Every year it is joyfully celebrated with Fourth of July speeches, fireworks, and all kinds of amusements. These celebrations reach a climax on special occasions, as, for instance, in 1876 on the hundredth anniversary of the Declaration. For that occasion, patriots of the land that to many symbolized the New World asked Richard Wagner, whose *Festspielhaus* in Bayreuth was opened that year and who, after the publication of Robert Schumann's *Neue Bahnen,* was considered the creator of a new type of opera, to compose a march celebrating the Fourth of July. He cheerfully accepted the commission and did not show himself anti-American when he later remarked that the best thing about that march was the $5,000 he received for composing it. In 1976, on the occasion of the bicentenary, several composers were commissioned to present something for the celebrations. The best piece probably was the opera *Paradise Lost* by the Polish composer Krizysztof Penderecki, which was completed late and saw its first performance in 1978 in the Lyric Opera House of Chicago. There was such a mass of commemorative music that in 1977 two books were published on it, Richard Jackson's

United States Bicentennial Music and *The Bicentennial Parade of American Music,* a compilation listed in the catalogue under "American Revolution Bicentennial 1776–1976." Furthermore, there were veritable parades celebrating the event in other respects.

The bicentenary celebrations were not only concerned with the Declaration of Independence. They extended to the formative period, climaxing in 1987 and 1989, commemorating the drafting and ratification of the Constitution. While Americans celebrate the Fourth of July like a birthday, they cherish the Constitution not just on a specific day but in a more timeless fashion, many of them perhaps not even knowing when and under what circumstances it came about. The Declaration of Independence is celebrated, the Constitution is honored. An American writing of the constitution of one of the fifty states may well refrain from capitalizing the word. If he has in mind the Constitution of the United States, capitalizing is expected, as in the case of God. As a matter of fact, the Constitution of the United States probably approaches divinity more than constitutions do in other countries. Whenever I walked by the Harvard Law School and saw Bracton's words, Non sub homine sed sub deo et lege, engraved, I thought of the high prestige of the American Constitution. Americans are proud to still have their first Constitution, thinking that its age is proof that it has the blessing of God. Many Americans take the fact that it is the oldest of existing constitutions as a sign that they live in God's own country. Edward S. Corwin's *The "Higher Law" Background of American Constitutional Law* begins with the words: "The Reformation superseded an infallible Pope with an infallible Bible; the American Revolution replaced the sway of a king with that of a document." The author of the most read short commentary on that document had the Constitution in mind.

There has been high praise for the Constitution and the men who made it. The literature is unanimous in stating that the fifty-five delegates to the Constitutional Convention were of high caliber, that there never has been an assembly of that quality in America ever since. Jefferson, at the time of its formulation ambassador to Paris, in March 1789 wrote David Humphreys: "The Constitution . . . is unquestionably the wisest ever yet presented to men." Speaking in Springfield, Massachusetts, Daniel Webster said on September 29, 1847: "We may be tossed upon an ocean where we can see no land—nor, perhaps, the sun or stars. But there is a chart and a compass for us to study, to consult, and to obey. That chart is the Constitution." William Gladstone, the Grand Old Man of the Liberal party, considered the Constitution "the most wonderful work ever struck off at a given time by the brain and purpose of man" ("Kin Beyond the Sea," *North American Review,* Sept./Oct. 1878). Two generations later the former governor of New York, Alfred E. Smith, on June 22, 1933, said at Harvard: "Keep your eye on the Constitution. This is the guarantee, that is the safeguard, that is the right watchman of democratic representative government—freedom of speech, freedom of the press, the right to public assembly and the right to petition the government. Save all these things in the Constitution and let the Supreme Court stand behind it, and then you can get off all the hot air in Congress and in the Senate that you want to." His successor, Franklin D. Roosevelt, said on March 2, 1930: "The United States Constitution has proved itself the most marvelously elastic compilation of rules of government ever written." In his first speech as president, he remarked: "Our Constitution is so simple and practical that it is possible always to meet extraordinary needs by changes in emphasis and arrangement without loss of essential form."

Smith and Roosevelt praised the Constitution, but each did it his own way because each had his own opinion of it. Smith saw in it something rigid, and Roosevelt, something flexible. For Smith, it was rather immune from human manipulation; for Roosevelt, the contrary was the case. This about corresponds to later different evaluations by Edwin Meese, Reagan's attorney general, and William J. Brennan, associate justice of the Supreme Court. The former saw in the Constitution a work that in principle had to be interpreted the way its creators interpreted it. The latter favored a wider interpretation, adjusting it to the present and thus seeing in it a tool for the satisfaction of existing desires. It must be kept in mind, however, that these differences are not as clear-cut as it may appear at first sight. Of course, a constitution is a work and can as such be respected and honored. But it is a work differing from, for instance, a building or a statue, which hardly change and have something static about them. A constitution, rather, can be compared to a musical composition, something living and vibrating. As a constitution of a society in movement, it is not just something silently standing there to be admired. It is full of action, setting modes of behavior by its application, setting norms through its interpretations. Just as people dance to interpreted music, they behave according to interpreted constitutional provisions. Thus a constitution is in a certain sense a tool some people will bend to their advantage, while others will view it as a dignified work that is itself to be served. For some, a constitution constitutes a barrier, for others, an opportunity: a red light or a green light or even a yellow light. The provisions of a constitution determine who sees what in it, and under a liberal constitution, more people will see more in it than under another one. With liberalism, there grow the ability and temptation to see many things.

The thought has been that the attitude of Roosevelt, the creator of the New Deal, a plan considered by many to demonstrate a new conception of the Constitution, amounted to something new because Roosevelt planned to replace the rights of individuals, especially those of an economic nature, by the right of the majority to regulate these rights. This obviously was the opinion of George Bernard Shaw, who was enthusiastic about that plan and, shortly after the inauguration of Roosevelt, said in New York on April 11, 1933: "When you came to examine the American Constitution, you found that it was not really a constitution, but a Charter of Anarchism. It was not an instrument of government: it was a guarantee to the whole American nation that it never should be governed at all. And that is exactly what the Americans wanted." It also was the opinion of Frank J. Hogan, president of the American Bar Association, when at its congress in San Francisco he attacked Roosevelt's attitude on July 10, 1939: "If the Constitution is to be construed to mean what the majority at any given period in history wish the Constitution to mean, why a written Constitution and deliberate process of amendment?"

Actually, Roosevelt's conception was not new. At the beginning of the Civil War, Lincoln had construed the Constitution to suit his desires. In the name of the majority he had done many a thing incompatible with the supreme law, even in clear contravention of its wording. He had enlarged the military, made certain financial transactions, and suspended the writ of habeas corpus, all of which only Congress was entitled to do. Other things he did have been considered dubious from a legal point of view, such as calling up the militia and ordering a blockade of the southern states. Having called Congress into session July 4, 1861, in an atmosphere laden with emotion Lincoln asked the legislators to approve his actions, whether they were legal or not, emphasizing they had been necessary in order to save the Union and, with it, the Constitution.

Now it may be argued that Lincoln's measures must be seen in the light of the emergency of the war and, under the principle *inter arma silent leges,* on account of their exceptional nature were not relevant for normal situations. However, already in normal times, Chief Justice Marshall, whose interpretation of the Constitution became important in many other respects, had made a decision that for future development probably was his most important and far-reaching one, namely, that the Constitution was to be interpreted flexibly. The justice, generally known for his conservatism after having favored judicial review and a wide protection of private property, in *McCulloch v. Maryland* (1819) opposed too narrow an interpretation of the Constitution. He stated that "we must never forget that it is a constitution we are expounding . . . intended to endure for ages to come, and, consequently, to be adapted to the various crises of human affairs." In view of the fact that at that time the United States could hardly be said to be in a crisis and a narrow interpretation of the Constitution would hardly have brought about a crisis, Marshall, when speaking of crises, seemed to have had in mind ordinary problems of society to which the Constitution had to be adjusted. This probably also was the opinion of Henry Clay when on February 6, 1850, he stated: "The Constitution . . . was made not merely for the generation that then existed, but for posterity—unlimited, undefined, endless, perpetual posterity." T. B. Macaulay even went so far as to write on May 23, 1857, to H. S. Randall: "Your Constitution is all sail and no anchor."

As far as the flexibility of the Constitution is concerned, Marshall hardly went further than his political opponent Jefferson, known to be more liberal. The latter indicated to Samuel Kercheval on July 12, 1816, that he was content with having the Constitution amended through the difficult way prescribed by it, writing: "Some men look at constitutions with sanctimonious reverence, and deem them like the ark of the covenant, too sacred to be touched. They ascribe to the men of the preceding age a wisdom more than human, and suppose what they did to be beyond amendment." He added: "I am certainly not an advocate for frequent and untried changes in laws and constitutions. . . . But I know also, that laws and institutions must go hand in hand with the progress of the human mind. As that becomes more developed, more enlightened, as new discoveries are made, new truths disclosed, and manners and opinions change with the change of circumstances, institutions must advance also, and keep pace with the times." Jefferson spoke of "amendment," specifically used for formal changes of the Constitution, but also for alterations in general. If indeed he used it in the latter sense, the suggestion that the Constitution can be changed simply by judicial interpretation, by a *Verfassungswandlung* in the sense of Georg Jellinek, could be said to go back to Jefferson. This thought may well be justified, given the general flexibility of that politician.

It admits of no doubt that relatively easy changes in the Constitution were eyed even prior to the crises of the Civil War and the Depression and were actually carried out. It also is beyond doubt that from an early time it was recognized that the difficult formal procedure of amending the Constitution, classifying that law as rigid, would jeopardize its longevity. After all, the Constitution was not perfect. I always have been impressed by the fact that the Founding Fathers humbly did not consider their work perfect, even though they may have considered it to be the best possible under the circumstances. On November 13, 1787, Jefferson, who had not participated in the deliberations in Philadelphia, wrote W. S. Smith: "There are very good articles in it, and very bad. I do not know which preponderate." On July 31 of the following year he wrote James Madison: "I sincerely rejoice at the acceptance of our new constitution by nine States. It is a good canvass, on which some strokes only want retouching." As mentioned above, in 1789 he felt that the Constitution was "unquestionably the wisest ever yet presented to men." This does not necessarily contradict the remarks just quoted. It reminds one of Churchill's words, made in 1947 in the House of Commons, that democracy was the worst form of government, except for all others. Jefferson's compatriots who participated in the Constitutional Convention shared his opinion.

The two major authors of the *Federalist* admitted that the work they advocated was not perfect but the best that could be achieved under the circumstances: "I never expect to see a perfect work from imperfect man. The result of the deliberations of all collective bodies must necessarily be a compound, as well of the errors and prejudices, as of the good sense and wisdom, of the individuals of whom they are composed." According to Madison, "a faultless plan was not to be expected." The convention was "compelled to sacrifice theoretical propriety to the force of extraneous considerations . . . forced into some deviations from that artificial structure and regular symmetry which an abstract view of the subject might lead an ingenious theorist to bestow on a Constitution planned in his closet or in his imagination. . . . The Constitution, blending inconveniences with political advantages" and at points being faulty, as compared with the Articles of Confederation, provides for "the GREATER, not the PERFECT, good." It is an "experiment" made for the "glory of America," one of "the numerous innovations displayed on the American theatre, in favor of private rights and public happiness" (essays 85, 37, 41, 43). In a proposed address to Congress, Washington remarked in 1789 concerning the Constitution: "I will not pretend to say that it appears absolutely perfect to me, or that there may not be many faults which have escaped my discernment." Still, he praised it in his First Inaugural Address.

Lincoln entertained similar thoughts. In an opinion on draft law he wrote on August 15, 1863: "I believe truly, that the Constitution itself is not altogether such as any one of its framers would have preferred. It was the joint work of all, and certainly the better that it was so." He was not opposed to amendments yet repeatedly warned of them. On June 20, 1848, he said in the House of Representatives: "As a general rule . . . we would [do] much better [to] let it alone. No slight occasion should tempt us to touch it. Better not take the first step, which may lead to the habit of altering it. Better, rather, habituate ourselves to think of it as unalterable. It can scarcely be made better than it is. New provisions would introduce new difficulties, and thus create and increase appetite for still further change." On December 28, 1860, he wrote Duff Green: "I do not desire any amendment of the Constitution. Recognizing, however, that questions of such amendment rightfully belong to the American People, I should not feel justified nor inclined to withhold from them, if I could, a fair opportunity of expressing their will thereon." Thus prior to the Civil War, in spite of his opinion that the Constitution was not perfect, he had no desire for amendments. In his First Inaugural, he confirmed this idea: "I make no recommendation of amendments." Even after he had transgressed certain constitutional provisions in the beginning of that war, he justified his actions by saying they were prompted by the necessity of preserving the Constitution as a whole.

The "in spite of" appears to be important. Perhaps the American Constitution can be called an in-spite-of Constitution. First, in the sense just mentioned: in spite of its shortcomings, it always has enjoyed great prestige and, in spite of formal amendments and alterations by interpretation, did not lose its high standing, irrespective of whether it was considered a work or a tool, a *Werk* or a *Werkzeug*. Secondly, it came about in spite of many difficulties and, later on, mastered many difficulties. Many of its provisions were greeted by some and rejected by others, be it in the Constitutional Convention, in the ratifying conventions of the thirteen states, or later on. Thus with all its amendments and interpretations, the Constitution has probably increased its compromises as to moral, political, economic, legalistic, and other problems. In their attempts to solve present problems by manipulations of the Constitution, Americans in liberal fashion made use of discussion and compromise. Solutions of problems amounted to compromises. One arrives at equations such as *Solution of constitutional problem = Constitutional compromise,* or *Constitution = Compromise.*

Already the original Constitution was known as a compromise. On December 20, 1787, Jefferson wrote Madison from Paris: "I am captivated by the compromise of the opposite claims of the great and little States, of the latter to equal, and the former to proportional influence." He had in mind the best-known compromise of the Constitutional Convention, the Connecticut Compromise favoring equal representation of the states in the Senate and an unequal one in the House of Representatives. Beyond that compromise were others. After proposals were offered from the extreme of one-year terms for representatives to life terms for senators, they finally agreed on two years for members of the House and six for members of the Senate. As to elections, a compromise was reached between those who wanted suffrage to be restricted to property owners and those opposing such qualifications: regulation of suffrage was left to the states. States in which there were many slaves wished them to be counted for purposes of representation, other states rejected that idea. The result of this disagreement was the provision that three-fifths of the slaves were to be counted. Most of the states seemed to favor a prohibition of the slave trade, but the southern states indicated that they would not ratify a constitution providing for that. As a result, Congress was prohibited from forbidding the importation of slaves before 1808 yet was permitted to impose an import tax not exceeding $10 per person.

There were other compromises. The Virginia Plan called for election of the national executive by Congress, the New Jersey Plan, by a body in which all states were equally represented. The solution was an election by an electoral college, to which each state could send as many delegates as it had in Congress. With the acceptance of this compromise, the original plan of electing the president for seven years and to exclude his reelection was dropped. It was decided to elect him for four years and not to mention reelection, thus leaving that possibility open. As to the relation of the president to Congress, views varied from that expressed by Roger Sherman to that favored by Hamilton. The latter proposed a president serving during good behavior and possessing an absolute veto over acts of Congress. Sherman, who considered the executive nothing more than an institution for carrying out the will of the legislature, wanted it to be appointed by, and accountable to, the legislature. The delegates finally agreed to a plan that was close to that of Madison, giving the president a veto over acts of Congress, which could be overridden by a two-thirds majority of the legislators in each chamber, and subjecting him to impeachment in certain cases, with the House accusing and the Senate judging.

More than anybody else in the Constitutional Convention, Madison tried to reconcile factions and for that reason became known as the Great Compromiser. Edward M. Burns subtitled a book on Madison, *Philosopher of the Constitution*. At the end of *The Constitution of Liberty*, Hayek referred to Madison as the father of the Constitution. He usually is given this attribute, which is also justified in view of the fact that as one of the major authors of the *Federalist* he played an important role in the ratification of the Constitution. The literature has always emphasized that the Constitution is a compromise. More compromises than those here mentioned can be found in Benjamin F. Wright, *Consensus and Continuity* (1958). In 1913 Max Farland, who in 1911 had brought out the best edition of the records of the Constitutional Convention, called the Constitution a "bundle of compromises" (*The Framing of the Constitution of the United States*, p. 201). In his article on the nature of the Union, published in 1950 in the *Political Science Quarterly*, Alpheus Mason also spoke of the "bundle of compromises," as did Wright in the work just mentioned.

Now the fact that a constitution is a compromise does not at all imply that it will not fulfill its purpose as supreme law. The way a law comes into existence need not detract from its honor. This is generally assumed whenever deliberations on a bill and legislative procedure are considered irrelevant to both the application and the quality of the law—whenever it is thought that the law is wiser than those who make it. This attitude can be found in dictatorships as well as in liberal states. It can be argued that laws coming about after long and free discussions must be good because they are the result of mature consideration and stand in contrast to decrees, often made on the spur of the moment. Especially in Western liberal democracies, care has been taken to make the process of legislation a long one in order to prevent hastily made and, thus, bad laws (initiative, referendum, and passage not just by one but by two chambers, plus approval and publication by the executive branch of government, etc.). There prevails the principle: the longer the legislative process, the greater the probability of good laws.

The making of the American Constitution took its time. The Constitutional Convention deliberated more than three and a half months. It convened in secret; the public was excluded. Its members were supposed not to talk about the proceedings to the outside world. This way it was hoped delegates could deliberate without being disturbed or pressured by the public. The process of ratification also took a long time. The pros and cons of the Constitution were carefully debated in conventions called in the thirteen states. Not until 1790 was it ratified by all states. Therefore, it could be expected that as a bundle of compromises—and compromises take their time to be agreed upon—the Constitution would and could be considered a well-formulated document and gain prestige accordingly. It could be assumed that, once the hurdles of the process of ratification had been overcome, there would be clear sailing. However, this was not the case. And this is not surprising.

Liberal constitutions call for discussion and criticism, for discussion and criticism are essential features of liberalism, as are compromises and the compromised compromises resulting from them. The admission by the creators of a constitution that it is not perfect but a mere compromise made possible by conciliations of opposing views is a veritable invitation to critical discussion. The compromise appears as compromising, leading to disapproval.

All this applies to the American Constitution. As a matter of fact, such an invitation may well be greater here because in the United States it is customary, when interpreting laws, to take into consideration how they came about, the *traveaux préparatoires*. People seem to be especially inclined to do so with respect to the Constitution—perhaps because America does not have a long history. The drive for criticism is one for freedom. The latter probably being greater in America than in other nations, the drive for criticism probably is too, pushing, like the quest for more liberty, for something new. As to the Constitution, this means that people will be very much interested in seeing it in new ways and in altering it accordingly. There exists, then, a good probability that the antagonisms leading to the original compromise, as well as their variations, will come to the fore again and again and be complemented by additional ones. And just as originally differences of opinion led to the "bundle of compromises," in a similar manner later opposing and differing ideas, whether or not they are bundled as new compromises, are likely to result in new interpretations and desires for changes, leading to further discussions and criticism and compromises, and so on and on. For they all—discussions, criticisms, and compromises—are characteristic of liberalism, especially in a country devoted to liberalism.

Perhaps such a development could have been slowed down and mitigated had there existed, from the beginning of the validity of the Constitution, a clear and unambiguous commentary. But such a commentary never has come into existence. For a good part, this is due to the fact that the best-known commentary, one considered classic, namely the *Federalist*, is ambiguous to such a degree that it literally invites different interpretations of the Constitution. These differences go so far as to have prompted Alpheus Mason, following Douglass Adair's 1944 essay on the disputed authorship in the *William and Mary Quarterly*, to bring out an article on the split personality of the *Federalist* in the *American Historical Review* eight years later. The commentary's major authors, Hamilton and Madison, interpreted the Constitution differently! This was seen from the very beginning. On December 2, 1787, Madison wrote Edmund Randolph, enclosing two issues of the *Federalist:* "You will probably discover marks of different pens." On August 10, 1788, he wrote to Jefferson: "Though carried on in concert, the writers are not mutually answerable for all the ideas of the other, there being seldom time for even a perusal of the pieces by any but the writer before they were wanted at the press, and sometimes hardly by the writer himself." In his reply, Jefferson remarked on November 18 of that year on what he had read of the *Federalist:* "I read it with care, pleasure, and improvement, and was satisfied that there was nothing in it by one of those hands, and not a great deal by a second. It does the highest honor to the third" of the three authors. In 1830, John Mercer stressed that "from different numbers of this work, and sometimes from the same numbers, may be derived authorities for opposite principles and opinions." Six years later, John Quincy Adams remarked that "written in separate numbers, and in unequal proportions, it has not indeed that entire unity of design, or execution which might have been expected had it been the production of a single mind."

As long as it was deemed compatible with their plan to recommend the Constitution, Hamilton and Madison interpreted that supreme law quite liberally the way each of them saw fit. This is obvious in the evaluation of the relation of the Constitution to the Articles of Confederation. According to Madison, the Constitution amounted merely to a revision of the Articles; according to Hamilton, to a complete break with them. Madison saw in the United States under the Constitution something close to a *Staatenbund* with far-reaching rights of the individual states; Hamilton, on the other hand, a *Bundesstaat* considerably reducing these rights. While Madison wrote that the Constitution would be ratified by the American people living in the different states, Hamilton asserted this would be done by the people irrespective of state boundaries. Hamilton emphasized that under the Constitution the happiness of the people would be best secured under a strong federal government. On the other hand, Madison thought the states would play an important role in doing so.

Similar differences can be noted with respect to the institutional division of powers in the federal government. Hamilton showed more skepticism toward the legislature and favored a stronger executive than did Madison. He advocated judicial review, whereas Madison was silent on it. Just as he did with respect to that division, the New Yorker favored a greater concentration of power in connection with federalism, that is, the national government, be it represented by the president or by the federal judiciary. Madison was more in favor of a genuine territorial and institutional balance, one between the national government and the states as well as among Congress, the president, and the Supreme Court.

These are but a few examples showing the split personality of the *Federalist*. Others could be added. The different interpretations of the Constitution often are subtle, but they are there. This can hardly be expected to be different. Both authors showed good political instinct. Their respective commentaries were compromises and thus resemble the Constitution itself. One cannot help but feel that, as far as the concentration of governmental power is concerned, Hamilton actually would have liked to go further than he did, whereas Madison would have liked to do so with respect to power balances. But that would have been risky and might have lost votes. Therefore Hamilton, in spite of all his advocacy of a stronger national government, left no doubt that such a government still was in tune with the federal principle, thus assuaging the fears of those who saw states' rights as guarantees of their freedom. Madison, while emphasizing these rights, left no doubt that the Constitution provided for a stronger national government. He made concessions to national power, and Hamilton, to states' rights. The voters could take from all that whatever they wanted. Nobody, they hoped, would really feel disappointed! Similarly, Hamilton, who on the national level favored a strong president, let it be known to his readers that the Constitution provided for a separation of the powers of the federal government. Madison, while emphasizing such a separation, did not miss admitting that the new chief executive would be stronger than under the Articles of Confederation, one that hardly had any authority at all. Recommending judicial review, Hamilton avoided the impression that this institution was incompatible with popular government. On the contrary, he maintained that whenever judges put a constitutional provision above that of an ordinary law, they gave preference to an act of the constitution maker, of the people as the master, before an act of the ordinary lawmaker, the delegates of the people in the legislature, the servants of the people. And while Madison was silent on judicial review, it nevertheless followed from his contribution that the Constitution as the supreme law was binding upon lawmakers. Here, also, readers could take whatever they felt like taking. The same is true of other comments by Hamilton and Madison: something for everybody.

The *Federalist* is a pragmatic, genuinely American work. On the whole, it is not particularly systematic. One can grab from it what one momentarily desires and needs, not only by preferring one interpretation over the other but, also, by picking one particular essay or group of essays out of the total of eighty-five composing the commentary. Often the editors published only a selection of essays they considered important at the time. This increased the probability of specific emphases as well as that of distortions and one-sided interpretations. The one aspect of the *Federalist* that has impressed me as the most unequivocal, one in which all three authors seem to be in agreement, is that the Constitution guarantees a free government in which the ruling majority must protect the rights of the minority. Yet even that version of free government appears in different nuances and shades.

From among the commentaries on constitutions known to me, the *Federalist* is the only one bringing different interpretations. In a typically American way, its authors took great liberties in their interpretations. In his essay on the authorship, Adair showed that particular essays were written in a great hurry. In a memorandum entitled "TF" written by Madison after his presidency, we read that it often happened that, while the first parts of a contribution were being typeset, the following parts were not yet even written. Obviously, there were no deliberations among the authors as to what should be addressed in a particular essay. Due to its diverse authorship, the work is *schizogen*. The pseudonym "Publius," under which all the essays were published, does not change the fact that they basically are bare of unity and thus are schizoid. It will always be an interesting question why the somewhat dubious Hamilton looked for collaborators in the enterprise he conceived. Perhaps he did so not only because Jay and Madison were better known than himself or because he wanted to put at ease the minds of as many voters as possible by as many interpretations as possible but also because he desired to leave open the possibility of different interpretations of the Constitution even after ratification in order to secure its viability for a long time. After all, he admired the flexible English constitution. His letter of February 7, 1802, to

Gouverneur Morris leaves no doubt that Hamilton was interested in the longevity of the Constitution. Is the *Federalist* schizophrenic? According to Mason's article, Hamilton's and Madison's different opinions on the nature of the Union planted a time bomb, which in 1861 exploded at the beginning of the Civil War. In that case, the *Federalist* would be schizophrenic indeed, for a healthy commentary does not endanger the constitution it explains. Perhaps the *Federalist* is schizophrenic not just with respect to federalism.

The London *Economist* of December 17, 1960, considered the *Federalist* a sacred text, the document that, next to the Declaration of Independence and the Constitution, Americans honor the most. This corresponds to Corwin's opinion, comparing the Constitution to the Bible. Perhaps these three stars of the American Revolution can be regarded as the American trinity. Many Americans seem to think so. Aside from its religious trimmings, we are here faced by a trinity of liberalism that appears to be natural in the United States. However, in view of the fact that the drive for freedom is one to do good or evil, the holiness of that trinity, including that of the *Federalist,* is at least open to doubt. One asks oneself whether or not a bundle of compromises can be sacred. A fortiori, one must harbor doubts as to the sacredness of a commentary that is nothing but a bundle of compromises interpreting a bundle of compromises, that as a compromise comments on a compromise, doubts arise about a sacredness that goes beyond that of liberalism.

But mentioning the earliest part of the American trinity, the Declaration of Independence, raises the question about its relation to the Constitution and, especially, the question whether that Declaration, similar to the *Federalist,* increases the possibility of liberal interpretations of the Constitution. In the following, that question will be answered in the affirmative.

11 The Constitution in Old Dress

Time and tide make constitutions come and go. Their being is co-being. They come out of the past, come about in the present, and move into the future. Since constitutions are tied to past and present, their being is being tied up. Liberal constitutions being tied to freedom and its growth, their being is being associated. The co-being of a constitution is assumed to be a compromise. It appears to be a compromise toward what is possible under existing circumstances. A liberal constitution is, above all, tied up with the necessity of fighting factors considered unfortunate because they restrict freedom. A liberal constitution is, above all, associated with everything that is conducive to the freedom it promotes, be it in the past, or the present, or the future. A new constitution may confirm or emphasize older formulations by what it says. The makers of liberal constitutions probably always are out to revive old ideas cherishing liberty.

Being associated, being tied up, and co-being are features of the liberal American Constitution. Whether the latter was as originally made or later changed or moderated, people always adjusted it to existing circumstances by making compromises. However, it always remained tied to restrictions of freedom felt to be unfortunate, such as slavery or limitations of the suffrage, which today is reserved to those eighteen years old or older. The Constitution also always remained associated with ideas on the emancipation of man, be they expressed in the distant or recent past.

If the American Constitution is seen as a result of the American Revolution, it appears to be associated with the liberties asserted by the inhabitants of the thirteen colonies even before the Declaration of Independence, liberties known as "rights of Englishmen." These rights associate it with the great events of liberal development in England, such as the Bill of Rights, the Petition of Right, and the Magna Carta. In tune with this association, the American Revolution often has been considered a continuation of the Whig Revolution in the seventeenth century—even as the American version of the *diffidatio* against King John at Runnymede in 1215. Wendell Phillips said in a speech in Boston in 1861 that everything of value in the American Constitution was a thousand years old. One can see this as an exaggeration but also as a sign of how Americans trace the liberal values of their Constitution far back into the past. To a large extent, English common law is still valid in the United States. Its evolution has demonstrated the steady growth of the emancipation of man through centuries, and Americans are proud of that continuity. He who observes the visits of members of the ruling house of Britain in the United States cannot help but wonder if so much fanfare would be possible in the absence of a feeling among many Americans that their liberties have their roots in England.

Be this as it may, there can be little doubt that the American Constitution is regarded as having been influenced by that great American document of liberty, the Declaration of Independence. Liberals, who in their drive for freedom always look forward, on account of their association with liberty also like to look back, for looking back encourages looking forward. Although national pride will make many an American reluctant to consider another country the cradle of his liberties, that pride will also prompt him to look for American beginnings and sources of these liberties. What, then, is more natural than to think of the Declaration of Independence, based upon the unanimous declaration of the thirteen united colonies of America? On July 3, 1776, John Adams wrote to his wife after independence had been agreed upon: "Yesterday, the greatest question was decided, which ever was debated in America, and a greater, perhaps, never was nor will be decided among men." Many freedom loving Americans have felt that way to this day.

The influence of the Declaration was evident when in 1787 the Constitution was drafted. James Wilson of Pennsylvania quoted from it on June 19 in order to persuade the Convention to follow its ideas. Several delegates to the Constitutional Convention who signed the Constitution had earlier signed the Declaration of Independence. Others also were aware of the latter's importance. The Declaration was, after all, the outstanding document produced so far in the New World, not just in the thirteen colonies. Unlike the Articles of Confederation, it was not up for revision. Its text, known for its good literary style, was never criticized, and there was nothing to criticize with respect to its content. It was generally praised and honored.

One has juxtaposed the Declaration to the Constitution and asserted that the latter was a reaction to the former. One has pointed out that the

Declaration was followed by a veritable flood of new state constitutions, as many as seven in 1776, another two in 1777, and finally one in 1780; that under some of these constitutions, there often existed legislative despotism. The desire for a new federal Constitution, it was added, was primarily prompted by the hope of remedying these evils. All this is correct. However, it is wrong to hold the Declaration of Independence responsible for these occurrences in some of the states. Aside from the fact that three states had adopted new constitutions prior to the signing of the Declaration, the latter did not prescribe the kind of legislative governments that made their appearance in some of the states. It must not be overlooked that, according to the Declaration, the consent of the governed is nothing but a means for the protection of inalienable human rights: "We hold these Truths to be self-evident, that all Men are created equal, that they are endowed by their Creator with certain unalienable Rights, that among these are Life, Liberty, and the Pursuit of Happiness—That to secure these Rights, Governments are instituted among Men, deriving their just Powers from the Consent of the Governed."

The author of these words left no doubt that he disapproved of the development of legislative powers in some of the states. In his *Notes on Virginia,* Jefferson wrote: "One hundred and seventy-three despots would surely be as oppressive as one. . . . As little will it avail us that they are chosen by ourselves. An *elective despotism* was not the government we fought for." Like the men who drafted the new Constitution, Jefferson favored a free government under which the ruling majority had to respect the rights of the minority. The idea of the Declaration of Independence, that self-government is a means for the protection of individuals, also guided the Constitutional Convention in Philadelphia.

Much of what occurred in particular states can be explained by the enthusiasm over their just-won freedom for self-government. After all, Americans for centuries had been unable to make their own constitutions, had needed the approval of governors appointed by the king for the laws they made. Their condition worsened during their struggle with Parliament, which imposed laws upon them in the making of which they were not permitted to participate and, thus, were increasingly considered oppressive. Given these facts, it can be understood only too well that, with their independence from Britain, many Americans would lose a sense of measure and indulge in making constitutions providing for self-government. Every liberty can intoxicate and make presumptions, especially a new one and one that allows people self-determination. He who is free to make laws often feels freer that he who is free according to the laws. And he who is free to order others around or make rules about how they are to behave certainly is freer than those for whom he makes the rules, even if his rules leave these others certain liberties. The danger of hybris is likely to grow with the dimension of freedom as measured by its novelty and the extent of oppression preceding it. Americans during their colonial period hardly suffered as much as did the French under the ancien régime. This may explain the absence of excesses due to newly won liberties, such as the Jacobin terror. But there was a mania of legislation.

In this atmosphere of general enthusiasm, Americans were not too particular and acted quite liberally with respect to the constitutions of their states. As an ability to do good and evil, liberty often results in the inability to do good, and that inability is likely to grow with the enthusiasm over newly won liberties. The procedures for the formulation and adoption of the new state constitutions showed erring and changing, and the same applies to the substance of the constitutions. They often lacked juristic precision and clarity. With the exception of the constitution of Massachusetts, the last to be adopted during the Revolution, they all were made in a hurry, often by people who on account of the war did not have much time. There was a certain agreement on specific principles, but people in the different states went different ways concerning the transmutation of these principles into legal norms. The democratic principle of self-government stood in the foreground, and next to it was that of the separation of powers. One gains the impression that the constitutions were written as enthusiastically as the Declaration of Independence, that they were as general and, as far as many of their provisions are concerned, were not really suited to legal application. Although it does not necessarily follow from the texts of these constitutions that, in the enthusiasm over self-government, it was overlooked that this type of government was nothing but a means for the protection of the individual—something clearly emphasized by the Declaration of Independence—this important fact often was ignored in the application of these constitutions. And although these laws prescribed a separation of powers, in practice it actually often was ignored that this separation was meant to protect individuals. As in Montesquieu's home nation, it was interpreted to imply the supremacy of the legislature.

Without any doubt, independence and, in its wake, the emancipation of Americans brought about many a dubious thing in particular states. Whether the Declaration of Independence can be held responsible for them is another question. Perhaps a certain responsibility can be attributed to that document on account of the overwhelming impression made by its language and its appeal to the laws of nature and to God. An elegant, appealing style is impressive not just in situations following centuries of dependence, and neither is an appeal to God and to natural law. While these had an impact upon the emotions and the thinking of Americans feeling liberated that is not to be underestimated, and while they helped to produce a kind of hybris due to an exaggerated self-confidence, it must not be forgotten that those who applied the new constitutions often did not realize that the Declaration of Independence makes plain that popular self-government is nothing but a means for the protection of the rights of the individual.

The Declaration is a mixture of propaganda and enlightenment. As a broad appeal it prefers general rhetoric to concrete enumerations of positive measures. This preference can be seen in the organization of the document. It first states that "in the Course of human Events, it becomes necessary for one People to dissolve the Political Bands which have connected them with another, and to assume among the Powers of the Earth, the separate and equal Station to which the Laws of Nature and of Nature's God entitle them." Thereupon one reads that "a decent Respect to the Opinions of Mankind requires that they should declare the causes which impel them to the Separation." There follow some general "truths" of natural law. Only then we read of the specific accusation that the king planned "an absolute Tyranny," as well as an enumeration of facts supposed to justify that accusation. After that enumeration the Declaration in the end stresses the signers' "firm Reliance on the Protection of divine Providence" when they "mutually pledge to each other" their "lives . . . Fortunes and . . . sacred Honor." The appeals and explanations of natural law thus precede specific oppressions based upon positive laws. Furthermore, they conclude the enumeration of such oppressions. They thus form the framework of the whole document. Brought in at both the beginning and the end of the Declaration, these appeals and explanations are emphasized. The American Declaration of Independence is an appeal to humanity for the sake of securing human rights by democratic means. An authorization to elevate the means over its end cannot directly be concluded from its text.

One has spoken of the significance of general clauses in the law. Still more important are the generalizations of propagandistic appeals. Just as people have forgotten the specific accusations against the Bourbons but remember the slogan Liberty, Equality, Fraternity, one forgets beyond the general, hymnal remarks of the Declaration of Independence the enumeration of the misdeeds of George III. American schoolchildren learn only the former by heart. They can be considered sublime, encouraging truths; the latter, on the other hand, unpleasant tirades. On August 9, 1856, Rufus Choate wrote E. W. Farley of the "glittering and sounding generalities of natural right" in the Declaration. This probably goes too far, ignoring as it does the specific accusations against the king, which after all make up the better part of the Declaration. But it shows what most Americans see in the document best known to, and most honored by, them.

In *Der Streit der Fakultäten* (1798), Kant, a contemporary of Jefferson, defined enlightenment of the people (*Volksaufklärung*) as "the public education of the people concerning its duties and rights within the state to which they belong." From this point of view, the Declaration of Independence is *Volksaufklärung,* for it instructs Americans of their rights and also of their duties (not to make revolutions without thinking about it twice). On the other hand, the Declaration addresses the whole earth and thus appears as propaganda. This assumption is supported by the fact that Jefferson was officially asked to draft it, making the Declaration an official document, whereas Kant wanted *Volksaufklärung,* the enlightenment of the people, to be in the hands of free teachers of the law, or philosophers, not in the hands of men who were appointed by, and in the pay of, the state. It will be argued that the signers of the Declaration of Independence, being delegates, hardly could be considered the kind of officials Kant had in mind; that men like John Adams, Benjamin Franklin, Jefferson, and Rush were considered philosophers by many. The document they signed thus appears to be a combination of popular enlightenment and propaganda. It is difficult to draw the line between the two. Even if *Volksaufklärung* is mentioned first, this does not mean that propagandistic aspects could not predominate. Certainly the practice has shown that enlightenment has been diminished by propaganda and often serves as camouflage for it.

In the case of the Declaration of Independence, the possibility of its propagandistic aspects' pushing aside its enlightened ones could be increased on account of the fact that, aside from concrete, clear provisions, the document contains more general terms subject to rather extensive interpretations usable for purposes of propaganda. And they are the ones that fascinate the most. References to the "Laws of Nature," to "Nature's God", to the belief that "all Men are created equal," "that they are endowed by their Creator with certain unalienable Rights," the use of terms like "the Pursuit of Happiness," "the Consent of the Governed,"—they all make a bigger hit than sober statements such as the king's refusing to assent to laws desired by the colonists, creating a multitude of new offices, keeping standing armies in times of peace, turning Indians against the colonists, and so on. A register of sins has a hard time asserting itself against glamorous predictions. The light future always wins out over the dark past, even among those who by nature are not as optimistic, as liberally driving toward the new, as are Americans. There just can be no doubt that, especially in America, preference is given to whatever people can do due to their inalienable rights under a generously conceived law of nature, over what ought not to have been done by a former monarch, who with the passing of time has moved deeper and deeper into the past and thus has become less and less significant to the living.

Even if the propagandistic did not push aside the enlightening, it still always would be equal to it. The chances that the latter will overshadow the former are quite slim. To realize this fact, one need not be of the opinion that we have moved away from the age of enlightenment in time and that as a result of the extension of the suffrage ever broader masses have tended away from rationalism toward emotionalism. Thus in all probability the Declaration of Independence will remain a hybrid. Its enlightened and propagandistic ingredients are likely to provoke a great many interpretations, especially among people who are as much oriented toward liberalism as Americans are. This provocation will be aided by the fact that the Declaration is a famous document of liberalism, the most famous in the New World, and that, besides, it stands at the beginning of the sovereignty of the United States, initiating free government in that country.

These features can hardly miss an impact upon the Constitution. One always goes back to the beginning. Genesis is a charismatic force. Few people succeed in escaping its pull. The Constitution itself stresses the importance of the beginning when it stipulates that only born Americans can become president and thus reduces all naturalized Americans to second-class citizens. By providing for free government, the Constitution makes it inevitable that, when interpreting it, people will think of that document standing at the beginning of the nation, the Declaration of Independence. French constitutions also have adhered to the best-known first document of the French Revolution, the Declaration of the Rights of Man and Citizen. When in the constitutional laws of the Third Republic no reference was made to that declaration, it was assumed to be part of these laws. It must be added that the Constitution was supposed to guarantee free government through a more perfect Union. Also from that point of view, it can be assumed that later generations, when interpreting the Constitution, would not ignore the Declaration of Independence—which Jefferson, in an 1825 letter to Dr. James Mease, spoke of as "This holy bond of our Union," and which coined the term *United States,* a term taken over by the Constitution.

When people consider the Constitution a reaction to the Declaration, they probably think less of the document itself and more of the conditions that came about after it had been made known to the world. Actually, the Constitution is in agreement with the Declaration with respect to important principles. This was emphasized by Edmund S. Morgan in *The Birth of the Republic 1763–1789* (1956) as well as by the study by Benjamin F. Wright, mentioned above. The most important point of agreement probably was that concerning self-government. It is mentioned in essay 40 of the *Federalist,* quoting from the Declaration by speaking of "the transcendent and precious right of the people to 'abolish or alter their governments as to them shall seem most likely to effect their safety and happiness.'" This reflects an old English idea. Even prior to independence, in the First Continental Congress of 1774, John Adams and James Duane had considered the right of the people to participate in legislation as the basis of every kind of free government. The Declaration expresses this idea as "Consent of the Governed." It was recognized, after having been emphasized by the constitutions of the various states, by the federal Constitution, which came about with the consent of the governed and prescribes a government by the people. The guarantee of human rights is another point of agreement. It can be seen in the Declaration, in the bills of rights and the constitutions made by the states, and in the federal Constitution. The latter was framed for the protection of these rights and, to make doubly sure these rights would be protected, soon complemented by a Bill of Rights. These rights of the individual for the most part can be traced to England, some of them back to the Magna Carta and even to earlier coronation oaths. Often they varied from document to document, their protection going further in some than in others. Thus freedom of the press is guaranteed more often than freedom of religion, and freedom of petition and assembly can be found only in some longer bills of rights.

It cannot escape attention that the unanimity on self-government seems more convincing than that on guarantees of human rights. As to the latter, there was agreement in principle but not so much with respect to detail. One gains the impression that the Constitutional Convention was more unequivocally influenced by the general desire for self-government than by the obviously more obscure and more divided opinions concerning the way the rights of individuals were to be secured. The former can be compared to a united phalanx, the latter, to a divided balance. One cannot help feeling that the thrust of the phalanx was so great as to allow the delegates to refrain from formulating a bill of rights. On the other hand, we know that in documents preceding the Constitution self-government was seen as a means for the protection of individuals from the government; that in Philadelphia there was created a Constitution establishing federalism and the separation of powers with a view of protecting these rights. According to essay 84 of the *Federalist,* that protection went so far as to make the Constitution a bill of rights without the addition of a formal Bill of Rights.

There can be little doubt that the Constitution was made in order to curtail democratic excesses in some states, infringing upon the rights of citizens. A fortiori, it may be concluded that such excesses were to be excluded on the national level also. The Constitution thus appears to be a supreme law that, while recognizing the principle of popular government, warns of the latter's excesses and thus limits it. It has been called antidemocratic, restricting democracy for the sake of the individual's protection. The government it creates is generally considered a constitutional democracy. However, it must not be overlooked that references to the people can be found in important places in the Constitution. The preamble reads: "We, the people of the United States, in order to form a more perfect Union, establish justice, insure domestic tranquility, provide for the common defense, promote the general welfare, and secure the blessings of liberty to ourselves and our posterity do ordain and establish this Constitution for the United States of America." And at the end of the Bill of Rights, which can be considered an integral part of the original Constitution because it was ratified by some states only under the condition that such a bill would be added, the Tenth Amendment reads: "The powers not delegated to the United States by the Constitution, nor prohibited by it to the States, are reserved to the States respectively, or to the people." The first words of the Constitution are "We the people," the last ones, "the people." This is significant.

It is even more significant in view of the fact that things are similar with the Declaration of Independence. Its very first sentence speaks of the people, as does its last paragraph. At the end of the latter we also find the word *we* when it reads, "for the support of this Declaration, with a firm Reliance on the Protection of divine Providence, we mutually pledge to each other our lives, our Fortunes, and our sacred Honor." The *we*, standing for the delegates of the people, mentioned as it is at the end of the Declaration, leads to the *we* at the beginning of the Constitution, standing for the people of the United States. There is thus indicated a transition from the representatives of the people to the people themselves, showing an ideological unity between Declaration and Constitution, which was not put in jeopardy by democratic experiments in some states between 1776 and 1789.

The Declaration of Independence sees in the consent of the governed a means for the protection of individuals from the power of the state as exercised by the majority and thus indicates a limitation of democracy. But all this is done within the framework of confessions to the American people at the beginning and the end of the document, under the spell of which the whole text can be said to be. These confessions constitute a recognition of the authority and the rule of the people, of popular government, whether it is called democracy or not. These emphases on the legitimate will of the people are the buttresses of the Declaration. It is not different with the Constitution. As a matter of fact, it appears to be even clearer, because first, the *we* stands for the people themselves and not just for their delegates; secondly, the confessions to the people and their authority are not found just in the first sentence and in the last paragraph but are the first and last words of the Constitution and its Bill of Rights. Irrespective of how many articles there are in between with all their enumerations of the authorities of the various branches of the government, of their limitations for the sake of citizens, and of their emphases upon human rights, there can be no doubt that they all are framed by the recognition of popular sovereignty. Both the Declaration of Independence and the Constitution are associated by the *we* of the representatives of the people and the *we* of the people themselves. In view of this association and the common emphasis upon the people as the legitimate source of governmental authority, the Declaration of Independence appears as some kind of a pre-Constitution, as a *Vorfassung der Verfassung*. As such, it is certain to be considered for the interpretation of the supreme law.

Since the first part of the Declaration, due to the greater appeal of its general axioms, is more impressive than its later enumeration of the king's misdeeds, the question arises whether or not, being made prior to the Constitution, it also enjoys priority before the Constitution with respect to the importance of the two documents. That question appears to be the more justified in view of the fact that the Constitution restricts itself to mere statements on governmental authority. I am inclined to give an affirmative answer. Just as for the English their first great document, the Magna Carta Libertatum, overshadows later ones, for most Americans the earlier Declaration of Independence is probably more important than the later Constitution, which is considered the result of independence and, with the exception of its preamble, appears to be rather cool and sober. Furthermore, since this preamble, with its strong emphasis upon the sovereignty of the people and upon general, attractive, constitutional aims, is likely to overshadow the rest of the Constitution, it cannot be seen why the general truths on human rights, as they are obvious in the Declaration, would not do likewise, especially in view of the fact that the end of the Declaration forms a clear transition to the preamble of the Constitution, associating both documents.

The Declaration, by contrasting the general principles of free government to concrete infringements upon certain aspects of liberty, shows these principles in an especially compelling manner. The Constitution does not quite succeed in doing so. Except for its preamble, it by virtue of federalism and the separation of powers merely creates means supposed to guarantee a specific version of free government. Only a few specific rights can be found in the original document, and the Bill of Rights, added like an afterthought, also enumerates just a certain number of rights. By contrast, the Declaration of Independence brings, fanfarelike, the basic idea of human rights at its very beginning, clearly and unmistakably. Even its name sounds more unequivocally liberal than does the word *Constitution*. For under the term *Declaration of Independence* people would not understand just the independence of the thirteen colonies from the mother country but, more generally, the independence of men from despotism as such—a confession against tyranny. Such an uncompromising meaning is not characteristic of that bundle of compromises, the Constitution.

When the Constitution was up for ratification, questions were raised concerning its protection of human rights. Such questions need not be asked with respect to the Declaration of Independence. The document written by Jefferson reflects liberalism as a whole, liberalism as such; that in the drafting of which Madison played an important role merely shows a concrete, visible aspect of liberalism, one among its many aspects. The Declaration thus corresponds more to pure liberalism, whereas the Constitution rather reflects one of liberalism's many appearances. And just as the drive for freedom spawns and nourishes concrete liberalisms, an early document that corresponds to it (the Declaration) will influence the later one (the Constitution), whether one likes it or not. People thirsting for freedom as much as Americans do will be inclined to rather like it.

The influence of the Declaration upon the Constitution will probably grow even further because the man who drafted it is considered America's outstanding political philosopher. Jefferson seems to have approached pure liberalism more than any other American leader.

12 Jefferson and Pure Liberalism

The Declaration of Independence precedes the Constitution just as its father Jefferson precedes the father of the Constitution, Madison. Madison was born after Jefferson. After Jefferson had made himself known as the author of the Declaration, Madison helped frame the Constitution and wrote his commentaries in the *Federalist*. He succeeded Jefferson as president. He died after him without having, unlike his predecessor, the good fortune of doing so on a national holiday. For Americans, Madison comes after Jefferson. There are three major monuments in their capital named for former presidents: the Washington Monument, the Lincoln Memorial, and last but not least, the Jefferson Memorial. There is no comparable monument for Madison. "Little Jimmy Madison," as he was called, must be consoled with the Madison Building erected a few years ago as the second annex to the Library of Congress. In a large measure, I attribute the general preference for Jefferson to the fact that he drafted the first American document of freedom and is identified with it. As Lincoln remarked in his speech in Springfield, it is the beginning that counts and makes immortal.

However, Jefferson's great popularity probably is not just due to his authorship of the Declaration, although he wanted his authorship engraved on his tombstone. I think it may well be due to the fact that for many he symbolizes the typical American. Much as the compromiser Madison may be liked by Americans and other liberals, Jefferson probably is closer to them. For he was not only, as Madison was, a landed squire who devoted himself to politics, always ready for a compromise, but the polymath Jefferson engaged in many walks of life, often on a high level. This corresponds to the professional mobility of Americans, their versatility, which has its roots in that self-reliance characteristic of the days of the pioneers and, while it is not always crowned by success, always allows for new chances and possibilities. And if someone even succeeds in becoming president, his example encourages people to try again, try something new. The variety of Lincoln's experiences before he became a moderately successful lawyer in his home state is well known. A more recent, less well-known example is Harry Truman. Up to the age of thirty-seven, he had done nothing but fail. He wanted to be a professional soldier but came to be an assistant in a drugstore, a paper wrapper for a Kansas newspaper, a bank clerk, a farmer, an unknown pianist, an officer in the field artillery during World War I, a partner in a haberdashery shop that went bankrupt after a year, a road overseer, an administrator with the right to call himself "judge," a follower of the notorious boss of Kansas City, Thomas J. Pendergast, through whom he was chosen as United States Senator for Missouri, then vice president as a compromise candidate at the Democratic convention of 1944, and, upon the death of Roosevelt, president, to be confirmed in the election of 1948 for another four years. For Truman, the American Dream came true, the pursuit of happiness showed its fruits.

When I lived in the Colonnade Club, the oldest pavilion of Jefferson's design at the University of Virginia, I sometimes met William Faulkner, and we admired the beauty of Jeffersonian architecture. Visiting Jefferson's home, Monticello, one is impressed by his ideas and inventions, his versatility: "Thomas Jefferson was a lawyer, politician, revolutionary, the author of the Declaration of Independence, wartime governor of his native state, writer of epoch-making bills, American minister to France, secretary of state, vice-president and, for two terms, president of the United States, founder and directing spirit of the University of Virginia. He was an assiduous farmer in the extensive manner of big eighteenth century landowners, supervising not only agriculture but also a sprawling home production of almost everything needed in a community of several hundred people. He was a great builder and creative architect, a manufacturer of nails, an enthusiastic gardener who gave much of his time to procuring plants and experimenting with them. He was a student of mathematics, an inventor of practical devices and gadgets, a naturalist, a meteorologist who made observations year after year, a collector of records about the Indians. He assembled the biggest private library in America and possibly of his age, and gave much time to its organization and cataloguing. He wrote so many letters that those hitherto published fill a score of volumes; he estimated that in one year their number amounted to twelve hundred. . . . All this is the record of only part, though a major part, of his interests and activities" (Karl Lehmann, *Thomas Jefferson*,

American Humanist, 1947, pp. 9–10). Jefferson has been considered the American coming the closest to the Renaissance man.

The literature has not only dealt with the politician Jefferson, on whom there is an enormous number of books, articles, and tracts. In only the past decades there have been published such works as Eleanor Davidson Berman, *Thomas Jefferson Among the Arts* (1947); Edward T. Martin, *Thomas Jefferson: Scientist* (1952); Robert M. Healey, *Jefferson on Religion in Public Education* (1963); Roy Honeywell, *The Educational Work of Thomas Jefferson* (1964); C. Randolph Benson, *Thomas Jefferson as Social Scientist* (1971); William Howard Adams, *Jefferson and the Arts: An Extended View* (1976); Frederick Doveton Nichols and Ralph E. Griswold, *Thomas Jefferson, Landscape Architect* (1978). There probably is no other American about whom so much has been written in so many respects. For his compatriots, Jefferson is the most many-sided of their great men. They are deeply impressed by his universality. Jefferson symbolizes their liberal inclination to try their hands in many fields, to look for their luck everywhere, in a steady pursuit of happiness. His way of life confirms their belief that every job can bring new liberty and that people can succeed everywhere. Jefferson is, as he was called in the title of a best-selling book by Gilbert Chinard, the apostle of Americanism. He is like the enterprising all-American George F. Babbitt, described by Sinclair Lewis.

Since Americanism implies a drive for more freedom, for the new, the letting go of the old, it could be called apostasy, and Jefferson, as the apostle of Americanism, an apostate. There was something restless in him, something fleeting, a steady desire for something new. He wanted to get away from what was, look for something new, seek freedom from the old. Right after his death he was seen as an apostle of freedom and prior to the Civil War was so called by Benjamin F. Hallett, a New England leader of the Democratic party (Merrill D. Peterson, *The Jefferson Image in the American Mind*, 1960, pp. 9, 208), and later by President Roosevelt on the occasion of the inauguration of the Jefferson Memorial in 1943; by Herbert Bayard Swope and W. Warren Barbour in a volume edited by James Waterman Wise that year, *Thomas Jefferson Then and Now, 1743–1943;* by Benson in the work referred to (p. 271). Although it usually followed from the context that Jefferson was seen as *the* apostle of freedom (sometimes the definite article would be used), people went further and applied superlatives. Anson Phelps Stokes called Jefferson "the greatest liberal who took part in founding our government" (*Church and States in the United States*, 1950, vol. 1, p. 338). At the beginning of *The Living Jefferson* (1936), James Truslow Adams wrote that Jefferson "was, and still is, the greatest and most influential American exponent of both Liberalism and Americanism . . . bound to insist upon freedom."

Did liberalism, equaling Americanism, did American liberalism go further than liberalism did in other countries? Jefferson was called the First Emancipator. This can have a mere historic meaning and be connected with a specific period: his Declaration of Independence emancipated Americans from England, and men, from despotic government nearly a century before Lincoln, known as the Great Emancipator, abolished slavery. It also can have a broader meaning, indicating that the slave owner Jefferson, as far as the scope of emancipation is concerned, was an emancipator prior to the emancipator of the slaves. Lincoln only emancipated slaves; Jefferson emancipated man. The latter was not content with liberating Americans from Britain, of liberating men from tyranny. He also emancipated man inside his society by fighting prejudices existing there. More still: he liberated man from restrictions imposed by himself. Jefferson liberated men from their autolimitation. He emancipated all the way. That's what the superlatives mentioned indicate. Jefferson appears as superliberator, liberating man from himself.

The author of the Declaration of Independence demonstrated the life of an independent man who in the pursuit of happiness always was out for liberation. On May 26, 1792, Hamilton, at the end of a long letter to Edward Carrington, called Jefferson "A man of profound ambition and violent passions." On January 11, 1831, John Quincy Adams entered in his diary: "He tells nothing but what redounds to his credit. . . . Jefferson, by his own narrative, is always in the right. . . . If not an absolute atheist, he had no belief in a future existence. All his ideas of obligation or retribution were bounded by the present life. His duties to his neighbor were under no stronger guarantee than the laws of the land and the opinions of the world. The tendency of this condition upon a mind of great compass and powerful resources is to produce insincerity and duplicity, which were his besetting sins through life." In tune with this evaluation, Jefferson, when entering the Virginia Assembly in 1769, could propose to give slave owners the unlimited right to emancipate their slaves while he had relationships with his female slaves, who came to him through a subterranean tunnel he designed, and fathered children, who inherited the slave status of their mothers. Jefferson's writings, especially his letters, are full of moral exhortations. But in Thomas Hamilton's *Man and Manners in America* (1843) we read: "The moral character of Jefferson was repulsive. Continually puling about liberty, equality, and the degrading curse of slavery, he brought his own children to the hammer, and made money of his debaucheries." Obviously, Jefferson's drive for freedom went so far as to liberate himself from moral inhibitions, which he may have had as a husband or as someone who in 1770, in *Howell v. Netherland,* emphasized that all men are born equal.

Jefferson hardly felt obligated or tied down. In 1874, David Wasson wrote in *North American Review* that "there was no special strength in Jefferson's character or mind. He had an eager curiosity to know something of all that was going on in the world; he dabbled in *omne scibile* of his day, but he studied nothing thoroughly. He soon tired of a subject and turned to another. He was a smatterer of the dangerous kind who feel that they have arrived at truth. Believing firmly in his intuitions, revelations of reason, he never knew when the oracle was *medizing*. When he changed his mind he rearranged his principles or invented new ones." Obviously, Jefferson's was the liberal motto, As I Like It, Even if You Don't. James Truslow Adams, who in 1931 published his widely read song of praise, *The Epic of America,* wrote at the beginning of *The Living Jefferson* that "Jefferson had a far broader range of interests—political, religious, economic, agricultural, aesthetic, and scientific—than did any other of the leaders. His curiosity was insatiable." Yet "Jefferson never set forth his views in any formal treatise. . . . His ideas have mostly to be patched together from scattered remarks in public and private papers, each written for an occasion. For that reason many of them have assumed a form at once somewhat exaggerated and confused. His nature was markedly sanguine and affectionate. Particularly in his private letters he often expressed himself with heavy over-emphasis. It is quite unfair to treat many of these statements as though they had been deeply pondered and carefully worded for those who, unlike his friends, did not know the background of his mind and understand his mode of expression." This leaves the impression of a remarkable variety of what was thought in many places on many occasions, of a never-ending desire to keep abreast of things and to liberate oneself from whatever one is concerned with. This obviously missing constancy cannot well just be attributed to Jefferson's wide range of interests. He simply was an unruly, unsteady liberal.

The attorney's legal arguments increasingly became political ones, tinged with natural law. Jefferson became a politician, rising from a delegate to the assembly to governor of Virginia, from the revolutionary author of the Declaration of Independence to the ambassador of the newly independent nation in Paris, where he welcomed the Declaration of the Rights of Man and Citizen of 1789, observed the Revolution, and was influenced by it. Upon his return he became secretary of state, vice president, and president. He advanced in a career requiring ever new adjustments and ingratiations with voters. While he never tired of praising liberty, he took care of never defining it and thus infinitely increased its potential. It is difficult to find out where he really stood. Only one thing seems to be clear: he was a liberal. Consequently, he always took the liberty to discard old positions and take new ones. Practically every American politician can support his arguments by quoting Jefferson. The possibilities of selection are great indeed. Jefferson expressed certain ideas prior to the French Revolution, others during that event, still others thereafter; some prior to his presidency, others during his administration, and still others thereafter. And in each of these periods, his thoughts deviated a great deal. Said Stuart Gerry Brown: "Jefferson's mind was, above all, flexible and open. It is in this sense that he was a great liberal, the greatest of the modern era, not because of any specific programs he advocated or opposed" (*Thomas Jefferson,* 1966, p. vii).

Jefferson thus turns out to be a liberal who very frequently took the liberty to just do whatever he liked, by changing his opinion or activity; be it in private or public life. He obviously felt justified in adjusting his behavior to his own wishes or to those of others, if it was in his interest. He said whatever people wanted to hear and often made remarks that deceived people as to his real intentions. He showed himself to be an ever changing observer and adjuster who made out of opportunities whatever he could and again and again found himself back on his feet. He appears as an opportunist making the most of opportunities. One arrives at the conclusion that basically he was faithful only to the principle of freedom and its extension.

Whatever may be said about Jefferson, there is general agreement on his drive for liberty. On January 8, 1813, Henry Clay called him "the second founder of the liberties of this people." In Nicholas Biddle, *Eulogium on Thomas Jefferson* (1827), we read that "the life of Jefferson was a perpetual devotion . . . to the pure and noble cause of public freedom. From the first dawning of his youth his undivided heart was given to the establishment of free principles—free institutions—freedom in all its varieties of untrammeled thought and independent action." In Jacksonian democracy, Jefferson's memoirs were considered textbooks of liberal principles. In 1838 the Democratic Young Men's Convention resolved that in Jefferson's life and writings "we learn the great lessons of human rights" (Peterson, *The Jefferson Image,* p. 107). On April 6, 1859, Lincoln wrote to Henry L. Pierce and others: "The principles of Jefferson are the definitions and axioms of a free society." In these remarks, the use of the plural is striking: "liberties of the people," "free principles," "free institutions," "freedom in all its varieties," "lessons of human rights," "the principles of Jefferson are the definitions and axioms of a free society." This indicates that people were aware at an early stage of Jefferson's many concepts of freedom. It was clearly seen that the apostle of freedom knew of freedom's enormous possibilities, using them for himself and for others and operating in the wide field of general freedom and its many particular aspects.

Robert Healey stated that Jefferson's "consistency lay in his continued striving for freedom" (*Jefferson on Religion,* p. 79). Since this hardly can be said of any other American president—certainly not with respect to the broad scope of liberty—one arrives at the conclusion that Jefferson's consistency can be seen in his inconsistency. For the principle of the drive for freedom is bare of all principles that could hinder it in ethical, moral, legal, or other ways. It brings to mind pure freedom and pure liberalism, which is only out for an extension of freedom, be it conducive to good or evil, and thus can be reproached for being value-free. And with the reproach of value-freeness comes that of insincerity. If I stand up for something today, for something else tomorrow, and for still another thing the day after tomorrow, then it will be assumed that I was not honest from the beginning. And if I make such a behavior, thirsting for the new, into my way of life, this impression will be strengthened.

As a matter of fact, Jefferson has been considered insincere. In the passage quoted from the diary of John Quincy Adams, he is accused of insincerity as well as of duplicity. On July 29, 1836, Adams added that Jefferson's writings "show his craft of duplicity in very glaring colors. I incline to the opinion that he was not altogether conscious of his own insincerity, and deceived himself as well as others. His success through a long life, and especially from his entrance upon the office of Secretary of State under Washington until he reached the Presidential chair, seems, to my imperfect vision, a slur upon the moral government of the world."

This reproach can be considered justified as well as unjustified. It all depends from what point of view Jefferson's behavior is seen. Obviously, the standards of Adams differed from those of Jefferson. The son of the latter's predecessor in the White House, Adams shared many of his father's moral views. While John Adams, known for his conservatism, had stated that popularity never was his master, Jefferson was out for popularity, cared for the opinions of others, and arranged himself accordingly. Furthermore, John Quincy Adams of Boston was ambassador to Berlin and St. Petersburg. Between these two cities was Königsberg, where Kant emphasized categorical imperatives. The apostle of freedom from Monticello could feel relatively free from such restrictions of liberty, being closer to pure liberalism. Under the smile of pure freedom's goddess of fortune, at times probably a grin, he could, full of lust, enjoy its sun and give himself up to the delights of the earth, just as he pleased. He could afford to follow present moods and to be carried away in the pursuit of happiness by the drive for freedom. Smiling spitefully with an air of superiority or derision, he could reject any criticism of his behavior, based upon ethical, moral, legal, and other values. For according to pure liberalism such values are not relevant if they hinder the drive for greater freedom. Of course, Jefferson could maintain that, whenever he acted unethically or immorally, he obeyed the laws, although pure liberalism, not recognizing any restrictions on the drive for freedom, did not even require that. For pure liberalism is exclusively interested in liberation, liberation in all respects, including all kinds of license. In the drive for liberty, Kant's categorical imperatives turn into categorical liberations of so enormous proportions that they cannot be categorized.

Jefferson is considered the American who advocated the most far-reaching extension of freedom. He has been contrasted to John Adams, who also fought for independence from Britain but was beaten by Jefferson in the 1800 election for the presidency. Just as Kant grew up in a strictly pietist home, Adams was brought up in a strictly Puritan way. At age twenty-one, he wrote in his diary on June 14, 1756: "He is not a wise man, and unfit to fill any important station in society, that has left one passion in his soul unsubdued . . . passions should be bound fast, and brought under control. . . . From a sense of the government of God, and a regard to the laws established by his providence, should all our actions for ourselves or for other men primarily originate." On August 14 of that year he added: "God has told us . . . that this world was not designed for a lasting and a happy state, but rather for a state of moral discipline; that we might have a fair opportunity and continual incitement to labor after a cheerful resignation to all the events of Providence, after habits of virtue, self-government, and piety; and this temper of mind is in our power to acquire, and this alone can secure us against all the adversities of fortune, against all the malice of men, against all the operations of nature." Adams lived according to these principles. He fought for freedom but, more than Jefferson, saw its dangers; he wanted to combine it with responsibility, to control passions by reason, to balance lust by modesty. He did not seek the far-reaching liberty Jefferson sought. His quest for liberty was attenuated by strong ethical and moral considerations.

The latter went so far as to let Jefferson's supporters in the presidential election of 1800 depict him as a potential tyrant. At any rate, they left no doubt that Jefferson was closer to freedom, singing:

> Rejoice! Columbia's sons, rejoice!
> To tyrants never bend the knee,
> But join with heart, and soul, and voice,
> For JEFFERSON and LIBERTY.

Right after the Stamp Act, Adams's dissertation on church and feudal law left no doubt about his love of freedom. On account of that act he attacked the mother country, emphasizing that the rights of the people were prior to any government established on earth; that the people may defend themselves against injustices of the state; that Americans had settled there from love for universal freedom: "Tyranny, in every form, shape, and appearance was their disdain and abhorrence." He considered the Stamp

Act a plan to enslave America, urging his countrymen to "dare to read, think, speak, and write" so as to "let every sluice of knowledge be opened and set a-flowing" against "encroachments upon liberty." Adams remained a friend of liberty later on, but in a more measured way than Jefferson. Likening him to a tyrant may well have been due to the fact that friends of liberty often depict those favoring freedom in a more measured way as advocates of despotism.

Jefferson's election to the presidency has been referred to as the Jeffersonian revolution. Since both he and Adams were friends of liberty, it obviously was a revolution within the framework of American liberalism, as was made plain in Jefferson's First Inaugural Address. Still, Jefferson represented more than just a new dimension of American liberalism. His disagreements with a man like Adams, whose moral imperatives resemble those of Kant, did not merely influence American liberalism, but liberalism in general, creating, as it did, a new view of the drive for freedom. It is not surprising that this was done in the New World by a man who stood at the beginning of the independence of that world's most powerful nation. Since Jefferson's concept of freedom included a growing participation of the people in the government and since the Virginian usually is considered the father of American democracy, we may assume that this concept was going to influence American democracy in all its enormous proportions. America's democratic rulers were likely to desire to free themselves, and to feel free, from ethical and moral inhibitions as much as did Jefferson himself.

Now it cannot be denied that Jefferson's writings abound in moralistic exhortations. They may be picked out and considered facets of his liberalism. Jefferson then may appear as one of many popular liberals, such as Montesquieu, Adam Smith, and Kant, said to represent the eighteenth century, a century known for its moral writings. If this aspect of Jefferson is stressed, his type of liberalism seems to be as limited by moral considerations as the liberalisms of the authors mentioned. On the other hand, the latter were not accused of insincerity and a dubious way of living. In *Persian Letters,* Montesquieu described morals and manners in a way that amused some and shocked others. He was not believed to have led an immoral life. People have spoken of the "Adam Smith problem" and have asked whether or not his *Wealth of Nations* was compatible with his earlier *Theory of Moral Sentiments.* There was no talk of immoral behavior, of duplicity. In the case of Kant such questions were not raised at all. They always were with respect to Jefferson.

Jefferson lived in the nineteenth century not for just four years, as did Kant, but for over twenty-five. Less than the Prussian's was his tie to the eighteenth century. In that predominantly authoritarian century, liberalism appeared more modest and restrained than in the following one, known as the liberal century. Therefore, it is not surprising that Jefferson would be more generous as to liberty and popular government than Kant, who voiced doubts about both. In contrast to Kant, Jefferson also put the pursuit of happiness here on earth above duty. The difference between the liberalism of Kant and that of Jefferson brings to mind that between Adam Smith and the Manchester school. Just as the latter desired more laissez-faire than did Smith, Jefferson favored pure liberalism more than did Kant.

Jefferson's duplicity was not seen just by John Quincy Adams. It also is indicated when some people praise, and others criticize, him. On April 26, 1834, Charles Francis Adams entered into his diary, following a reading of Jefferson's letters: "The phrases always appear to outrun the man." On August 19, he added: "You cannot think the man great." On May 23, 1857, T. B. Macaulay wrote H. S. Randall: "I have not a high opinion of Mr. Jefferson. . . . I cannot reckon Jefferson among the benefactors of mankind." Woodrow Wilson was of a different opinion when on April 13, 1916, he stated in Washington: "The immortality of Thomas Jefferson does not lie in any one of his achievements, or in the series of his achievements, but in his attitude towards mankind and the conception which he sought to realize in action of the service owed by America to the rest of the world." But however much Jefferson may be considered good or evil, there exists general agreement as to his love of freedom. When in 1903 Senator George F. Hoar told the Thomas Jefferson Association that Jefferson was an expansionist of freedom, he expressed a general opinion, which can also be seen in President Roosevelt's remarks on April 13, 1943, on occasion of the dedication of the Jefferson Memorial, celebrating the bicentenary of the Virginian's birth: "Today, in the midst of a great war for freedom, we dedicate a shrine to freedom. To Thomas Jefferson, Apostle of Freedom, we are paying a debt long overdue." The words "shrine to freedom" indicate the drive for more and more liberty.

In praise of the dead Caesar, Shakespeare let Anthony say that the evil that men do live after them, whereas the good is often interred with their bones. With Jefferson it has been different. Increasingly, the way he used freedom in an evil way has been ignored, and all the good things he did have been emphasized. In the land of the free, people tend to overlook that liberty also is an ability to do evil. I again and again have been struck by the fact that Americans tend to forgive their countrymen and to forget about their sins. People who have served time in prison are elected to public office, even though it appears to be difficult to get a confirmation by the Senate if there are doubts about a candidate's behavior. So far, no one with a criminal record has resided in the White House, although there was talk about Truman's connection with a shady boss in Kansas City. After Chappaquiddick, one could read that Edward Kennedy cheated on an exam at Harvard—something that did not prevent his election to the Senate. Chappaquiddick eliminated Kennedy as a presidential candidate in 1972, it is true. However, when he announced in 1987 that he would not be a candidate in 1988, the Speaker of the House of Representatives stated that Kennedy would have won the nomination. I do not attribute the willingness to forgive so much to Christian ideas, for their influence has considerably subsided—certainly in the media. I rather attribute it, to a large extent, to the drive for freedom. For forgiving results in liberty, and liberty demands forgiveness.

Jefferson and his ideas are as alive today as they were at the time of the New Deal, when James Truslow Adams published a book with the telling title *The Living Jefferson.* In his introduction to the papers of Jefferson, Julian P. Boyd wrote in 1950 that they should be regarded as the embodiment of the idea of freedom and self-government. Three years later, Caleb Perry Patterson stated: "Wherever man exists and has the aspirations to be free, he derives new hope and inspiration from the political philosophy of Thomas Jefferson" (*The Constitutional Principles of Thomas Jefferson,* p. 62). In 1960, Merrill D. Petersen called Jefferson "freedom's most inspiring American voice." He added: "Into whatever remote niches the historians pursue Jefferson, they help to illuminate the American faith in freedom. Of freedom, Jefferson speaks to the present with the same urgency as to his own time, and with a voice as affirmative as it is authentic. . . . When so many of Jefferson's values have slipped away, he may yet go on vindicating his power in the national life as the heroic voice of imperishable freedoms" (*The Jefferson Image,* pp. 442, 456, 457).

In the subtitle of his volume of a collection of statements by Jefferson, Bernard Mayo in 1970 spoke of "a Many-Sided American." This is correct in a double sense. Jefferson displayed many interests and tried his hand accordingly. On the other hand, he showed himself to be quite unsteady and of so many different sides that he was accused of duplicity. Now it is conceivable that he always desired good and moral things and simply was unable to carry out these desires because he could not stand restrictions on his freedom that might obstruct his pursuit of happiness, with its materialistic overtones; that, wavering back and forth, he again and again took the liberty of succumbing to the temptations of the pursuit of happiness. In that case he basically would have been good and moral even if he was content with just obeying the ethical minimum of the law: an average citizen with above average achievements. However, it also is possible that he wanted to take it easy and for that reason did not recognize imperatives beyond those of the law, especially if his own interests were concerned. In that case his exhortations to obey the demands of morality and of natural law would be nothing but hypocritical tirades perhaps having the purpose of making a good impression on his fellowmen. For we know he cared about the opinion of others. This reveals him as an average politician with obviously great gifts, who wanted to be popular, who knew where the votes were and how the voters must be worked on. Mayo wrote in his introduction that Jefferson wrote his letters "in the warmth and freshness of fact and feeling." Indeed, his letters show the brains and the heart of the man, and it is difficult to find out what comes first. There is a great variety of thoughts. Lincoln was right when he spoke of Jefferson's principles in the plural, principles that "are the definitions and axioms of a free society." A free society is bursting with principles, definitions, and axioms—and seldom are priorities clear. Only the priority of freedom is undisputed.

Whatever kind of a man Jefferson may have been, one thing appears to be certain: his remarks and actions encouraged his countrymen to pick from them whatever appeared opportune for the particular moment. Jefferson's "as I like it" could in a democracy become As We Like It. Thus the ruling majority can be similar to its teacher, Jefferson: it can be basically good and moral and yet succumb to the temptations of the pursuit of happiness and, accordingly, capitulate before uninhibited, easy, smooth, and often ruthless pursuit; it can quite openly and liberally approach pure freedom—without ethical or moral inhibitions. Therefore, everything seems to be possible under popular government in the land of unlimited opportunity, impossible as it may appear from a moral point of view. And this opportunity is likely to increase with the growth of those making up democratic government, that is, with the ruling majority of the voters.

13 From Elitist to Egalitarian Democracy

As popular government, democracy implies the identity of the ruled and the rulers, of all those governed with their government. The sequence of the syllables of the word *democracy* ought not to be overlooked. People come first, rule second. The people as the source of their self-government have primacy. Only then comes the rule derived from the people and legitimized by them. Thus the word *democracy* putting *demos* before *kratia,* is more correct as a symbol than are Lincoln's words at Gettysburg, often considered a definition of democracy. Lincoln, speaking of "government of the people, by the people, for the people," put government ahead of the people. On the other hand, his explanation is right in pointing out that popular government for a long time was captivated by the idea that the government comes before the governed. Furthermore, it expresses the hope that the government of the people will, by the people, govern for the people. Scheidemann's exclamation, "The German Reich is a Republic. State authority emanates from the people," made at the end of World War I, while putting state authority before the people, mentions first of all the republic, a form of government that implies popular government for the sake of the people.

Taking democracy in its literary sense makes any attribute unnecessary, for the word *democracy* clearly states its nature. The adjective *egalitarian* is redundant, because the term *popular government* does not indicate any restriction on the people and comprises all members of the people irrespective of age, sex, and so on, all of whom are equal because of their being part of the people. An elitist democracy is a contradiction in terms, because in it only an elite rules, only part of the whole people, much as such a rule may be based upon the drive for equality.

Democracies as concrete forms of government known to us so far are mere steps toward democracy proper. They show that whereas more and more people participate in the process of government, all of them do not yet do so. Due to various types of restrictions on the suffrage of certain strata of society, that is, due to the denial of the suffrage to some groups, there has not yet existed a democracy proper, that is, a democracy in which all people, without any exception, rule. Until now, democracy always has been something merely hoped for by the people. They have known monarchies and aristocracies and rejected them. Since in contrast to these forms of government democracy has never been totally realized, it supposedly is something better and is adorned with some kind of halo. For what has not been experienced often is aspired to, and what is considered ideal often is more powerful than what is real. However, the nonexistence of democracies proper does not mean that systems of government that have moved toward democracy and today are considered democratic in principle might not prove themselves the way they are and should not be classified as democracies. In the study here presented, I have called these systems democratic, following general practice. Still, I want to draw attention to what I just said. For whenever we speak of concrete democratic governments, seeing them living and working, we must be aware that we are faced not by full-fledged democracies, but by steps toward democracy proper, by mere aspects of democratic evolution.

That evolution demonstrates growing democratizations. In analogy to Kant's remarks on the Enlightenment it may be said that we are not yet living in a democratic age, but in one of democratization. The latter has increasingly moved toward democracy proper, in which all members of society, that is, all people, enjoy an equal right to participate in government. It is not surprising that so far that aim has not been reached. If, as in the great democratic revolutions in England, America, and France, democracy is seen as a means for the extension of the freedom of the individual, if it is realized that it is a long way to absolute freedom, then it will hardly be expected that a perfect democracy has been accomplished. Whatever is not perfect exists because the means for its perfection are not perfect.

The identity of the ruled and their rulers indicates that governing is inherent in those who are governed. However, in view of the fact that such an immanence does not yet totally exist because not all of those ruled can vote, it may be assumed that transcendent conceptions of previous forms of government, forms that were prevalent prior to the process of democratization, are still alive. This is indeed the case. The process of the emancipation of man is a gradual, evolutionary one. Even revolutions cannot get rid of what has been. Just as the concept of God demonstrated God's transcendence vis-à-vis the world, the sovereignty of the absolute monarch in the seventeenth and eighteenth centuries showed its transcendence over the state and its subjects. True, the democratic revolution elevated subjects to citizens. Nevertheless, a certain transcendence remained. It survived not just because many people remained excluded from the suffrage, with the result that new governments, elected by those who could vote, kept possessing transcendence vis-à-vis those who could not vote, so that in practice monarchy was replaced by aristocracy. It also survived because the divine right of kings was replaced by the principle of *vox populi vox Dei,* the political thought of Hobbes by way of Rousseau—the absolute monarch by the absolute *volonté générale,* that democratic deity, the general will.

However, both Hobbes and Rousseau were conscious of the strength of the individual and of his drive for freedom. Hobbes had seen how that drive had brought about a pluralism in which parties and sects and other splinterings of English society moved his country toward anarchy, threatening the nation. The nationalist Rousseau wanted to save France from such a fate. Hobbes tried to counter pluralism with a strong monarchy, Rousseau, with a strong general will, that is, with a strong united society. However, the fact that such a society was composed of many individuals had its consequences. People striving for freedom were not satisfied with the replacement of a transcendent monarchy by a transcendent *volonté générale.* They remained conscious of their own plurality and were interested in breaking up the monism of the general will and to annihilate this fiction in an individualistic manner. Their attempts were crowned by success, for fictions fall prey to realities. What is real in the general will, namely, that will's composition of the wills of a plurality of individuals, became increasingly realized. More and more individuals qua individuals claimed the right to individually codetermine popular government. When during the polemics of the French Revolution against the church as an ally of the monarch, Notre Dame de Paris was made into a temple of reason and reason elevated to the new God, it is not surprising that in the end many people reasoned that in the long run they had, in the service of reason, to liberate themselves from the chains of that fiction called *volonté générale.* The liberation came, although in the beginning the government's transcendence remained to a certain extent even after the liberating democratic revolutions. Descartes wrote Mersenne that a king makes the laws of his realm just as God makes those of nature. To Elizabeth he wrote in September 1646 that God makes those being right whom he gives might. After these revolutions, the lawmakers kept this in mind, and their power had the aura of divine law. Basically, the democratic lawmaker was elitist and still was the one and only *législateur.* Growing democratization has firmly reduced that elitism. However, it has not yet completely liberated itself from it. Democracy has become more egalitarian; it is not yet egalitarian. Democracy has been increasingly approached but not yet reached.

This approach was brought about by extensions of suffrage, coming with the replacement of the transcendent image of democratic government by conceptions of the immanence of individuals. In the course of this development people moved away from Hegel's philosophy of immanence, which retains the concept of God, and attacked belief in God as the clearest expression of government and its unity. Major figures in this struggle were Proudhon, who was under the influence of Comte, German Hegelians of the Left, and Bakunin. Discreditation of the church on account of its alliance with the absolute monarch, as well as of the aristocracy and the bourgeoisie due to their rejection of great art and literature, all contributed to the decline of transcendental beliefs among the educated. One no longer looked for aid from above, but from below. Atheism was advancing; the new immanence, pantheism, approached anarchy. Along with belief in God there was also lost belief in the state as a God-willed institution, even in the republican state. Young Engels wrote that religion and the state were due to humanity's fear of itself (*Schriften der Frühzeit,* ed. G. Mayer, 1920, p. 281). This fear declined with the extension of the suffrage, considered by many a confirmation of the godliness of the voters even in the lower strata of society.

It has been argued that the substitution of republican forms of government for monarchical absolutism elevated subjects to citizens. Actually, it created first- and second-class citizens, full and half citizens, citizens and quasi- or near-citizens. While all inhabitants enjoyed certain rights to be left alone by the government, such as free speech, freedom of religion, freedom of assembly, only part of them had the right to vote and to participate in government. Therefore, the development of popular government tended toward extending suffrage to broader segments of the population in order to make full citizens out of half citizens. The process of democratization is one of naturalization in the sense of citizen-making. Generally speaking, it proceeded from abolition of property qualifications to abolition of education, sex, and age. Given this trend, sooner or later youths and even children will have the right to vote. It will be argued that in democracy proper all the ruled must be rulers and that it cannot be seen why children should not have the same rights that childish old people have.

Minimal as the democratic element may have been in the beginning, it was, above all, the introduction of elections that created modern democracies. In most monarchies, the ruler was not elected. He inherited the throne and ruled, as was often said, by the grace of God, not that of the people. Uniting all power or authority in his hands, he usually stood at the head of a monolithic state in which existing pluralisms, characteristic of all societies, basically were ignored by the ruler. Such pluralisms became reflected in governments upon the introduction of elections—although by no means all of them. The extension of suffrage increased pluralism within the government because a greater number of pluralisms in the population was recognized.

On the whole, this extension probably took place at the cost of rationality. As long as suffrage was restricted to males, its extension from property owners, taxpayers, and educated people to poorer and less educated parts of the population amounted to an increase of the irrational in the democratic process, assuming that the former people usually are more rational than the latter. The meaning of the word *Vermögen* supports this opinion. The increase of the irrational was further aided by extending suffrage to women, if one accepts the widespread opinion that women are more emotional than men. If one further considers the fact that young people are more erratic and less mature than older ones—milder penalties for crimes and prohibitions of alcoholic beverages are indications—another factor favoring irrational behavior is added. The democratization of society seems to be in a reverse relation to its rationalization. It will be argued that with the extension of suffrage to greater parts of the population there came education for more and more people, as desired by Jefferson. Robert M. Hutchins, president of the University of Chicago, countered this argument by saying that education for all is no education at all.

Aside from the extension of suffrage, the process of democratization shows, with a growing recognition of the right of association, a growing number of groups, parties, and other types of association. As early as the second half of the sixteenth century, the English clergyman Richard Hooker regretted the many religious sects that had come about in his country as a result of the Reformation—the importance of which for the democratic process ought not to be overlooked. The English Revolution added quite a few political and other factions, prompting Hobbes to write his *Leviathan,* proposing a strong monarchy for the sake of peace among the subjects and their security from foreign attacks. With the Glorious Revolution, the political philosophy of Locke won out over that of Hobbes, paving the way for new associations.

The situation was similar on the European continent following the revolutions of 1789 and 1848. Originally, the politically relevant groups were the aristocracy and the church. With the emancipation of the third estate, there were formed associations within that estate. In the nineteenth and twentieth centuries, labor organizations were added as well as those of women and youths. They were more liberal and radical than the earlier estates, which had been tied in with the existing order. In contrast to Great Britain, with its two-party system, many parties came into existence on the continent, representing the interests of specific, small groups with an often dogmatic zeal.

Now it is characteristic of democratic development that associations outside political parties were not content with making their wishes known through the media of parties officially represented in government by suggesting to their members what party they should vote for. Since it can be assumed that the necessity for extraparty associations diminishes with the growth in the number of parties, this discontent could be expected to have been larger in Britain, with its two-party system, than on the continent, with its many parties. However, even on the continent extraparty associations have grown, putting parties and governments under pressure.

These groups demonstrate the insatiability of democratization. People no longer are satisfied with a mere extension of the right to vote for parties, with the opening of ever more polling places for ever more voters, with a popular government elected under official rules. In addition, they wish to influence the government in irregular ways, by letting their demands and desires slip through back doors. Such procedures are not incompatible with the democratic process, for in a strict sense, democracy means nothing but popular government. The word says nothing about the workings of that government. It merely indicates government by the whole people without any qualification, that is, equal rule by all. Therefore, it can be argued that democracy is not sufficiently realized as long as it is run just by parties, that party government must be complemented by that of extraparty associations, especially in view of the fact that not all individuals have the right to vote. It can be added that this is especially necessary in countries where there are only a few parties. Furthermore, it can be said that the word *party* is derived from the Latin *pars*, meaning part, and that it cannot be seen why in a democracy only organizations called parties should participate in government, but not other associations. One might go so far as to maintain that a democracy defined as party rule, like that under the Bonn Basic Law, is a contradiction in terms and perhaps not much better than the rule of a single party in a one-party state.

Be this as it may, there can be little doubt that with the extension of suffrage to individual citizens, with the coming of parties and other associations, pluralism in society has grown and become more relevant. Pluralism was promoted by other factors, confirming the rule that the political relevancy of pluralism grows with the diversity within a nation. That relevancy probably is greater in a territory broken up by mountain ranges, such as Switzerland, than in one consisting of a mere plain, such as Holland. It is likely to be greater still in the case of a nation like Germany, partaking of both features. Pluralism will grow with the number of climatic zones, religions, types of employment, and so. Montesquieu, following his compatriot Bodin, dwelt on this in his major work on the spirit of the laws. He also indicated that pluralism would be greater in a federal than in a unitary state.

The outstanding French observer of England wrote about a hundred years before the outstanding French observer of democracy in America, whom he strongly influenced. In his time, there were still the thirteen American colonies, which in many respects already showed a great deal of pluralism. But that pluralism was insignificant compared to the one Tocqueville could observe. And the latter was small in comparison to the one we can see in the United States today. When Tocqueville visited America, it had thirteen million inhabitants. Today, there are a quarter of a billion. There were twenty-four states then. Today, there are fifty. The territory then stretched over 1,753,500 square miles; today, this figure is 3,618,770. These are enormous increases.

As to the broadening of suffrage, that occurring in America was similar to that in other nations. In Tocqueville's time, the individual states no longer had property qualifications. In 1870, the Fifteenth amendment gave blacks the right to vote; in 1920, women received that right under the Nineteenth Amendment; in 1971 it was given to those eighteen years of age under the Twenty-sixth Amendment. In spite of the rather difficult amendment procedure, in all these cases the time from the introduction of the bill to its final passage was relatively short. The amendments were proposed in 1869, 1919, and 1971. Prior to 1971 it occurred only twice that proposals for amendments were ratified the same year, namely, in the cases of the Thirteenth and Twenty-first Amendments. The former abolished slavery in 1865, and the latter, the prohibition of alcoholic beverages in 1933, inviting the sarcastic comment that an amendment to the Constitution took about as long as the opening of a bottle.

The development from a more elitist to a more egalitarian popular government is seen not just with respect to suffrage. It can be observed in other connections, making pluralism ever more relevant. In spite of the transformation of an agrarian society into an industrial society, the two-party system basically survived, with a few exceptions here and there. The programs or platforms of the major parties are not very different. It is as if each of them was afraid of daring too much and to touch a hot iron. Even after considering new issues—usually introduced by more courageous third parties, which on account of that have proven to be short-lived—and incorporating them into their platforms when it no longer appeared dangerous to do so, the principles of the two major parties have continued to be rather similar. They are as comprehensive as they are colorless and quite different from the colorful *variété* of the national party conventions that nominate candidates for the presidency every four years. The basic agreement of America's big parties to a large extent seems to be due to the fact that the American tradition is a liberal one. For among white inhabitants feudalism never existed. Thus juxtapositions such as absolute ruler versus liberal citizen, powerful capitalist versus powerless worker never really came into existence. For a long time, Marx was not listened to because there were labor unions before he spread his doctrines. Basically, everything remained within the scope of liberalism.

However, this does not mean that a great number of variations and variants would not have come about within that scope. In view of the many facets of American liberalism, their coming into existence is not surprising. They are powerful and attempt to exert influence on the local, state, and national levels. With the growing role of the federal government, more and more national headquarters of such pressure groups moved to the national capital, following the march of power to Washington. He who has lived there for some time no longer is surprised to observe the arrival of ever new organizations. In the telephone directory of 1986, I noticed after the words *American Association* the following: of Museums, of Preferred Providers, of University Professors, for Adult and Continuing Education, for Budget and Program Analysis, for Clinical Chemistry, for Continuity of Care, for Counseling and Development, for Dental Research, for Ethiopian Jews, for Higher Education, for Hospital Planning, for International Aging, for Marriage and Family Therapy, for Medical Systems and Information, for the Advancement of Science, for World Health, of Advertising Agencies, of Airport Executives, of Black Women Entrepreneurs, of Blacks in Energy, of Children's Residential Centers. This is only half of those organizations whose names start with "American Association." The list goes on and on. Following American Association of Mental Deficiency and American Association of Teachers of Italian, there come American Astronautical Society, American Astronomical Society, followed by a great many other associations beginning with the word *American*. The American Bar Association, American Federation of Labor, and American Medical Association belong to that group, a group even more numerous than the one beginning with American Association. And the associations mentioned constitute only part of all the others existing in the United States, where the number of parties and other groups relevant to the democratic process is much greater than in other countries, possibly even greater than in all of Europe. I hope that my reference to a telephone directory will not bring upon me the criticism leveled against members of American legislatures who, trying to prevent the passage of laws, exercise their freedom to promote or prevent laws, filibustering by reading such directories. The multiplicity of associations in America impressed Tocqueville. It was small compared to that of today. It is an aspect of the democratization he envisioned.

The question why, next to the extension of suffrage, there came about so many associations relevant to democracy can be answered by saying that the United States fulfills conditions conducive to pluralism. It is a federal state, not a unitary and even less a centralized one. It is a huge federal state with a great number of inhabitants. Switzerland and Germany also are federal. However, their ethnic and geographic diversity lags far behind that of the United States. Where the latter also exists, for instance in Australia and in Canada, the population is much smaller. If one accepts the rule that pluralism grows with the extension of country and its population, then the United States appears as a nation of pluralism *par excellence*.

This impression is strengthened by the fact that America, more than any other nation, is the land of the free and that pluralism is furthered by freedom. In colonial times, Americans basically were free of feudal restrictions. At the end of the age of absolutism they declared their independence in the very year Adam Smith urged the end of mercantilism. After independence, America, promising freedom, became the home of immigrants yearning for freedom, to a larger extent than any other nation. They came from all over the world, brought along their specific characteristics, and made the United States more and more pluralistic. In the land of the free they and their descendants were given the opportunity of driving for ever greater degrees of liberty, together with the rest of the population. In view of these facts, it is not surprising that in the process of democratization, being an aspect of liberalization, there would come about along with political parties a great mass of associations with definite aims, first on local, then on broader, levels. After all, the *Federalist* already had considered "factions" an outstanding feature of the American scene.

All this makes the American development toward egalitarian democracy unique. Nowhere else in the world was the discrepancy between the number of political parties and that of other organizations and pressure groups as great. Nowhere else are the delegates of the official parties worked on, influenced, and tricked by as many unofficial agents. In contrast to nations on the European continent, there is, for party delegates, no imperative mandate. There is not much party solidarity, little party cohesion. A counterpart to the English party whip does not really exist, and delegates usually get away with voting the way they like. Basically, there is no real party line, for party platforms are conglomerations of the most diverse desires and requests, the priorities of which constantly change, as far as the particular party members are concerned. In elections, people vote for a certain candidate rather than a party on both the local and the national levels.

Those elected, who less and less can be said to be the highly selected, find little support from their party organization and always are worked on by pressure groups. Pulled back and forth, they move from one position to another. They often do not even go along with what President Nixon called "the silent majority" but rather follow the loud drums of ever newly emerging agitators and demonstrators. Even those known for their constancy, those elected by an overwhelming majority, at times waver. President Reagan, probably the most popular president since World War II, originally had planned to visit a cemetery of German soldiers killed in that war rather than the site of a former concentration camp. Some organizations protested vehemently: "If he goes to a cemetery, he also must go to a concentration camp!" Reagan agreed to that request. But requests are insatiable. It was now demanded that the president should only visit Bergen-Belsen and skip the visit to the cemetery in Bitburg altogether. The pressure groups succeeded in getting the majority of the House of Representatives to support them. Thereupon, the plan for Bitburg was altered. The visit was limited to a few minutes, and neither national anthem was played during the visit. Under the Twenty-second Amendment, Reagan at that time could not even be reelected. And yet he gave in to pressure. One can well imagine that a president eligible for reelection, especially one not known for his firm attitudes, would have done so even more and virtually succumbed to pressure. Such changes of behavior usually are considered quite normal. They are hardly criticized at all. They are part and parcel of American politics: politics is not only, as Bismarck would have it, the art of the possible; it is to a large extent a way of convenience. In the land of the free, a politician does not lose face by taking the liberty of just doing whatever is opportune at the time. A liberal land is a land of opportunity and thus of opportunism. For the line between opportunity and opportunism is difficult to draw. The similarity of the two words indicates that it is more difficult to draw than the one between genius and insanity mentioned by Nietzsche.

In *The Deadlock of Democracy: Four-party Politics in America,* published the year Kennedy was assassinated, James MacGregor Burns made the point that there actually were four parties in the United States, because the two official parties were divided into two groups each, concentrating on Congress and the White House. Chapter headings speak of "The Splintering of the Parties," "The Pulverization of Party," "The Dilemma of the Democrats," "The Whirlpools of Change," and (thrice) "Which Republican Party?" Furthermore, the dilemma of American party politics is that all parts of both parties are constantly subject to the decisions and influences of a great many pressure groups—to a degree that they perhaps, as so many things in the United States, are "thrown" (in the sense of Heidegger). It is not by chance that it was in America where the discipline of behaviorism, concerned with the behavior of political parties, was created. Given the amazingly high number of groups and associations as well as individuals influencing politics, there came about a great many analysts examining politics on the local, state, and national levels. I have always been impressed by the fact that their analyses differed a great deal even when they observed the same thing. Thus, in spite of the general publicity given to it, American politics, due to its unpredictability, appears highly enigmatic. It can be compared to a sphinx with its smile, which perhaps resembles the grinning of pure liberalism, that deity of the New World in which Americans and their politicians seem to sunbathe in their pursuit of happiness.

Now it cannot well be denied that many things are being held together by patriotism, to which tribute is often paid in more or less serious confessions and lip service. However, it is dubious whether that feeling actually welds together the many parts of the people. Just as individuals think of liberating themselves from the *volonté générale* in their own interest, groups of individuals are likely to entertain similar thought—especially in a liberal society and even more so in one that approaches pure liberalism to a high degree. Democratization thus basically amounts to a growth of the ability to realize one's self. According to Lincoln's famous definition, a government of the people, by the people, may indeed be one of all the people, by all the people—remindful of the general will. More probably it will appear as one of whirlpools making up a pluralism in which everyone individually or with the help of parties or associations or the majority is out to promote his own interests. Everything is likely to turn round the idea "for the people," emphasized as it was by Lincoln. And again, that idea may be interpreted in a singular or pluralistic way, because one does not get around the fact that a people, after all, is composed of many individuals.

In view of the danger that individuals, parties, and associations in the pursuit of happiness may harm the community and lead to disintegration, republican governments have been interested in rationalizing popular government by means of representation. However, the *ratio* of democracy proved to be opposed to thus rationalizing popular government. The first dimension of democratization—extension of popular participation in the political process—increasingly was complemented by a second one: the development from representative to direct democracy.

14 From Representative to Direct Democracy

Assuming that democracy means the identity of rulers and ruled, the question arises whether a representative popular government is a contradiction in terms. Representation obviously differs from presentation. Presentation of a people means its presence at a particular location. By contrast, representation does not mean, as is often believed, that the people meet again at a certain place. Quite to the contrary: it means that they do not meet but prefer to have their delegates or representatives take care of their wishes. The syllable *re* is transformed from its original meaning, *again,* to the different one, *instead.* The actual presence of the people becomes a fiction. And fictions are something merely assumed, supposed, invented. They may be ideal, but they are not real. One arrives at the conclusion that representation amounts to falsification, that representative democracy is a falsified democracy, not a real one.

When the concept of democracy came into existence in ancient Greece, it was understood to mean the assembly of the city-state's citizens for government purposes, that is, direct, immediate, popular government, an undisputed identity of citizens and rulers. Similar democracies still exist today in Swiss *Landsgemeinden* and New England town meetings. Rousseau observed this kind of government in his home state of Geneva. He saw in it the only true popular government, and he opposed representation (*Contrat social,* bk. 3, chap. 15). Without doubt he was right. Representatives, being mere delegates of the people, are less likely to express the real intentions of the people as a plurality of persons than representatives of a particular individual or firm will be able to stand in for their respective employers. Yet even a provision like that of the German Civil Code, according to which those represented are bound by the acts of those representing them, is not without risk, even though it can be assumed that the representative will act in the interest of the ones he represents, especially in case he represents just one natural or juristic person. The number of those represented increases the probability of misrepresentation. This means that representative democracy is a pseudodemocracy because the representatives of the people are unable to exactly express the will of all those they represent. Even with all good will—and it is open to doubt whether this can be expected from politicians—it is not possible for a representative to truly represent the wishes of as few as ten or even less people, to say nothing of a hundred, a thousand, or still more. He could not do so even in case of the imperative mandate.

Although representative democracy is not a real popular government because there is no identity of the rulers and the ruled, it can, from the democratic point of view, be defended. It can be argued that when in the word *democracy* the concept of the people precedes that of government, this is merely a matter of linguistic formulation. In substance, the adjective *popular* is subordinated to its subject, *government*. In view of the importance of the people, the important thing is that it governs. This presupposes its ability to govern, to rule people. And the possibility of popular government points to its effectiveness. In order to have an effective popular government, there must be a popular government that can effectively rule the people. Since, however, a direct rule by numerous people hardly is possible, one must put up with an indirect, representative government. In order to secure government by the people, direct democracy must, for practical reasons, be sacrificed to representative democracy. What is right in theory does not necessarily work in practice. Much as direct democracy may be desirable from a theoretical point of view, it cannot, like many other desired ideals, be realized. It may thus be argued that for practical reasons the ratio of democracy itself demands a curtailment of direct popular government by a representative one—that the people must pay that price for their own self-government in order that the latter be effective. Direct democracy is, so to speak, rationed insofar as the people rule in rations of themselves, namely, their representatives. The rationing of the people by their representatives can be seen as a rationalization of democracy for the sake of the realization of democracy. For instance, it is not possible that ten thousand people be ruled by ten thousand people. When in the United States there is talk of the upper ten thousand as the virtual government of America, one has in mind the regiment of these relatively few over the whole, much larger, population, not just over themselves. However, even a ration of ten thousand men and women ruling over a quarter of a billion people does not appear practicable. A rule by one hundred families (of which one has spoken in the case of Peru) would appear to be more practicable. At any rate, in most democracies the number of elected representatives is lower than a thousand. The word *regiment* is similar to *rex*. Elected representatives constitute the rule of one or a few over more or many, whatever the proportions may be in any particular case.

Representation is more than just a means for the realization of effective popular government. It has been asserted that representation rationalizes democracy because representatives constitute a representable elite thinking and acting more rationally than the people. Indeed, we think of someone who represents something as of someone blessed with rank, that is, one who enjoys greater status and prestige than those he represents—someone who is better than they are. He is the presentable, admirable representative, the pride of those he represents. Representation is here not understood in the sense of commercial business—a commercial agent seldom is called a representative—but in a more elevated social one, implying refined society manners. It can be considered the price society is willing to pay for an effective rational government. The ratio of representation appears as a rationalization of democracy due to its refinement of public opinion.

Edmund Burke's words in a speech of 1774, addressing electors at Bristol, are well known: "Certainly, gentlemen, it ought to be the happiness and glory of a representative, to live in the strictest union, the closest correspondence, and the most unreserved communication with his constituents. Their wishes ought to have great weight with him; their opinion high respect; their business unremitted attention. . . . But his unbiased opinion, his mature judgment, his enlightened conscience, he ought not to sacrifice to you, to any man, or to any set of men living. These he does not derive from your pleasure; no, nor from the law and the constitution. They are a trust from Providence, for the abuse of which he is deeply answerable." According to Burke, a representative of the people has the duty to freely and conscientiously exercise his office to the best of his ability. He does not fulfill that obligation if he acts contrary to his conviction in order to please his constituents or others. In a speech prior to the elections in Bristol, made in 1780, Burke answered in the negative the question as to whether, if elected to Parliament, he would execute the wishes of his voters. Referring to his opponent for the seat, he stated: "My worthy colleague says, his will ought to be subservient to yours. If that be all, the thing is innocent. If government were a matter of will upon any side, yours, without question, ought to be superior. But government and legislation are matters of reason and judgment, and not of inclination; and what sort of reason is that, in which the determination precedes the discussion; in which one set of men deliberate, and another decide? . . . To deliver an opinion is the right of all men; that of constituents is a weighty and respectable opinion, which a representative ought always to rejoice to hear; and which he ought always most seriously to consider. But *authoritative* instructions; *mandates* issued, which the member is bound blindly and explicitly to obey, to vote and to argue for, though contrary to the clearest conviction of his judgment and conscience; these are things utterly unknown to the laws of this land, and which arise from a fundamental mistake of the whole order and tenor of our constitution. Parliament is not a *congress* of ambassadors from different and hostile interests; which interests each must maintain, as an agent and advocate, against other agents and advocates; but parliament is a *deliberative* assembly of *one* nation, with *one* interest, that of the whole; where not local purposes, not local prejudices ought to guide, but the general good."

As did Hooker and Hobbes before him, Burke tried to prevent a growing disintegration of his country on account of local interests. He obviously saw the evil potential of liberal factions and desired to keep them limited with the help of the greater rational judgment of elected representatives of the people. The elitism he attributed to his parliamentarians is especially remarkable on account of the fact that then only a small percentage of the people had the right to be represented. This did not worry Burke at all. According to him, only those who stood out due to their ability and possessions were supposed to vote and be represented in Parliament by those whom they had elected, who also represented those without suffrage. In 1792, Burke, in a letter to Sir Hercules Langrishe, distinguished "virtual" from "actual" representation, clearly coming out in favor of the former. He saw in virtual representatives "a communion of interests, and a sympathy in feelings and desires between those who act in the name of any description of people and the people in whose name they act, though the trustees are not chosen by them." For Burke, representation rationalizes popular government in two ways: those unable to vote are virtually represented by those who can vote, whose representatives in turn are, for the sake of the nation, subject only to their conscience and sound judgment. In view of the fact that *representare* means to make present what actually is absent, Burke's double dimension of representation appears to be quite justified. Two guarantees are better than just one.

Burke's ideas, supposed to rationalize popular government, actually are opposed to democracy. If it is assumed that property owners are more rational than have-nots, and British estate holders, more than people with fewer possessions, a virtual representation of the latter by the former indeed seems to be more rational than the representation of all by virtue of elections in which all may participate. If, furthermore, it is assumed that those elected to be representatives judge and act more rationally than their constituents, then the absence of the imperative mandate must appear as something rational indeed. On the other hand, Burke's kind of representation is incompatible with democracy. This is obvious with respect to virtual representation. If a large part of the population cannot vote, it is, as Burke admits, actually not represented. As to the representation of voters without an imperative mandate, they are not really truly represented, much as they may be represented in a refined way. All this proves that Rousseau was right when he maintained that representation means a falsification of the popular will. A refinement of the people's interests and desires amounts to its falsification, good as it may be considered. For like freedom, falsifications exist for good and evil.

Since in the last analysis democracy means rule by the whole people and since representation curtails that rule, it appears natural that with growing democratization and approaches to unlimited democracy, curtailments of democracy by representations would be considered as untenable as, for instance, those of limited suffrage. Therefore, with extension of suffrage, Burke's idea of virtual representation was increasingly rejected, much as it still exists on a small scale as a result of remaining restrictions of suffrage. Likewise, the absence of an imperative mandate was increasingly viewed as undemocratic. In practice, Burke's concept thus turned out to be a dream. By his time it was obvious that most members of Parliament were doing what the members of the landed aristocracy wanted them to do. The latter did not even have to make their desires explicit. Their representatives in Parliament sensed them. In our century, Robert de Jouvenel was not wrong when he remarked that the members of the legislature cared, above all, about getting reelected (*La république des camarades*, 1914, p. 22). It also is open to doubt whether or not the representatives of the people are really more rational than those they represent. One need think only of the fact that successful businessmen, whose ability to think rationally hardly can be doubted and who often are more reasonable than politicians, usually refrain from entering politics. But even if representatives were more rational than those they represent, there would remain the question whether Burke's argument is not based upon the wrong assumption that political decisions are rational. Actually, they often are not, certainly not predominantly. And finally, there is the problem whether or not it is admissible from a democratic point of view to go about rationalizing the desires and interests of the people. For this could amount to weakening or falsifying them, to a disregard or neglect of emotions. Thus it is not surprising that in the process of democratization, characteristic of democracies, one dimension of that process—extension of suffrage—was supplemented by another one, namely, the development from representative to direct democracy.

Early under the Swiss constitution of 1848 there spread in the various cantons the quest for direct democracy in the form of initiative and referendum. In the 1860s that quest became so common that the general revision of the constitution in 1874 provided for these institutions on the national level. Given this trend from representative to direct popular government, it obviously was felt that concessions to the latter were right and required by the democratic principle. If all this happened in a small country like Switzerland, where, especially in the small cantons, the representatives of the people were pretty close to their constituents, it was, a fortiori, likely to occur in bigger nations, where the distance between representatives and those represented was much greater and where the former often were hardly known to the latter. Following Napoleon I, who in his youth was an enthusiastic admirer of Rousseau, saw himself as the executor of the *volonté générale* and loved plebiscites, the French constitutions made after World War II acknowledge the referendum. The constitution originally planned for the Fourth Republic, providing for a one-chamber legislature, was rejected in a referendum. The constitutions of the Fourth and Fifth Republics were accepted by a referendum. President de Gaulle often made use of the plebiscite. Following his proposal, a plebiscite in 1962 introduced the direct election of the French president, who under the Third and Fourth Republics was elected by the legislature and, in the beginning of the Fifth Republic, by an ad hoc electoral college. The Weimar constitution and the Bonn Basic Law provide for initiative and referendum in certain cases. These institutions of direct democracy, together with that of recall, also exist in the United States.

The fact that in America there was added the institution of recall, which has been used frequently, prompts the question whether in the United States the inclination toward direct democracy is especially great. The recall not only adds to the methods of this type of popular government, it goes further than initiative and referendum. The latter bring about laws. They take time, for the legislative process is a slow one. A recall does not take so much time. It makes elected officials—including judges—dependent upon the grace of the people even before their term is up. Great concession indeed to the idea and practice of direct democracy!

Emphasis upon that form of government existed early in America. The colonists rejected virtual representation, thus taking a clear position against a dimension of representation favored by Burke, one the British put up with for a long time. After independence, it was an American state, Massachusetts, that held a referendum for the first time—in 1778, years before it was used in France and Switzerland.

In tune with the revolutionary slogan No Taxation without Representation, the constitutions of the newly independent states provided for representative governments. Still, the practice soon showed that the representatives of the people, close as they were to the voters, were strongly influenced by them. This flirtation with direct democracy contributed to the desire for a new Constitution, creating a more perfect Union, one that saw to it that all the states had a representative form of government. Article 4 prescribes "a republican form of government," the term *republican* being understood to mean representative. It was contrasted to *democratic,* implying direct democracy.

In essay 10 of the *Federalist,* Madison defined "a pure democracy" as "a society consisting of a small number of citizens, who assemble and administer the government in person." A "republic," on the other hand, is "a government in which the scheme of representation takes place." He continued: "The two great points of difference between a democracy and a republic are: first, the delegation of the government, in the latter, to a small number of citizens elected by the rest; secondly, the greater number of citizens, and greater sphere of country, over which the latter may be extended. The effect of the first difference is, on the one hand, to refine and enlarge the public views, by passing them through the medium of a chosen body of citizens, whose wisdom may best discern the true interest of their country, and whose patriotism and love of justice will be least likely to sacrifice it to temporary or partial considerations. Under such a regulation, it may well happen that the public voice, pronounced by the representatives of the people, will be more consonant to the public good than if pronounced by the people themselves, convened for the purpose." Madison explained why the representatives in a large republic are likely to be of a higher caliber than those in a small one: more voters have a greater choice and thus a better chance to elect highly qualified delegates.

Madison expressed ideas similar to those of his contemporary Burke. He hoped for a rationalization and a refinement of popular government by means of representation. However, he also voiced doubts about that mode of governing. He spoke of the "scheme of representation." A scheme reminds one of intrigue. And he became more outspoken when, following the quotation just given, he wrote that the effect of representation "may be inverted. Men of factious tempers, of local prejudices, or of sinister designs, may, by intrigue, by corruption, or by other means, first obtain the suffrages, and then betray the interests, of the people." In other words, the idea of representing the people is a good one. The probability of first-rate representatives grows with the size of the republic. But the representatives can also be evil fellows who betray the interests of the people, and even the large size of a republic does not preclude that possibility. To his praise of representation Madison added his warning—in the same paragraph, so to speak, in one breath. The opinion of the father of the American Constitution on the value of representation is somewhat ambiguous.

Madison's warning did not go unnoticed. Representatives of the people "may . . . first obtain the suffrages, and then betray the interests, of the people." The people come first, and only then come their representatives. This is important. A refinement of public opinion through representatives for the sake of the public well-being is desirable. A betrayal by representatives of the people must be condemned. Clever, shrewd and rational as the representatives may be, the people come first. Madison's compatriots always kept that in mind. They always have been skeptical about their representatives in the government. Therefore, it is not surprising that, after Switzerland demonstrated how representative systems could be complemented by modern institutions of direct democracy, they set out to do likewise. From the beginning of the twentieth century, more and more states and communities tried to protect their people from corrupt politicians and their machines by means of popular initiative, referendum, and recall. There is general agreement that these institutions were primarily seen as means for correcting the abuses and inefficiencies of representatives. This attitude has not changed to this day. Politicians still are viewed with caution. Decent people stay away from them. The expression "it's politics" has a peculiar ring to it. It probably is telling that an experienced observer of American politics, James MacGregor Burns, at the beginning of the volume mentioned, wrote that "politics has not engaged the best of us, or at least the best in us." He added: "Anyone active in everyday politics knows of concerned, civic-minded people who give hundreds of hours and dollars to fund drives, the Red Cross and other worthy local causes but will have nothing to do with politics." He mentioned the "politics of the cave." That is a far cry from the politics of those heights conceived by Burke's and Madison's hopes for representation. Given the many serious disappointments of the people in their representatives, it was only natural that they increasingly should look for aspects of direct democracy as remedies. In most of the states, constitutional amendments today must be approved by plebiscites. The same is true, in many states, of the enactment of ordinary laws and communal rules and regulations.

The introduction of democratic means such as the initiative, referendum, and recall soon met with resistance. It was argued that they were not compatible with the provision of the Constitution guaranteeing to all states a republican form of government. This argument was not without foundation. As was said, republican government originally meant representative government, in contrast to democracy, meaning direct popular government. Furthermore, the Constitution was made as a reaction to democratic excesses in the states. However, the drive toward democracy is powerful and can hardly be checked. In 1912, the Supreme Court, in *Pacific States Tel. and Tel. Co. v. Oregon,* decided that significant additions of institutions of direct democracy did not make states unrepublican. It thus went along with democratization and provided another example of not shying away from adjusting the Constitution to popular desires, rather than defending the supreme law against such desires.

In contrast to state constitutions, the federal Constitution does not mention initiative, referendum, and recall. However, this does not mean that on the national level important concessions to direct democracy would not have been made. The decision just mentioned shows that the United States no longer guarantees representative government to the states the way it used to. In 1913, the Seventeenth Amendment to the Constitution transferred the election of United States senators from the state legislatures to the people of the state. Only formally is the president still elected by the electoral college. Since the introduction of the direct ballot, he has practically been chosen directly by the people in the various states. These examples show how aspects of representation were eliminated. The general trend seems to be obvious: replacement of representative popular government by a direct one.

This trend did not just exist officially. It has been obvious for a long time that, in spite of all emphasis upon the absence of an imperative mandate, representatives to a large extent listen to their constituents and primarily think of their reelection. When in 1952 I attended Harvard, my eye was caught by campaign posters showing John F. Kennedy with the caption, He Will Do More for Massachusetts—more than his opponent, Senator Lodge, who for some time had engaged himself in the national interest. Later on, when during the Kennedy administration John's brother Edward was running for the Senate, word was spread that, if elected, he could do more for Massachusetts. Edward also was elected and reelected. These are only two instances showing the dependence of representatives upon their parties and the different pressure groups in their respective electoral districts and how they permit themselves to be influenced by the desires of the voters.

And then there is the enormous influence the media, at the prompting of individuals, parties, and associations, or out of their own interest, have on the representatives of the people, especially if they belong to the ruling party. That influence is great even if it does not reflect the opinion of the majority. It is even greater if it does, carrying along (or seeming to do so) the masses. Elected representatives of the people waver to and fro in order to please their voters. They seldom seem to overcome their egos by asserting themselves vis-à-vis their constituents. The few American politicians who succeeded in doing so were honored in John F. Kennedy's *Profiles of Courage* (1956). Again, Reagan's visit to Bitburg in May 1985 comes to mind. In *Essays in the Public Philosophy,* Walter Lippmann wrote: "The unhappy truth is that the prevailing public opinion has been destructively wrong at the critical junctures. The people have imposed a veto upon the judgments of informed and responsible individuals. They have compelled the governments, which usually knew what would have been wiser" (p. 19f.).

Such warnings changed little in the American development from representative to direct democracy, an aspect of democratization that has been proceeding under the aegis of pure liberalism, as if driven by an invisible hand. In his reflections on the French Revolution, Burke sharply criticized the democratic trends of that revolution, hoping they could be undone. By contrast, Kant, who admired Rousseau and, similar to Madison, rejected democracy and advocated republican government, wrote in *Der Streit der Fakultäten* that the French Revolution was an event that could never be forgotten. The arguments of the father of that revolution against representation also were not forgotten. They have been clearly advancing compared to those of Burke and Madison, favoring representative popular government.

Having mentioned Rousseau and the French Revolution, we think of a third dimension of democratization, namely, the development from limited to unlimited popular government.

15 From Limited to Unlimited Democracy

Democratizations prove the incompleteness of democracy, for a complete democracy can no longer be democratized. Every kind of democratization demonstrates a move from limited to unlimited popular government, for the purpose of democratization is to reduce and abolish limitations on democracy. A broadening of democracy presupposes curtailments on democracy. The achievement of unlimited popular government makes democratization unnecessary; it loses its rationale. We do not know whether democratization will ever achieve its end, much as its aspirations to do so seem to be obvious. Trends prove that something is not yet achieved. People have complained that democracy has been pushed too far. Actually, total popular government is still quite distant. This does not mean that forms of government that today are generally known as democracies, could not already have gone far toward the democratic or that one could not be concerned with their actual existence and their potential.

Developments from an elitist to an egalitarian, from a representative to a direct democracy, running parallel as parts of the process of democratization, demonstrate the progression from limited to unlimited popular government. An elitist democracy, limiting the right to participate in government to a small part of the population, is more limited than one extending that right to larger segments of the population. Similarly, direct democracy, on account of its greater immediacy is less limited than a representative one, for representation means limitation of the will of the people, be it for good or evil. All these developments show approaches to complete democracy. Therefore, they could easily be dealt with under the heading "From Limited to Unlimited Democracy." I have dealt with them in the preceding chapters under the titles "From Elitist to Egalitarian Democracy" and "From Representative to Direct Democracy." I did so because, under these titles, quantitative elements of the right to participate in government stand in the foreground and because they can, accordingly, be easily subsumed under the general title "From Limited to Unlimited Democracy."

Under that title, a rather qualitative dimension of democracy can be discussed, one concerned with the acting rather than the being of popular government, one considering popular government not so much from the point of view of its basis, but rather from that of its organization or want of organization, its workings, its function, its possibilities, and its impossibilities. It does not ask how many people participate in government and what the nature of this participation is, whether it is direct or indirect. It asks how this kind of rule manifests itself, how far it goes. So far, I have examined ways toward democracy. Now I want to show what roads were taken under this form of government, as it has been realized so far—or under its name, and what roads could be taken, either openly or clandestinely.

I start with the word *democracy*, for in the beginning was the word. The word is likely to give the best indication of what it means. I will show what active people have made of democracy and what they can make of it. Democracy is more problematic than aristocracy and monarchy. The latter can simply be explained as the rule of one called a monarch. An explanation of aristocracy is more difficult. A class rules in its plurality. One can speak of either a singularistic and a pluralistic concept of aristocracy. Under the former, aristocracy can be seen as a collective leadership, a closed unit vis-à-vis the governed. The senate of a hanseatic city is an example. Under the pluralistic concept, the aristocracy does not pose as a concrete, closed unit. It is not seen and respected as such. It is, due to its being composed of several people, split. Members try to get the upper hand over other members. Disintegrating features appear, weakening the rule of the privileged class over the numerically greater and broader mass of the people. Examples such as the Holy Roman Empire and Poland come to mind.

In the case of democracy, everything is still more problematic. It is, as far as its rule is concerned, more pluralistic than aristocracy. With increasing democratization, its pluralism is likely to grow. As long as property owners ruled in it, it came close to aristocracy. Its major difference from hereditary aristocracy was that the latter would be rejected and replaced by what, with different emphases, has been called natural aristocracy, from which aristocrats on account of birth were increasingly excluded. In his appeal from the Old to the New Whigs, Burke included among natural aristocrats all people of means. He thought of the English landed nobility, which had a great deal of leisure, was educated, and lived by the principle of noblesse oblige; he thought also of jurists, scientists, artists, and merchants whose successes demonstrated that they were clever, diligent, law-abiding, and constant. Burke's American contemporary Jefferson praised the natural aristocracy on October 28, 1814, in a letter to John Adams. To him, aristocrats of birth and riches belonged to an "artificial aristocracy," one without virtue and talent, although he conceded that if these people had virtue and talents, they would qualify as natural aristocrats. Thus with Burke the artificial aristocracy was complemented by the natural one. In the opinion of Jefferson, it was pushed aside by it. As a result of the march of democracy and the elimination of property qualifications for the right to vote, the distance between democracy and aristocracy in the traditional sense grew. Democracy became more pluralistic, and this trend was supported by additional extensions of the right of the people to participate in government. The fact that in modern democracies there still exist leading elites does not disprove this development. For these elites are elites on account of achievement and thus differ from artificial aristocracies. In the latter there existed, in spite of quarrels among the aristocrats, a greater *corps d'esprit,* a greater cohesion than in modern democratic elites, because the former, as they became ever more anachronistic, increasingly felt on the defensive against the rising popular government. Democracy's elites-through-achievement, those natural aristocrats, show less cohesion. Their members are aggressive in pursuing their own interests. Their will to succeed, to ever growing success, is not conducive to such cohesion, for each individual will consider it aristocratic to be better than other natural aristocrats and to be ahead of them. By their very nature, democracies are pluralistic.

The pluralism of a form of government decreases the probability of its effectiveness. Therefore, this probability must be the smallest in the case of the most pluralistic of all forms of government, democracy. Consequently, people have looked for ways and means to restrain pluralism in order to secure the quality of democracy as a government. Limitations on suffrage and the institution of representation are some of them. However, as a result of developments toward egalitarian and direct democracy, both were reduced. In order to secure an effective government by the people, there was an attempt to arrive at a singularistic concept of democracy and, by a *tour de force,* to remodel pluralistic democracy.

Rousseau thought of the *volonté générale,* which he distinguished from the will of all. One may see in the former something objective corresponding to the general interest, the subjective element of will, the voice of reason, an organism thinking of its own well-being; all these cases, the invention of the great apostle of popular government, who rejected representation as a falsification of the sovereignty of the people, can be said to indicate the singularistic concept of democracy. Liberals, seeing in democracy a means for liberation, may have doubts about Rousseau's ideas, made in connection with the *volonté générale,* that the individual should not care so much about his own interests but rather think of the good of society; that he could be forced to be free. Other liberals will find those ideas quite appealing: if people feel thrown, lonely, and lost in society, they will attempt to improve their lot with the help of society. They will try to satisfy their egoism by arranging themselves within the general will. For that purpose, they will not mind involuntarily participating in that will, imposing it upon others under more or less hypocritical assertions, in order to liberate themselves. The *volonté générale* is the General Will, the General Will of the people. His orders are not subject to criticism. He can force individuals to accept his concept of liberty and to liberate them in the sense of that concept. Those following him, executing his orders, those going along, will force those who refuse to go along to do so under the parole, "If you don't want to be my brother, I'll smash your skull!" From the point of view of pure liberalism, such behavior cannot be objected to. For pure liberalism approves of all means serving at any one moment the desires of an individual, even if they hurt others.

The many possibilities of interpreting Rousseau's *volonté générale* did not harm the desire for a singularistic concept of democracy, for they left little doubt about the sovereignty of the people and its monism. The latter created a myth of the total rule by the people, a rule that on account of various interpretations of the *volonté générale* became enshrouded by a certain mysticism, something that strongly fascinated humanity. It led to people's seeing in the *volonté générale* the desired effective popular government, much to the encouragement of all those who desperately asked themselves whether, in view of a democratic pluralism tending toward disintegration, such a government was possible at all. Thus one could hope for a realization of a true sovereignty of the people, even if it was in the distant future and might never be achieved. Realizations of ideals are rare, and realistic advocates of democracy soon realized that, in order to make an effective rule by the people possible, one had to be content with a form of government that could be realized more easily than that of the general will. They settled for majority rule.

The ideal of the father of the French Revolution was considered perfect by many, as were many things that occurred in that event—to the disgust not only of Burke. John Locke, the outstanding liberal thinker in a nation known for its practical outlook, a nation whose liberty was admired by Montesquieu, offered a more down-to-earth plan, which could be realized more easily. In his second treatise on civil government, Locke identified popular government with majority rule. For the purpose of an effective popular government, he proposed the equation, *people = majority of the people.* In chapter 10, central to the nineteen chapters and thus perhaps the most important one for Locke, around which the rest turn, we read at the beginning: "The majority having, as has been shown, upon men's first uniting into society, the whole power of the community, naturally in them, may employ all that power in making laws for the community from time to time, and executing those laws by officers of their own appointing; and then the *form* of the government is a perfect *Democracy.*" Locke continued, saying that the majority may put the power of making laws in the hands of a few or of one and thus, just as it pleases, erect any form of government. Locke therefore identified majority and community. He made plain that every legitimate government, be it that of the majority, the few, or one, has its source in the community, respectively, its majority. He thus took popular government as a starting point, irrespective of its being run by one, a few, or the majority. Yet to him, only majority rule was a perfect democracy. It can be concluded that for Locke other forms of government, deriving their legality from the people, were also democracies, although not perfect ones. The defender of the Glorious Revolution, who is often considered the father of modern liberalism, left no doubt that to him popular government was the best means for the protection of the individual. In tune with that opinion, he considered the legislature, usually evaluated as the most democratic of the branches of government, the supreme power.

Locke, who lived a generation after Hobbes, did not try to solve the problems deriving from the pluralistic nature of popular government by taking recourse to monarchy. He did so in a democratic manner, by transforming the pluralistic concept of democracy into a singularistic one and by enabling the majority to operate effectively. Now, every government operation results in restrictions on those governed, for rule always implies restrictions on the ruled. In order to alleviate such restrictions and to make them bearable, limitations upon governments are necessary. Locke was well aware of that. While he made plain that the popular government he proposed possessed the quality of a government, ruling as it did as one united body even though the people were constituted of a great many individuals, he took care to prevent despotism. He divided governmental power into different branches and emphasized that the people, full of confidence in the government, entrusted the protection of their rights to it, considering that protection the purpose of government. Locke's position became reflected in William Blackstone's *Commentaries on the Laws of England,* which stated that Parliament had to respect the rights of the individual even though there was no governmental power above it. Montesquieu, who visited England at that time and was impressed by the liberty the English enjoyed, attributed this fact to the separation of powers and their checks and balances. The ideas of the authors just mentioned were shared by others who hoped that democracy and majority rule would secure the rights of man. That hope led to the great liberal democratic revolutions.

On the other hand, individuals could look for cover in the majority for acts they were unable, or did not dare, to do by themselves. They could attempt to indulge in their desires with the help of the majority and to extend their liberties with that help—even at a cost to others. To that end, they could follow a demagogue, submitting themselves to him in such a way that he could make himself a despot supported by the majority. For just as demagoguery is not far from democracy, the despot is not far from the demagogue. Thus majority rule may evolve from a limited to an unlimited one. This approaches the democratic equivalent of absolute monarchy, attacked by democratic revolutions, and arrives at democratic absolutism—at the despotism of the majority of the people. Now a ruler interested in taking the liberty to do whatever he pleases will want to do away with restrictions such as separation of powers and judicial review, because they are likely to slow down or even prevent his activities. Should he still think of human rights, he will attempt to interpret them his own way, going so far as to interpret them away. Those belonging to the majority will, out of egoism, go along, be it as agitators or just as more or less disturbed followers. Being liberals, they need not be ashamed of their attitude. Their behavior is quite compatible with pure liberalism, for that liberalism permits the individual to do everything that appears to him conducive to the extension of his liberties, irrespective of whether his desires are of an ideal or a material nature or of any other kind promising to make him feel freer, of whether new liberties bring about good or evil.

Just as pure liberalism may thrive under limited and unlimited majority rule, it may do so under those who reject that kind of rule. Many among those who go along with despots supported by the majority, who follow the masses, will ask themselves whether they can do so with a good conscience. Going along may be convenient for the time being but will not satisfy in the long run. A collaboration is about as problematic as a *codominium* or a *coimperium*. The temptation of getting something as part of the majority may be great indeed. Still, many people will not feel particularly happy in such a situation and not quite free even in the absence of scruples with respect to their taking part in the majority's oppression of the minority. Others may well have such scruples and for that reason attempt to seek distance from the majority. The range of liberals is big. Many of them detest the oppression of others, especially by the masses. Their motto is Freedom with Measure. And if even members of the majority entertain doubts about the potential oppression by the majority, such doubts can be expected a fortiori with those who do not belong to the majority and even feel oppressed by it. They will fight being imposed upon by the majority because they will consider the majority about as oppressive as a monarch, not to mention the combination of both, of which we have become aware in the twentieth century.

Such a resistance is conceivable in spite of a recognition of the principle of majority rule, for example, when recourse can be had to human rights guaranteed by a constitution; when the ruling majority permits free elections and shows a willingness to give up power in favor of a new majority that includes the previous minority. Under liberal constitutional government, minorities are a potential majority. However, majority government may well come under attack. This can be expected if it eliminates and even liquidates the minority, as the Bolsheviks did with the Mensheviks—the translation of these words is *majority* and *minority,* respectively. It can also be expected if the ruling majority refuses to jeopardize its dominance by refusing free elections or by falsifying elections, as occurred under Napoleon and Hitler. People may reject majority rule even under a constitution that prescribes free and regular elections and provides for far-reaching human rights. This was demonstrated not too long ago in so-called extraparliamentary oppositions, which were believed to have approached terrorism. Such oppositions were defended on the ground that regular parliamentary oppositions were too much part of the Establishment and thus no longer fought for freedom from majoritarianism.

It has been argued that majority rule is not genuinely democratic because the majority is, after all, not the whole people, especially if represented by delegates. It has been added that Locke's system is a n makeshift solution, a practical but a weak ersatz for Rousseau's *vol générale.* It can also be maintained that a singularistic concept of people is a contradiction in terms, that the transformation of people one unit is artificial and false, that something by its very nature plural cannot be singularistic. Finally, it may be said that democracy as a f of government necessarily implies restrictions on the individual's lib even though, under that form, protection of the individual can be pected and hoped for.

From the point of view of pure liberalism, the individual may re democracy as much as any other rule, because it constitutes, after a government, and the liberal resents being governed. Locke, favoring resentative majority rule, and Rousseau, favoring direct rule by the eral will, both believed that the government they suggested was cor cive to freedom. On the other hand, it can be pointed out that so fa democracies, be they approaching rule by the *volonté générale* or by majority, always have restricted the freedom of individuals. If one con ers democracy a means of liberalism, one will be inclined to consider pure democracy a means of pure liberalism. In that case, Rousseau, favoring the general will and direct popular government, will be preferred to Locke and his representative majority rule. Rousseau, then, would appear to be the titan amusing himself with the petty suggestions of Locke and being sure of his final victory over the Englishman.

Yet in view of the fact that democracy, reflecting the rule of the general will, that of the majority, restricts the behavior of individuals, and that from the standpoint of pure liberalism all restrictions of individuals are illiberal, one can go so far as to maintain that no democracy, thus understood, can really be a genuine democracy. For it will be argued that genuine democracy is of necessity rule by the people in their plurality and that, therefore, it is not feasible to make something singular out of them by means of such singularistic concepts as *volonté générale* and majority rule, in order to make the people an effective ruler. Such an artificial procedure of making democracy effective, it will be argued, is in practice likely to make it ineffective because people actually can rule only if each one of them can behave as he pleases without giving any consideration to others. Democracy thus appears as a state of nature, which can, but need not, be a war of all against all. In such a state of affairs, people have what Kant called wild freedom, which corresponds to the definition that slipped from the pen of the famous English liberal John Stuart Mill because it was obviously unavoidable, namely, "liberty consists in doing what one desires," that is, without any inhibition or restriction. The General Will is within every individual, exclusively within him alone. And just as Rousseau lurks behind Locke in order to finally kill him off, there are behind these two, waiting more or less patiently for their hour to arrive, Bakunin and Max Stirner, longing impatiently to realize, in the name of liberty, anarchy as the only true and genuine popular government.

For the promotion of freedom, democracy offers to the people many possibilities of ruling. But of which there is much, there will be little that is excellent, and plenty of what is cheap and common. The English word *vile* comes to mind, derived from the Latin *vilis,* which means cheap, common. Given the similarity of the word with the German *viel,* meaning much, the comparison seems appropriate. Now, the word *common* does not just mean bad, for otherwise the community of Plato's beloved *polis* would be something bad. *Common* can also imply what is common to all, as in the case of the common law, a law common to all of England. It can point to the community. Similarly, *cheap* is not necessarily *bad;* it can also be used in the sense of *right.* When the Germans say something is *recht und billig* (right and cheap), they mean it is right, good, worth its price, because it enjoys recognition in the community. On the other hand, the Germans say something is *recht und schlecht*—right and bad. And in view of the fact that freedom is an ability to do good and evil, "ein Vermögen des Guten und des Bösen," according to Schelling, to do what is *recht* and what is *schlecht,* it can be expected that popular government, being a means for the promotion of liberty, will secure the latter in a manner that is both *recht und billig* and *recht und schlecht.* And the people will decide what is *recht und billig* or *recht und schlecht* at any particular time. The people can be seen as one unit, be it in the sense of Hobbes, led by a monarch, or of Rousseau's *volonté générale,* or of Locke, led by the majority. However, the people can also be seen in their plurality, as Bakunin and Stirner saw them.

In view of the fact that Hobbes wanted the individual protected by a monarch, it is quite natural that after the victory over the Stuarts and the idea of the divine right of kings, Locke would revive the identity and individuality of the individual, something that to a large extent had been lost in the work of Hobbes. In tune with the Glorious Revolution, Locke glorified the individual. Much as he emphasized majority rule, he left no doubt that, in the last analysis, authority remains in the hands of the people who in case of abuse and misuse of governmental power can get rid of the government. His political theory leaves no doubt that the singularistic concept of democracy in the form of majority rule basically is an artificial transformation of the pluralistic concept of popular government. This means that the former, compared with the latter, must appear unnatural and inferior. Thus Locke opened up prospects for the restoration of the state of nature described by him, under which individuals live according to moral imperatives, a state not far removed from the one Hobbes lamented, one without even moral imperatives. As to Rousseau, he saw in the absolutism of the general will a means for the security of the members of a community, just as Hobbes had considered a monarch such a means. Yet on the face of it, pluralism is more clearly expressed in the republican system of Rousseau than in the monarchical one of Hobbes. After the liberal writings of Locke, this is not surprising. If in addition it is taken into account that the French Revolution, with its Declaration of the Rights of Man and Citizen, emphasized the identity and the individuality of the individual, the ideas of the father of that revolution contained the seed for the individualistic teachings of Bakunin and Stirner. The types of government spawned by that revolution—*gouvernement d'assemblée, de la Convention, de la majorité*—all are essentially not too different from the English Parliament, containing as they do possibilities of transforming singularistic concepts of democracy into pluralistic ones. *Honi soit qui mal y pense* (Those who think bad about it, think too well of human nature). For that nature attempts whenever feasible to win individuals more freedom. And the individual will try in all possible ways to gain more freedom for himself, be it by means of constitutional protection from the government, by his participation in government, or by his rejection of all government.

Being a reaction to the despotism of absolute monarchy, liberal democracy originally was conceived to be a popular government in which the ruling majority of voters was bound to respect the rights of the minority. This changed with increasing democratization on account of extensions of suffrage. A majority of only a few voters, faced as it is by the possibility that the minority of voters will be backed by all those who cannot vote, is likely to respect the rights of that minority. On the other hand, if the majority of the people can vote—and especially if that majority is great—their ruling majority will be less inclined to honor the rights of the minority because the latter cannot expect a substantial backing by those who cannot vote. Bills of rights, which seldom provide for an absolute protection anyway, can be interpreted by the ruling majority the way it sees fit. Therefore, members of the minority will increasingly try to belong to the majority.

Membership does not necessarily mean loss of individuality. Those belonging to an organization do not always go along with what they don't like. They can remain free by leaving the group. Integration into a community can amount to giving oneself up; it is only a matter of how much. Some people join others out of enthusiasm for a certain thing; others do so out of a mere desire for joining. Memberships usually are voluntary and without political relevancy. The situation is different with respect to political parties and groups. Now politics—with its falls, favors, likings and desires to be liked, its concepts of friend and foe, as well as its compromises—enters the field. It is a battlefield without need for war between nations, one that Clausewitz saw as a continuation of politics by other means. For politics is not just what is known as *Große Politik* among nations. It also is small-scale politicking within a particular nation, often of a truly petty nature. The latter will be most likely in a liberal community characterized by pluralism, for the pettiness of politics grows with the number, and thus with the smallness, of groups that make politics and are made by it to splinter further and further.

Joining the majority may be prompted by liking it as well as by expecting advantages from it. The latter motive shows an egoistic inclination, which may well signal moral decline. From the liberal point of view, it is quite defensible, for all that counts is what is of interest to the individual, be it good or bad. Some people belong to the majority because they are convinced of its program. Others join it out of opportunism. From the standpoint of liberalism, this also cannot be objected to, for liberalism urges people to grasp opportunities. Those convinced of the majority's aims are likely to be inclined toward giving up their individuality in order to better integrate themselves into the majority, whereas those merely going along with the majority out of opportunism usually will not give up their individuality, much as they might seem to—thereby deceiving the outside world. This does not mean that opportunists could not voice their desires more loudly than convinced people. Opportunists all too often will try to camouflage, and make up for, their lack of conviction by loud and ostentatious behavior if they consider such behavior opportune. For all too often overzealousness stands in a reverse relation to conviction. Yet however great the degree to which members of the ruling majority are integrated into the majority and to what extent they have given up their individuality, many of them will be, qua individuals, conscious of belonging to the majority. This is similar to an absolute monarch's being conscious of his majesty. As a matter of fact, it probably will be greater because, unlike the monarch, the majority is faced only by the minority. One can speak of the majesty of the majority, of a majestic hybris of the majority, of its lust for power and more power in the pursuit of extending the freedom of its members toward depriving the minority of its rights. From the standpoint of the majority, this again is compatible with liberalism, demanding as it does greater freedom for the individual irrespective of others. Thus democracy in the form of majority rule can end in far-reaching oppression. This is not surprising, for it is in the nature of every form of government to potentially be oppressive. Tyranny is the extreme of all forms of government, whatever their norms.

Aside from its despotic potential, majority rule has an anarchistic one, endangering its effectiveness. For it cannot be precluded that the feeling of power that the individual possesses as a member of the ruling majority develops so as to become all too much part of his ego. He may be taken in by his presumed power as a member of the majority to a degree that he considers that power inherent in himself. The belief in his own power may well induce him to arrogantly pursue his lust for power on his own and to separate himself from the majority. Such behavior would not be surprising. Just as the open hand appears to be natural, a hand closed into a fist, formed by the individual fingers for the purposes of greater power, is basically artificial. It returns to a more natural state by being opened again. Similarly, it can be maintained that individuals joining the majority for the purpose of the greater effectiveness of their activity join something artificial and that their leaving this condition is natural.

Such behavior may not even be considered unnatural by those who become integrated into the majority out of conviction. Those who join the majority out of opportunism will find it even easier to separate from it. They will have few inhibitions against harming society or their fellowmen, at least from the perspective of pure liberalism. Furthermore, it can be assumed that members of the minority will like such behavior, weakening as it does the majority. They will be only too willing to join anarchistic trends among members of the ruling majority if they had not already entertained such plans on their own, motivated by majoritarian oppression. All those turning against the government can argue that they are acting according to the principles of liberalism as well as democracy, because majority rule falsifies the will of the people and democracy proper implies a pluralism that demands the complete independence of all individuals. Thus the people assert themselves in their plurality. It will be argued that their primacy, following from the word *democracy*, must show itself in pluralism rather than in the artificial unity of majority rule. In support of this theses it will be said that for that very reason democracies known as liberal have limited majority rule through checks and balances—such institutional and territorial divisions of power as separation of legislative, executive, and judicial branches, federalism, judicial review, and bills of rights, all of which curtail sheer majority rule. It will be added that the attempts of the majority, often successful, to interpret these limitations out of existence, to circumvent and abolish them, are incompatible with a true democracy in which the people, and not just their majority, are supposed to rule.

Looking at forms of government known as liberal democracies, it can usually be seen that, due to democratization by extensions of suffrage and direct popular government, there occurred an increasing majorization of the minority. More and more the rule of the elected majority has been emphasized. This is indicated, for instance, in the reduction of second chambers to second-class chambers. In England, the House of Lords lost power in favor of the House of Commons. In France, the powerful Senate of the Third Republic was succeeded by the weak Council of the Republic. In Germany, the strong Bundesrat under the imperial constitution was replaced by the weak Reichsrat under the Weimar constitution. In spite of some reactions to their predecessors, the constitution of the Fifth Republic and the Bonn Basic Law did not establish strong second chambers. Too great is the general trend toward elevating first chambers because they are considered more democratic. As far as their importance is concerned, the name *first chambers* is not a misnomer. We thus have arrived at a situation in which upper chambers have become rather insignificant, whereas so-called lower houses rank high.

The might of majority government vis-à-vis the wealthier parts of the people was not only demonstrated in the so-called people's democracies, which imitated the victory of the Bolsheviks over the Menscheviks. It also was evident in the so-called liberal democracies of Western nations. The better-off parts of the population were legally deprived of a relatively large part of their possessions by majorities in accordance with their own interpretations of roads to freedom, many of which Hayek would have called roads to serfdom. This again demonstrates the many facets and ambiguities of freedom and the drive toward it, that is, liberalism.

In spite of all their power, ruling majorities have been increasingly challenged. There was the Prague Spring in 1968, and the Paris May. In the latter, there were few indications that the rioters belonged to the Gaullist majority. The same can be said of Prague, where the process of liberalization was supported by the government. On the other hand, in the Federal Republic of Germany education students and teachers demonstrated against Chancellor Brandt, whom they had helped bring to power. Their slogan was "Wer hat uns verraten? Die Sozialdemokraten!" There were signs of breakaways from the ruling majority. More and more, they led to challenges of the majority by its former members, who became an extraparliamentary opposition, some of them being drawn into terrorism.

In summary, it may be said that the development of popular government falls into different stages, as far as its competences and the exercise of its authority are concerned. Originally, there was a strictly circumscribed rule by the majority of voters. Later on, that rule became ever more unlimited. In the end, there came about, even within the ruling majority, disintegration and anarchical trends. The original intention of making democracy an effective government by means of majority rule was disputed. After that rule had turned out to be big government, it was argued that majority rule was no genuine democracy. The hybris of the majority came to be followed by that of individuals, irrespective of whether individuals condemned the behavior of the majority or considered it exemplary. Rousseau's *volonté générale* was replaced by the *volonté de tous,* the general will by that of all particular individuals. And the latter attempted to do whatever they happened to like, for their own pleasure, even at the expense of their fellowmen.

Democratic exercises of power demonstrate a great variety of possibilities. This is not surprising in view of the fact that popular government is a means of liberalism for realizing freedom and that liberalism, just as freedom, can mean many things.

It is even less surprising that this variety of possibilities has been evident especially in the land of unlimited opportunity, where pure liberalism is approached the most, where popular government as a means for realizing freedom was introduced first, and where it has been emphasized the most. If I am asked in what country the democratic cycle has run the fullest course, I answer: in the United States of America. Majority rule respecting or oppressing minority rights has existed everywhere, including the United States. Signs of anarchy, however, appear to me most evident in America, where the full cycle can be observed from the beginning.

The colonists revolted against Parliament and its government, representative of the majority of British voters. Some observers felt that the behavior of the colonists was justified because they felt oppressed. The school of George Louis Beer, on the other hand, stressed that the colonists no longer appreciated the good aspects of British rule due to their egoistic, ungrateful, and independent pursuit of happiness. Be this as it may, there can be little doubt that the colonists' behavior was considered rebellious and anarchist by the British—and not only by them. Many Americans shared their opinion in the beginning of the dispute with the mother country and even later on, when more and more colonists had come to favor independence. In the end, the Loyalists left the country and moved to Canada.

After the thirteen colonies had become independent states, they all established governments representing the majority of voters. Some of them were considered despotic. But there also were anarchical tendencies. Following Shays's Rebellion against the government of Massachusetts, the then Secretary of War Henry Knox wrote to Washington on October 23, 1786, "This dreadful situation . . . has alarmed every man of principle and property in New England. . . . What is to give us security against the violence of lawless men? . . . The men of property and . . . station and principle . . . are determined to endeavor to establish [a government that shall have the power to] protect them in their lawful pursuits; and, what will be efficient in all cases of internal commotions . . . they mean that liberty shall form the basis,—liberty resulting from an equal and firm administration of law." Knox juxtaposed freedom under law and the concept of liberty entertained by the rebels and proposed to counter the latter by the establishment of a stronger national government for the sake of "happiness, private and public." The fear of riots did not subside after Shays's Rebellion. Papers like *Gazetteer, Gazette,* and *Journal* published an article warning that a Shays on the federal level could be more successful than the one in Massachusetts. Widespread fear of the despotism of the majority and of anarchy led to the Constitutional Convention in Philadelphia, and, finally, to the adoption of the Constitution.

At the First Continental Congress of 1774, characterized by a moderate attitude toward Great Britain, Patrick Henry, later the first governor of independent Virginia, remarked that the government was dissolved and that the colonists were in a state of nature. Until the adoption of the Constitution in 1789, there were, in the various states, despotic and liberal governments by the majority of voters as well as anarchistic tendencies. Thus Americans, in the short span of fifteen years, experienced the various aspects of popular government. Under the Constitution, which was made in order to prevent both democratic despotism and anarchy, this did not change. A majority government respecting the rights of the minority increasingly became one in which these rights came under attack, until there came about anarchist trends, in part running parallel to an unrestricted majority rule, in part opposing that rule and government, generally.

The development from limited to unlimited democracy on the federal level appears to be most obvious in the increase in presidential power and national power and the decline in judicial review. Major features of the original Constitution—institutional and territorial separation of power as well as constitutional legitimacy—increasingly fell prey to the march of egalitarian democratism, to that of majorization, with its emphasis upon the mere legality of the law.

The event that greatly sped up this development was the Civil War. It is the most important incision in American history. One distinguishes the antebellum period from the postbellum period. For Americans, this event had an importance similar to what the English Revolution had for England, and the French Revolution, for France. Its wounds are not healed to this day. Yet the Supreme Court did not consider the secession of the southern States as incisive as those revolutions that replaced monarchical absolutism with governments by elected parliaments. According to *Texas v. White* (1868), the seceding states never left the "indestructible Union of indestructible states." It could be added that the federal Constitution never was left behind the way the rule of the Stuarts and the Bourbons was. Nevertheless, it was not the same after the Civil War. This was due not only to official formal amendments, the so-called war amendments (the Thirteenth, in 1865, abolished slavery; the Fourteenth, in 1868, made Negroes citizens and gave them certain rights; the Fifteenth, in 1870, gave them the right to vote) but also to a large extent to constitutional interpretations that changed the main tenor of the document by concentrating power in the presidency and the national government and by decreasing the authority of the courts. The Civil War, called by Lincoln a war for the "government of the people, by the people, for the people," enormously stimulated the process of democratization, giving American democracy new dimensions. As far as the power of the government is concerned, this process was, first of all, demonstrated by the march of power to Washington, replacing pluralistic aspects of the Constitution by monistic ones and characterized by growing majorization.

The main actor in the Civil War was Lincoln. His significance to the United States is, next to that of Jefferson, generally recognized. At the beginning of the War for Independence, Jefferson stood at the cradle of the new nation. With the Civil War, Lincoln saved that nation. Both men have certain things in common. They both were liberals. From 1832 to 1852, Lincoln supported Whig candidates for the presidency. He admired Jeffersonian principles, considering them "the definitions and axioms of a free society." Like Jefferson, he had several definitions of liberalism and believed in several principles of a free society. As did Jefferson, Lincoln emphasized them as they fit a particular situation. In 1947, James G. Randall published *Lincoln the Liberal Statesman*. In the volume *The En-*

during Lincoln, edited by Norman A. Graebner (1959), there can be found contributions such as David Donald, "Abraham Lincoln: Whig in the White House," and T. Harry Williams, "Abraham Lincoln: Pragmatic Democrat." All these publications fit nicely together. As liberals, Whigs were pragmatic democrats who adjusted themselves to existing conditions in order to see their wishes come true. And the politician Lincoln was one of them. At his funeral, another master in the art of politics whispered, "the Master Politician of the Ages" (quoted in George F. Milton, *The Use of Presidential Power,* 1944, p. 128). Lincoln saw to it that by adjusting himself more or less smoothly and shrewdly to existing situations he would emerge as a victor, be a success as a politician. Like Jefferson, he knew his way around in all kinds of circumstances. In liberal America, this endeared him to people, made him a national hero, "the enduring Lincoln." His emancipation of the slaves probably is the best-known example of his adaptability.

While there are few doubts that Lincoln, as a liberal democrat or a democratic liberal, basically acted pragmatically, it is more difficult to find out what prompted his behavior as a politician. Was it the good of humanity? Of his country? Was it personal ambition? We'll probably never know. His speech of January 27, 1838, made at the beginning of his political career before the Young Men's Lyceum in Springfield, Illinois, the place of his birth and burial, always will make us wonder. The speech emphasized the necessity of obedience to the laws and the Constitution, which made the American system the hope of all those who love liberty. He warned that men of ambition and talent might try to bring about changes and to destroy the established forms of government and urged his audience to frustrate such designs. On the other hand, the young ambitious politician said that those who "aspire to nothing beyond a seat in Congress, a gubernatorial or a presidential chair . . . *belong not to the family of the lion, or the tribe of the eagle,*" for these places would not "satisfy an Alexander, a Caesar, or a Napoleon." He continued: "Towering genius disdains a beaten path. . . . It *scorns* to tread in the footsteps of *any* predecessor, however illustrious. It thirsts and burns for distinction; and, if possible, it will have it, whether at the expense of emancipating the slaves, or enslaving freemen."

After he had become president, Lincoln did both. During the Civil War he emancipated the slaves and disregarded the right to a writ of habeas corpus, a right that for a long time had been considered one of the most important guarantees of the freedom of the person. He maintained that his actions had been motivated by the necessity of saving the Union and, with it, the Constitution. However, the speech of the young politician in Springfield makes one wonder whether his real motive was personal ambition, whether an unconscious or conscious drive got the better of him in a liberal quest for deeds that would make him one of the great men of his country, even of the human race, and assure him immortality. When at his funeral it was whispered, but not said aloud, that he was the master politician of the ages, it perhaps was indication that the liberalism of the time was restrained by ethics and morals, that a politician was not supposed to be without scruples. However, from the point of view of liberalism, it looks different: Lincoln was permitted without any inhibitions to curtail the freedom of the individual, whether such curtailment was permitted by the Constitution and the laws or not, just as he was allowed to emancipate the slaves, an act that has been compared to a tsarist ukase, amounting to the greatest act of expropriation in Anglo-American jurisprudence. It created a great deal of resentment and, according to other concepts of liberalism, of praise. As could Jefferson, Lincoln, from the standpoint of pure liberalism, could disregard all ethical, moral, and legal inhibitions. However, while Jefferson strictly obeyed the law, Lincoln, in the first weeks of the Civil War, did not do so. He broke the Constitution.

His behavior was not authorized just by pure liberalism. Lincoln also felt that the liberal Constitution itself justified his actions. He emphasized that under his oath of office, provided for by Article 2, section 1, of the supreme law, he had the duty of preserving, protecting, and defending the Constitution to the best of his ability. From this he concluded the right to disregard some constitutional provisions in order to save the whole Constitution. As did Jefferson, Lincoln considered the Constitution a compromise. On October 16, 1854, in a speech in Peoria, he praised "the SPIRIT of COMPROMISE . . . of mutual concession—that spirit which first gave us the constitution." In view of that compromise, Lincoln obviously did not worry too much about compromising details of the supreme law, if such behavior was deemed necessary by him. Compromises are invitations to being compromised. Furthermore, Lincoln could well have considered the Constitution imperfect because the American optimism of its creators had left it silent on who should rule in times of emergency and how such a rule was to be handled. The constitutional laws of the Third Republic had a similar deficiency, as was emphasized by de Gaulle in 1940.

In the emergency of secession, Lincoln gave high priority to the survival of the Union. His desire to save the Union was so great as to even make him willing to put up with slavery all over the United States, that is, in a territory by far larger than that of the so-called slave states. On August 22, 1862, he wrote Horace Greeley, the founder of the *New York Tribune:* "I would save the Union. I would save it the shortest way under the Constitution. The sooner the national authority can be restored; the nearer the Union will be 'the Union as it was.' . . . My paramount object in this struggle *is* to save the Union, and is *not* either to save or destroy slavery. If I could save the Union without freeing *any* slave I would do it, and if I could save it by freeing *all* the slaves, I would do it; and if I could save it by freeing some and leaving others alone I would also do that. What I do about slavery, and the colored race, I do because I believe it helps to save the Union; and what I forbear, I forbear because I do *not* believe it would help to save the Union." If it is taken into consideration that Lincoln, as a private citizen, always had been opposed to slavery prior to becoming a candidate for the presidency, this letter will disturb many people. On the other hand, it is in tune with the outlook of a liberal politician who resorts to many a means to achieve his purposes.

Under Lincoln's leadership, the North, constituting the American majority, won over the southern minority. Lincoln thus succeeded—but at the price of compromising the Constitution. He compromised that law not only because he liberally discarded some of its provisions; he compromised it also because he made plain that some of these provisions were more important than others. He thus relativized the provisions of the Constitution, opening up new possibilities of interpretation. These possibilities became evident not just in times of emergency but also in normal times, in which, depending on differing opinion, the Constitution could be interpreted and reinterpreted in new and different ways.

They became obvious in the growth of presidential power. For a long time and in many places, the American system of government was called presidential only in order to distinguish it from the parliamentary system, because the president was neither elected by, nor dependent upon, the legislature. As a result of American development, presidential government today implies an enormous power in the presidency. Up to the Civil War, the president was by no means the outstanding governmental power. The Founding Fathers were more afraid of a strong executive than of a strong legislature. Symbolically, they formulated executive power after they formulated legislative power. This was in tune with the philosophy of Locke, who wanted the legislature to be the most powerful branch of government. During the Civil War, it admitted of no doubt that Lincoln was at the helm. He was the one who was sovereign in a state of emergency. And this meant that in the last analysis sovereignty was vested in the president, for the sovereign is he who is sovereign in an emergency. France, which Jean Bodin considered the home of the concept of sovereignty, in 1940 had no sovereign. If, as was demonstrated in the Civil War, sovereignty basically resided in the presidency, this truth could not very well be ignored in normal times. Actual developments have confirmed this. They show a steady growth of the power of the man in the White House.

President Theodore Roosevelt, who held the high office from 1901 to 1909, a period characterized by an absence of major crises, one in which the United States even emerged as a world power, was not content with the traditional interpretation of presidential power, according to which the chief executive could only do things specifically authorized by the Constitution. He was of the opinion that the president could do everything the laws did not prohibit. In his autobiography, published in 1958 on the occasion of the centennial of his birth, we read on pages 197 f.: "My view was that every executive officer, and above all every executive officer in high position, was a steward of the people, and not to content himself with the negative merit of keeping his talents undamaged in a napkin. I declined to adopt the view that what was imperatively necessary for the nation could not be done by the President unless he could find some specific authorization to do it. My belief was that it was not only his right but his duty to do anything that the needs of the nation demanded unless such action was forbidden by the Constitution or by the laws. Under this interpretation of executive power I did and caused to be done many things not previously done by the President and the heads of the departments. I did not usurp power, but I did greatly broaden the use of executive power. In other words, I acted for the public welfare, I acted for the common well-being of all our people, whenever and in whatever manner was necessary, unless prevented by direct constitutional or legislative prohibition." In a large measure, then, Roosevelt defined the scope of his stewardship all by himself, just as he saw fit.

After further increases of presidential power in World War I, that power under Franklin D. Roosevelt became so extended that Corwin, reminding his readers of absolute monarchs, called him Roosevelt II, who flirted, as that author wrote in his commentary on the Constitution, with the Stuart theory, which Locke in chapter 14 of his *Second Treatise* described as the "Power to act according to discretion, for the public good, without the prescription of the Law, and sometimes even against it."

The growth of presidential power continued after World War II. A favorite book of President Kennedy was Richard E. Neustadt, *Presidential Power* (1960), considered a Machiavellian suggestion of additional powers a president could take on. Under President Johnson there came about, as a result of the war in Vietnam, a rich literature on presidential power. Arthur M. Schlesinger, Jr., published *The Imperial Presidency.* Presidential power had grown enormously ever since Lincoln had demonstrated who in a state of emergency was sovereign. Later on, when national survival was not in jeopardy at all, one went from the stewardship theory to the Stuart theory and, from there, to the imperial presidency.

It is, of course, possible to explain the latter via the Cold War. After all, uncertain international conditions usually bring about a strengthening of the executive. However, the power of the president had grown before. It grew especially under presidents with social programs, under

Theodore Roosevelt, the "trustbuster"; under Wilson, who for the sake of the common man announced a New Freedom; under Franklin Roosevelt, who championed a New Deal; under Kennedy and his New Frontier; under Johnson's Great Society. This indicates that the growth of presidential power is in part due to the fact that presidential activities no longer remained confined to specifically executive functions. Modern authors such as Wilfred E. Binkley, Richard F. Fenno, Louis W. Koenig, and Joseph E. Kallenbach indeed put the legislative activities of the president ahead of his executive ones. Louis Brownlow called the presidency "an inexhaustible fountain from which we may demand everything and anything that we desire" (*The President and the Presidency,* 1947, p. 73). If, in addition, we take into account that Franklin Roosevelt pressured the Supreme Court to approve social laws passed by Congress, we cannot help thinking of an absolute monarch. Even an observer like Corwin, who throughout his life described and stressed the growth of presidential power, in the end voiced doubt about that growth. In *The Presidency Today* (1956), coauthored with Koenig, doubts are expressed about the increasing elimination of Congress from the country's political leadership—in the introduction, as if meant to be some kind of a leitmotif. Upon the assassination of Kennedy, I dared to examine the question whether some day the highest office could be held by a tyrant who could prompt a tyrannicide. My article "Will the Presidency Incite Assassination?" which showed the enormous growth of presidential power, was denied publication for a long time. In the emotional atmosphere then existing, editors obviously were afraid to publish something on a theme that so far had not been touched. For even in liberal countries, even courageous people refrain from touching touchy topics, and in America civil courage has its limits. My old teacher, Alpheus Mason, encouraged me to go on looking for a publisher. After having been turned down by more than ten editors, the article finally, in 1965, made it into *Ethics,* published by the University of Chicago Press. Milton Friedman, an outstanding exponent of the Chicago school of economics and Nobel laureate in 1976, was on its editorial board.

I have never seen my article referred to in the voluminous literature directed against power concentration in the presidency following President Johnson's engagement in Vietnam. Perhaps those brought up in American democracy did not want to think of a president elected by the people as a tyrant, let alone of tyrannicide, even in a nation that approaches pure liberalism more than any other. Much as President Nixon may have been attacked because of Watergate, most Americans seem to have been glad that he was not impeached and that his successor, Ford, granted him immunity from criminal prosecution—for the president to a large extent is considered a symbol of the United States and its people, one of them who succeeded in making it to the highest office. As such a symbol, he is not supposed to be criticized too much. Although such criticism cannot be punished for lèse majesté in this classic republic, it is considered an insult to popular government and the majesty of the people.

American presidents always have emphasized this idea. Powerful as they may have been, they have stressed that they are men of the people even if they could not, as Lincoln could, point to the fact that they were born in a log cabin and came from a plain background. Theodore Roosevelt, the son of a millionaire, saw himself as the steward of the people. Woodrow Wilson came from a well-to-do family, was a respected professor and president of Princeton University, the alma mater of the sons of rich parents. When he was president of the United States, he left no doubt that he saw himself as the representative of the people. Franklin D. Roosevelt criticized the Supreme Court for opposing his social program, a program desired by the people. He also was the son of a millionaire posing as a man of the people. The same was true of Kennedy, the son of a millionaire, and by his successor, Johnson, a millionaire. The latter spent a good deal of his time in the White House honoring the principle "The Business of America is Business" by taking care of his business enterprises in Texas, his home state, where he had worked his way up. Kennedy—who in that state, riding in a motorcade with his erstwhile rival and present vice president, met his moment of truth—amused himself in the White House his own way. The behavior of both did not particularly disturb people, certainly less than the behavior of any one of their predecessors. After all, the people had increasingly become used to approaching pure liberalism, which permits any kind of behavior. The fifth edition of Corwin's *The President: Office and Powers 1787–1984*, published in 1984, has for an epigraph the remark of Lincoln's Secretary of State Seward: "We elect a King for four years, and give him absolute power within certain limits, which after all he can interpret for himself." Ever since, the prerogatives of America's people's king or tribune have expanded enormously. Still, he likes to identify himself with the people.

Without doubt, the American president represents the people as far as his position as ceremonial head of state is concerned. This is especially obvious when he is assassinated. The whole nation mourns. Everything he did wrong, all his sins, seem to be wiped out, certainly in the period immediately following his death. Also, in spite of his position as a controversial politician, he will usually be given the benefit of the doubt from his election through his first months in office, even by those who did not vote for him. Basically, Americans are trusting and not skeptical. But as time goes on, the president increasingly loses his image as the symbol of the nation. More and more, he becomes a mere political actor, subject to greater and greater criticism. Then it becomes increasingly obvious that he was elected merely by the majority of the electoral college, a majority that does not even necessarily reflect that of the people. He appears as the leader of his party, attempting to carry out a mere party platform against the opposition. And polemicists are subject to polemics. In spite of his strong position, he is not sure of being able to carry out his plans. Vis-à-vis Congress, the American president has gained in power, yet he still is not omnipotent. Even a "great communicator" like Reagan became aware of that. Congress still is a powerful force, much as its position may have declined compared to that of the man in the White House.

On the other hand, that decline was recouped to a large extent due to a substantial broadening of its powers vis-à-vis the particular states, leading to an increasing elimination of federalism and states' rights. The Tenth Amendment, to which, as the concluding provision of the Bill of Rights, special importance can be attributed, reads: "The powers not delegated to the United States by the Constitution, nor prohibited by it to the States, are reserved to the States respectively, or to the people." But as a result of constitutional amendments following the Civil War, the rights of the states were curtailed. In addition, they were decreased by judicial interpretation, for the provisions of the Constitution delegating powers to the federal government were interpreted broadly.

The interpretation of the commerce clause (Article 1, sec. 8, clause 3) is an example. Under it, "the Congress shall have the power to regulate commerce among the several States." In 1824, Chief Justice Marshall in *Gibbons v. Ogden* interpreted this provision to mean interstate, as contrasted to intrastate, commerce. In 1937 F. D. G. Ribble, a descendant of Marshall and for a long time dean of the University of Virginia School of Law, published *State and National Power over Commerce,* showing the enormous increase of the jurisdiction of the federal government. The difference emphasized by Marshall was to a large extent eliminated. In the Shreveport case of 1914, the Supreme Court had decided that whenever inter- and intrastate commerce are connected in a way that the regulation of one requires that of the other, Congress can regulate both. The Transportation Act, passed by Congress in 1920, broadened this principle even further. Yet the greatest concessions to the federal government came with Roosevelt's New Deal. At that time it also was decided that the commerce powers of Congress were no longer confined to the regulation of transport but extended to that of traffic.

In *United States v. Chandler-Dunbar Co.*, it was decided in 1913 that Congress had the right to regulate navigable rivers if it served navigation. In 1940, this right was extended in order to prevent inundations or to produce electricity by building dams. The Court even went so far as to say that the power of Congress to regulate was not confined to navigable rivers but extended to making rivers navigable (*United States v. Appalachian Electric Power Co.*, 1940). With respect to the authority of the federal government over commerce, the United States for all practical purposes has become a unitary state. In 1941, George C. S. Benson published *The New Centralization,* even before the Second World War brought further extensions of the national control over commerce.

Now it must not be assumed that the development toward a unitary state, observable also in other respects, moved in a straight line. In spite of the thrust inherent in liberalization and in its means, democratization, the ways of liberal democracies usually are roundabout. They are winding, adjusting themselves to temporary, often undecided majorities, wavering between good and bad will. In a liberal popular government such as that existing in the United States, there always will be, as a result of different concepts of liberalism, interruptions of existing trends as well as regressions. All too often it will be asked whether the road taken is the correct one, one conducive to liberty, for too many citizens have too many too different ideas on freedom and its promotion. Therefore, it is not surprising that along with judicial decisions extending the power of the federal government there were those that off and on put a brake on such extensions. This occurred under the doctrine of dual federalism, which emphasized that the Constitution, after all, reserved certain rights to the states that the federal government could not intrude upon. Still, the application of that doctrine could not prevent the growing elimination of those rights in the long run. This is indicated in the term *dual federalism* itself. Overemphases usually demonstrate that something no longer is in good shape. In case of a healthy federalism, which implies dualism anyway, it would not have been necessary to emphasize its dualism in so many words. On the whole, references to the federal character of the United States could no more prevent its development into a unitary state than relatively weak presidents could do anything to slow the growth of the power of their office.

Both trends are outstanding aspects of democratization and its assertion of majority rule on the national level as a means toward a liberalization of the whole nation. The latter actually came into existence only as a result of the Civil War. Although the word *national* can be found in the *Federalist,* there were, for a long time, debates going on concerning the nature of the Union and federalism. Did it amount to one sovereign nation composed of nonsovereign states (a *Bundesstaat*) or to a loose federation of sovereign states (a *Staatenbund*)? That question was, as in the case of Switzerland and Germany, solved only through iron and blood. The Civil War ended with a victory of the majority of states over the minority of states, that of the majority of the total population over its minority. John C. Calhoun's ideas on the protection of states' rights lost out. There came about a recognition of majority rule that was likely to make that rule omnipotent and to increasingly free it from its limitations vis-à-vis the rights of individuals, as these rights were originally prescribed by the Constitution.

The Civil War also resulted in a victory of northern economic interests over those of the South. Since this victory was connected with that of the abolitionists over the slaveholders, the combination of both victories could prompt further liberations in which economic considerations played a role that was not to be underestimated. There was not a great distance between the bad lots of slaves in the agrarian South, of the working proletariat in the industrial North, or of the poor all over the nation. It therefore appeared natural that in the twentieth century social measures were requested, often due to the influence of socialist immigrants. These measures were imposed by the poorer majority upon the richer minority. In that movement, presidents desiring greater power for their office played a leading part, using and abusing their power. Theodore Roosevelt, for the sake of the man in the street, moved against trusts. Woodrow Wilson continued his social policy with his program of the New Freedom. Franklin Roosevelt tried to solve the problems enhanced by the Great Depression with his New Deal. Harry S Truman, coming from a plain background, wanted a Fair Deal for all. In the campaign of 1948, he told Americans, "you never had it so good!" I can still see him beaming when in 1961 Kennedy emphasized his social program of the New Frontier in his inaugural address. President Johnson's Great Society was in tune with all these plans, although it was a far cry from the Great Society Adam Smith had in mind.

Still, all the social principles just mentioned did not reject those of Smith altogether. They only rejected social reform in the sense of socialism proper. American regulators of the economy remained tied to Adam Smith in about the way revisionist Marxists remained tied to Marx. The American attitude is even less surprising in view of the fact that Smith, in contrast to Manchester liberalism, emphasized fair competition. Yet although the United States basically has remained a country of free enterprise, there can be no doubt that the situation today cannot be compared to that prevailing in the nineteenth century; for the economy has been regulated to a large extent and, thus, been curtailed. The originally predominant concept of free government, favoring a far-reaching protection of the individual from the government, was increasingly replaced by one under which the ruling majority was free to curtail the rights of individuals. True, the principle, "The Business of America is Business" is still valid. However, while with Coolidge it meant as much freedom as possible from majority rule, today it implies that the majority may make it its business to promote its business through regulations and social laws.

For a long time, the Supreme Court opposed these trends. In the end, it approved them. Up until the New Deal, it defended the older concept of free government, acting as a bulwark against congressional infringements upon the rights of individuals and business enterprises. Between June 1, 1934, and June 1, 1936, thirteen provisions made by Congress were ruled unconstitutional and thus void. This attitude prompted President Roosevelt on March 9, 1937, in his first radio address after his second inauguration, to say that the Supreme Court was the branch of the government that, in contrast to the executive and the legislative, was opposed to the wishes of the people. The remark was part of his plan to pack the Court with judges who would be willing to accept New Deal legislation. The Supreme Court capitulated under pressure. Ever since, it has not dared to challenge national laws, at least not laws that were concerned with economic matters, out of fear of arousing the anger of the American majority. On May 3, 1907, the Governor of New York Hughes remarked in Elmira: "We are under a Constitution, but the Constitution is what the judges say it is." In 1941, Chief Justice Stone, in *United States v. Classic,* spoke of "the Constitution as a continuing instrument of government." Hughes, later on appointed chief justice by President Hoover, a strong advocate of free enterprise, conceived of free government in the sense of such enterprise. Stone, appointed the successor of Hughes by President Roosevelt in 1941, viewed free government as one in which the majority was free to regulate and thus restrict free enterprise. Hughes, opposing the New Deal, had differing ideas on freedom and the role of the judiciary to protect it from those of Stone, a friend of the New Deal, who desired that the Court go along with whatever the majority wanted.

To the two concepts of free government just mentioned there was added, in the 1960s, a third one. Its protagonists broke away from the then ruling majority as well as those who did not like that majority to begin with on account of its regulations and social legislation. Its birth was aided by the Vietnam War and the consideration that mere majority rule was not really a genuine and perfect democracy but, rather, a perversion of popular government. Its promoters tended to see in democracy a rule neither by the majority nor by the *volonté générale* but, rather, by the will of all, all of whom may follow their own individual desires. They are inclined to reject American government per se as an establishment incompatible with democracy. They consider themselves genuine democrats and genuine liberals.

After World War II the governments of the United States were close to the kind of free government under which the majority is free to impose its will upon the minority—certainly up until the 1960s (heralded by Kennedy as the Golden Sixties). Given the importance of economic matters in America, this meant that the poorer parts of the population could tell the richer ones how they had to behave and how much of their possessions they had to give up. The Eisenhower administration did not change much in basic orientation. Eisenhower, as well as his brother Milton, was considered a liberal Republican, that is, a man closer to the social program of the Democratic party than to the conservative wing of the Republicans under Senator Taft of Ohio, whose liberalism was more oriented toward laissez-faire and less toward spending government money for public welfare. The then-ruling majority, composed of voters from both major parties, favored programs of public welfare and a "big government" that could carry them out. It was supported by the young, notably students. However, when under President Johnson the war in Vietnam demanded more and more sacrifice, many of them changed their minds. They left the majority. Their attitude was simple and perfectly liberal: as long as they thought they could get something from a strong federal government, they were in favor of it; as soon as that government demanded sacrifices from them, they opposed it, denouncing it as "big government." So far, they had praised the state as a means for them to attain their desires. Now, when it demanded their services, they condemned it. Their behavior demonstrates that, except for its drive for freedom, liberalism knows no principles. As long as big government serves the interests of an individual, he favors it; as soon as it hurts these interests, he attacks it. It also was well in tune with liberalism when the former members of the majority allied themselves with those whom they previously had considered their foes, namely, those believing in laissez-faire and opposing the welfare state. The latter did the same when they joined the former, bringing about a coalition of the New Left and the Old Right. Politics, which especially in the United States is a merry-go-round or a logrolling for liberals, make strange bedfellows.

It is said that in war, the law is silent, usually having in mind theaters of war. But the Vietnam War had, far away from its theater, the effect of endangering law and order. There were demonstrations and confrontations. They prevented teaching in many a university. People demanded freedom for Vietnam and denounced the American engagement as imperialistic and immoral. Altruism, the well-being of others, was put into the foreground. Much less did I hear demonstrators speak of egoistic motives for their behavior, although I could not help feeling that fear of military service, especially in war zones, was very much on their minds, careful as they were in concealing to admit it, let alone emphasize it. All too many male students and their girlfriends confessed such thoughts to me under the seal of confidence, destroying whatever beliefs I still had in the willingness of American students to make sacrifices. The shirker mentality also is compatible with liberalism and not just as an aspect of moneymaking. When in the presidential campaign of 1968, none of the candidates clearly condemned the war in Vietnam, when even Vice President Hubert H. Humphrey disappointed hopes by showing himself a faithful follower of President Johnson in order to win the election, demonstrations and confrontation peaked. One no longer was content with attacking the existing majority rule; one attacked the American system of government as such, as an "industrial-military establishment." This attitude also was understandable from the point of view of liberalism. For liberalism is, above all, interested in greater freedom for the individual. It is much less concerned with the institutions of a particular country, even if they secure an abundance of liberties.

Now all this can be considered the result of the Vietnam War. Yet it also must be asked whether that war merely gave rise to feelings that had bothered many Americans for some time anyway. Due to my observations of the American scene during the past decades, I am inclined to answer that question in the affirmative. I see in the movement against the American democratic Establishment a new, prominent stage in the development from limited to unlimited democracy, as an aspect of a continuing process of liberalization.

In the United States, the ability of the ruling majority to emancipate has been demonstrated with special clarity. Originally, the individual sought membership in the majority in order to better protect and promote his own interests, even at the cost of others. He hoped to gain strength by means of that membership and, with it, greater freedom, for with strength comes freedom. The latter has two major effects, both being aspects of liberalism. There is, first, the effect of feeling secure. It is due to the absorption of the individual by the majority, resulting in his protection by it. It can be called the first emancipation effect. The second emancipation effect amounts to emancipation from the majority by getting out of it. At first sight, these two effects seem to be contradictory. If someone joins the majority in order to be more free, it will be argued, how can he leave it in order to be more free? This argument overlooks that the individual's drive for freedom can be strengthened by his membership in the majority to a degree that he wants to become independent of it. Membership is not necessarily blind allegiance.

When the individual looks for cover in the majority, he does so in the hope of gaining strength for the realization of his aims. He thinks that the main thing is to achieve these aims and that it is of secondary importance to do so all by himself. Membership in the majority strengthens his self-confidence, especially if he sees the majority get what it wants and thereby lets him get what he wants. This strengthened self-confidence can mean that it is being transformed into a feeling for the self. He will say to himself, What the majority can do, I can do. As its member, I am only a member, only part of it, not free. If, however, I part from it, I am, as an independent individual, one no longer tied to, and tied up, with the majority, free: a whole individual, a totally free man, a freeman! Thoughts such as these will be entertained by many belonging to a group, including that of the ruling majority. Perhaps this may be compared to the conquest of a mountaintop, which gives one a feeling of freedom. The individual climber will join, and tie himself to, other mountaineers, thinking that this will make it easier for him to get to the top. Once there, he will feel liberated from his desire to conquer the mountain, sharing this feeling of liberation with his associates. Later on, he may well separate himself from them in order to successfully climb all by himself so that he no longer need share his feeling of liberation with others, in order to be freer than previously, when he had to do so. Shared freedom is diminished freedom.

The drive to emancipate oneself by leaving the majority has always appeared to me to be especially great among Americans. I have explained it by the fact that they are immigrants or their descendants. Their steady migrations include, in the land of joiners, moving out of a majority as well as moving into it. And those who never sought protection by the majority should be strong enough to do without that protection anyway. Together with those who in their free pursuit of happiness left the majority, they probably will not just constitute a coalition of the Old Right and the New Left. They also will combine with other segments of the population in the multicolored prism of American liberalism. In their free pursuit of happiness, they all constitute a challenge to the existing system of government.

They have attempted to strengthen their liberalism by arguing that democracy, until now accepted as a means for a continuing liberalization in the form of majority rule, is a pseudodemocracy just as much as the representative democracy rejected by Rousseau; that also the latter's idea of a *volonté générale,* which can force individuals to be free, is incompatible with freedom. Consequently, there remains only the unlimited freedom of every individual, as manifested in *volontés de tous.* Only such a government can be that of all the people and, thus, a true democracy. It will be added that the Declaration of Independence does not mention majority rule and that the Constitution does not either, that the former emphasizes the idea of the people at its end, thus leading to the same idea in a place of honor at the beginning of the Constitution as well as at the end of its Bill of Rights. It will further be argued that emphasis upon majority rule derives from the English philosopher Locke; that it comes from the Old World and, therefore, does not belong to the New World because the essence of Americanism is its separation from the Old World. People will advance such arguments and similar ones without scruple in spite of the fact that most people may not share them. For from the standpoint of pure liberalism one need have no scruples and may feel quite free to reject traditional concepts of democracy. These arguments may appear simple and simplified. Yet what is simple often has a greater power to convince people than what is complicated and differentiated. The sheer, great thrust of pure liberalism, which has seen many complicated liberalisms come and go and has in its raw simplicity easily survived all of them, has demonstrated this only too clearly.

The free wills of all individuals are not only opposites of Rousseau's general will and Locke's majority rule; since they reject the American system of government as such, they can be seen, if one attributes to government legal order, as being *hors de la loi,* while not necessarily being outside of American society. This brings to mind the state of nature, be it that of Hobbes, of Locke, or of Rousseau, whose ideas on that state are the best known in America. Cruel and rosy as the state of nature may be, it cannot be denied that all those living in it rule themselves in their plurality insofar as each individual rules himself individually, all by himself. It is this kind of rule that in recent times has become increasingly popular with many Americans. In tune with the pragmatist William James they believe that the majority is composed of exclusive, egoistic individuals. They do not yet constitute a majority. But the liberal process of democratization has shown that minorities become majorities. The so-called Progressive Movement, beginning modestly at the turn of the century, came to blossom during the majority rule under the New Deal and its successors. Sociological jurisprudence, related to it and originally represented by the Brandeis-Holmes minority on the Supreme Court, later came to influence the majority of judges.

The new concept of democracy and free government is not without appeal. The critical spirit, emphasized by Hegel scholar Herbert Marcuse (in 1967 a *Festschrift* in his honor was published under that title, appearing, as did his works, in several printings), was suited to a nation characterized by migrations, agitations, and demonstrations. So was the growing literature produced by friends of a free market who resented too much government regulation of the economy. They allied themselves in many instances with those accused of procommunism, those favoring other types of socialism, and those favoring a planned economy. And everything was done in the name of liberty. In the land of unlimited opportunities, approaching pure liberalism more than any other country, this is not surprising. For the multiplicity of facets of pure liberalism is great, disturbingly stupendous, and all kinds of liberalisms can emerge from it.

Today, when the strongest nation in the New World enters its third century, the development from limited to unlimited democracy in the land of the free, a development showing democracy as a means for a continuing liberalization, can be divided into three major periods. The time from the beginning of the conflict with the mother country to the Civil War clearly was characterized by a limited majority rule protecting the rights of individuals. During that epoch, Emerson stated in *The American Scholar* in 1837 that the United States was the guardian of democratic civilization. In the hundred years following, majority rule became more and more unlimited. Since the 1960s, characterized by riots, attacks no longer have been directed against majoritarianism as the oppressor of individuals; they have concentrated on the American system as such. Those attacking have seen progress from the state of nature of Hobbes to that of Locke to that of Rousseau. The latter state, praised by the father of modern democracy as a peaceful golden age of equal people, no longer is considered utopian by these people. It is an aim to be realized, even in the form of anarchy. As a remedy, there may well come a fourth period under the dictatorship of one individual who in the name of his followers and under assertions to act in the name of the people will take liberties toward far-reaching oppressions, posing as a guardian of a democratic civilization that Emerson never imagined.

16 Potpourri in the Melting Pot

America, the liberal-democratic melting pot, today looks like a liberal-democratic potpourri. The land, the people, and their government show an enormous variety. Ethnic, political, economic, and other groupings of the people, their factions, groups, and parties, in tune with liberalism, have preserved their identities to a degree that justifies a comparison with a musical potpourri made up of many compositions having characters of their own to such an extent that one can wonder whether they really belong together. One need only turn on the radio or television to become aware of the colossal multiplicity in the American way of life.

This is especially evident in politics, showing a perpetual to and fro, up and down, here and there, now and again. Many are nauseated by it, many ingratiate themselves with its more or less dubious actors. In view of an extraordinary flexibility, the fronts often are blurred, the affronts hazy and of short duration in order to be followed by others. The division of American history just described does not mean that in the first period the generally accepted concept of free government, implying the freedom of the individual from the government, would not have come under attack at all; that during the second era, in which free government came to mean the liberty of the government to impose its will upon the citizens, there would not have been people who opposed that development.

History seldom shows abrupt solutions of existing problems. They do not even occur in the cases of far-reaching revolutions, as those in France in 1789 and in Russia in 1917, as is proved by the restoration and by Bonapartism in France as well as by the survival of dictatorship in Russia. In nations that, like Great Britain and the United States, had no revolutions comparable to the ones just mentioned, abrupt changes can be expected even less. This is especially true if one type of liberalism succeeds another, as in England in 1688, when liberalism in the sense of the Magna Carta reasserted itself, or in America in 1776, when English liberalism was succeeded by that of New England or that of America. Abrupt incisions can be expected the least when liberal continuity is guaranteed by steady immigrations and migrations prompted by the quest for freedom, as in the case of the United States, where, in that land of liberalism *par excellence*, perpetual changes for the sake of something new are the order of the day.

American pluralism has always shown a great variety of trends, even though just some of them may have been in the foreground. Even when a free government was preferred under which the ruling majority had to protect the rights of the individual, among which those of property ranked highly, voices could be heard protesting against a far-reaching protection of property and demanding social legislation. There was a Benjamin Hichborn who opposed any restriction on the will of the people to do anything it liked at any time. When unlimited majority rule came to the fore and, under the New Deal, won many a victory, there were groups, such as the American Liberty League in the 1930s and, after World War II, the John Birch Society, the Intercollegiate Society of Individualists, and the Foundation for Economic Education that opposed social legislation. The Republican party was reoriented from Eisenhower via Nixon to Reagan. The latter was a former admirer of New Deal liberalism who became a supporter of laissez-faire liberalism and who—in contrast to Franklin Roosevelt, who recognized the Soviet regime—strongly rejected that regime. In spite of attacks by those who conceived of free government and democracy as something their opponents denounced as anarchy, the existing American system of government has survived so far. In celebrations commemorating the bicentennial of the American Revolution, it usually was praised, whatever liberal variations there may have been. As a matter of fact, that praise often was due to the system's making all these variations possible, or proof of its ability to guarantee a free society. It remains to be seen whether it will prevail into the third century of the United States and whether Reagan's program of the new revolution actually will bring about a revival of the values cherished by the founders of the United States. The future is never clear.

On the other hand, it appears clear to me that the developments from an elitist to an egalitarian, from indirect to direct, from limited to unlimited democracy were parallel to developments showing the drive toward pure popular government. This indicates the proximity of egalitarianism and the plebiscite. Their combination has demonstrated an enormous thrust, which so far has asserted itself in majoritarianism. However, its trends toward anarchy challenge majority rule and, in the last analysis, the system of government that so far has been generally accepted. In view of the strength of pure liberalism, it must not be overlooked that majority rule as well as the rule of all possess an enormously broad scope of possibilities.

Oliver Wendell Holmes, the philosopher on the Supreme Court who, in analogy to the Grand Old Man of the Liberal party in Great Britain, Gladstone, often has been called the Grand Old Man of American jurisprudence, made remarks reminiscent of Hans Kelsen's Pure Theory of Law, showing the development from puritanism to pure democracy and pure liberalism. In 1881 he wrote in *The Common Law* (p. 41f.) that law "should correspond with the actual feelings and demands of the community, whether right or wrong." Three years later he remarked in "Law in Science and Science in Law" that "in these days the justification of a law for us cannot be found in the fact that our fathers always have followed it. It must be found in some help which the law brings toward reaching a social end which the governing power of the community has made up its mind it wants." In 1925, he stated in his dissent in *Gitlow v. New York:* "If in the long run the beliefs expressed in proletarian dictatorship are destined to be accepted by the dominant forces of the community, the only meaning of free speech is that they should be given their chance and have their way." He thus went so far as to maintain that the United States could become communist if the people wanted it. Holmes wanted to purify law of "every word of moral significance," adding: "We should lose the fossil records of a good deal of history and the majesty got from ethical associations, but by ridding ourselves of an unnecessary confusion we should gain very much in the clearness of our thought" (quoted in McKinnon, "The Secret of Mr. Justice Holmes," *American Bar Association Journal,* 1950, p. 264).

These words may be correct with respect to the clarity of laws. However, even the clearest laws are no match for confusions that come about as a result of floods of legislation. And when according to the pure theory of law there is no room in laws for ethics and morals, pure liberalism is approached, under which all noble and vulgar, good and bad legal measures are possible, depending upon the whims and calculations of those who can make and abolish such measures as they see fit, whoever may influence their decisions. The clarity of laws can be destroyed by inundations of laws. This was emphasized by Hamilton and Madison in essays 27, 62, and 85 of the *Federalist.* The United States today suffers from such inundations, for the quantity of laws made by the national government and by fifty state governments is enormous. It is due to all kinds of transmutations of liberal variants and variations into legal norms. Is this deluge of laws bred by sins? Certainly not from the point of view of pure liberalism, for the drive for freedom is one for the ability to do good and evil. On the other hand, it can hardly be doubted that all too many laws are all too few laws in the sense that people find it difficult to really know what the law is and what they may rely on. A multiplicity of laws confuses their simplicity in the search for clarity. A labyrinth of norms kills the norm, for it is difficult to disentangle. Because of too many trees, the forest cannot be made out. Yet in a liberal society, such a labyrinth appears to be normal, especially in one that, like American democracy, approaches pure liberalism.

In spite of their stupendous mass production, laws are a liberal minimum. Only a few of many different movements succeed in getting their present desires through the oftentimes consuming legislative process. The number of all these movements thus is considerably greater than is indicated by the laws a few of these movements succeed in having passed. Just as only a small number of crimes are discovered and even a smaller number punished, only a modest percentage of the desires of individuals or groups will become a bill, and a still more modest one, a law. Stimulated by the legal labyrinth, America has experienced trends toward permissiveness. They were aided by Holmes's statement in *Southern Pac. Co. v. Jensen* (1917) that the common law was "not a brooding omnipresence in the sky but the articulate voice of some sovereign or quasi-sovereign that can be identified." If one understands these sovereigns and quasi-sovereigns as the nation and the states forming it, those who reject the American system can especially argue that as individuals or groups they are at least about as quasi-sovereign as the states, if not as sovereign as the nation. After World War II, the Supreme Court decided that there was no common moral standard for the whole nation, leaving the setting of moral standards to local communities. In view of the supremacy clause of the Constitution, according to which national law supersedes that of the states, people could now argue: if there is no national moral standard, there can't be one in local communities. This opinion is popular with quite a few people, leading to the far-reaching permissiveness one can observe today in many places of the land of unlimited opportunities. On the other hand, many consider the extent of permissiveness impossible, making the land of possibilities one of impossibilities in the moral sense. It is characteristic of the United States that its melting pot is not just a potpourri from an ethnic point of view but in many other respects as well. A highly religious state like Utah can well border on Nevada with its gambling casinos and brothels, often controlled by the underworld. As an ability to do good and evil, beautiful and ugly, moral and immoral things, freedom can lead to all kinds of possibilities, impossible as these may be regarded. In America, all these things appear more in the open, and less camouflaged, than in other countries.

In the past years, I have been struck by the juxtaposition of efficiency and inefficiency. That juxtaposition is, of course, evident in all nations. But while in my travels all over the world, in most countries I came away with the impression that there was more inefficiency than efficiency, in the United States for a long time I was impressed by the emphasis upon efficiency. This has changed since the end of the 1950s. Perhaps President Kennedy had this change in mind when in his inaugural address he said, "But let us begin." However, this hardly was a beginning of greater efficiency. Inefficiency became worse and worse: I attribute the growing trade deficits to that fact. Since the loss of efficiency ran about parallel to the growth of permissiveness, which increasingly became reflected in the drug problem, in crime, and in the sexual revolution, the thought comes that there was an interrelationship, that the one complemented and instigated the other.

I could very well imagine that young Kennedy, when offering his program of the New Frontier, was as disappointed by the New Deal and its aftermath as was Reagan, America's oldest president, when announcing a new beginning. In the beginning, the welfare state that grew under the New Deal showed neither an increase in permissiveness nor a decrease in efficiency. Those active in the 1930s and 1940s had known and mastered the Depression and World War II. However, they were gradually replaced by an ersatz of those who had grown up either in a welfare society or in plenty. The latter took a more or less carefree life for granted and therefore no longer possessed the discipline and the willingness to do without things, characteristic of the older generation, which had considered government aid exceptional and stemming from the emergency of the Depression. It continued to regard efficiency highly. Its children and grandchildren, on the other hand, looked upon government aid as something normal and no longer cared so much about efficiency. Gifts distributed in times of need are likely to be claimed in subsequent normal times. It has seldom happened that social laws have been revoked. After the civil rights legislation of the 1960s, in a large measure constituting social welfare legislation, efficiency declined further. In view of growing permissiveness, identified by many with immorality, people over the past years have often mentioned the moral majority. But those feeling criticized and rejecting moral restrictions soon answered that the moral majority is neither, using bumper stickers to make their opinion known. In analogy, it can be said that the long-existing majority of those who appreciated efficiency by now probably has become a minority. These people may even be blamed by the inefficient for being inefficient, for the traditional concept of efficiency has, as have so many traditional concepts, been replaced by a new one that sees efficiency as getting as much aid from the government as possible and not efficiency in the traditional sense. Since from a liberal point of view both attitudes are defensible, both groups can well live side by side in the liberal-democratic potpourri of the melting pot.

Other attitudes showing liberal variations are hardly criticized either—for instance, acts that in other countries would be considered highly unpatriotic, if not treacherous. When American soldiers shed their blood in fighting North Vietnam, a prominent movie actress, accompanied by other Americans, paid a visit to that country. Upon her return, she praised the North Vietnamese to the applause of her audience, in which students predominated, who burned the very banner for which the soldiers gave their lives. When President Reagan, freely elected by an overwhelming majority, fought the Sandinistas in Nicaragua, American groups organized help for the Sandinistas. In the land of the free, all this is, again, not particularly objected to.

The far-reaching freedom of all individuals is so much taken for granted in the United States that people can hardly believe that others cannot be as free under regimes entertaining different ideas of freedom. Americans often think that these people do not really care to be free, and criticize them. For years I have answered the question why the Germans went along with Hitler and kept silent about his cruelties by pointing out that those asking probably underestimate the despotism of his regime, under which, even in time of peace, when foreign nations considered Germany a friendly nation, Germans who did not agree with Hitler and dared to oppose the regime were discriminated against and liquidated. When I added how in the war the situation worsened so that, for instance, a farmer who slaughtered a pig without reporting it would be put to death, they were quite amazed. Americans are all too inclined to think only of the anti-Semitic aspect of Hitler's tyranny and to emphasize anti-Semitism in the Soviet Union. As to the latter, I warned them not to underestimate the totalitarian aspects of proletarian dictatorship, saying that actually people who were not Jewish could not emigrate, either, because in the Soviet Union the standards of liberty simply differ from those in the United States. Most of those listening seemed surprised and skeptical.

The far-reaching freedom of American citizens, its use and abuse, the existence of extreme liberal-democratic variants, the different kinds of free government, and their cohabitation in the potpourri of the melting pot: all weaken the power and the policy of the government. Those who have lived for some time in Washington, D.C., are well aware of the competition for political influence—even among the staff in the White House. Everybody there knows that his position is dependent upon the president and seeks his ear. And the president listens to many, although in the case of Reagan it was joked that he only listened to his wife. The situation is similar in his cabinet. Unlike prime ministers under parliamentary forms of government, the American president need not fear that coalition partners will walk out and thus jeopardize the survival of the cabinet. He is not dependent on his cabinet members. He appoints and dismisses them at his pleasure. But he listens to them, and the differences of opinion probably are greater in his cabinet than they are among the leading members of the White House staff. In addition, there are the influences of his party, of the opposition, some members of which the president may want to win over for measures he proposes. Finally, there are the media and, quite generally, voices from the people, be they expressed by individuals or groups. The situation is similar with respect to the legislature and even, as Justice Benjamin Cardozo pointed out, in the case of the judiciary. In short, the government of the United States is truly one under a liberal-democratic system. It often shows the absence of systematicness and constancy.

One has spoken of the principle *divide et impera,* meaning that, by dividing the governed and by posing some parts against others, the government can stay in power. Machiavelli and Mazzini accused the papacy of preventing Italian unification in order to rule Italy. Great Britain promoted competition among the rulers of India to enable it to govern the subcontinent. Franco stayed in power because he was a master at juggling the army, the Falange, and the church. Since in democracies the people rule themselves, divide and conquer is applicable because the various segments of the people are reflected in a freely elected government. That applicability is likely to grow with the pluralism of society as well as with its liberalism. In a pluralistic democratic society such as the American, one characterized by migrations, demonstrations and vacillations, one approaching pure liberalism to a large extent, the people's domination of a government merely considered its agent is likely to be especially great. Such a domination is facilitated and symbolized by the separation of governmental powers and their checks and balances, and everything is part of the American concert of factions and fractions. That concert may be full of harmony and of dissonances; it may be tonal and atonal, as can be expected of a potpourri in a melting pot in which things have not yet been melted down into just one big mass.

The governance of the rulers by the ruled may, then, bring about an even greater deadlock of democracy than the one regretted by Burns. The principle of divide and conquer is not only useful to the American people. America's liberal pluralism is used and abused also by foreigners, who find willing help from Americans. For instance, after it had taken Americans hostage, the government of Iran, saying that blacks and females were oppressed in the United States, let them go. Those freed happily took off without making it plain that they were not oppressed in the

United States, the country they had been supposed to represent in Teheran. None of them went even further by refusing to be set free unless all the other hostages were liberated. I never even heard this possibility spoken of in America, where great understanding was shown for the attitude of those coming home. This shows that in the United States the desire to be free is given priority to the fulfillment of duty. Certainly those set free must have realized that their exceptional liberation was motivated by the desire of the Persian rulers to divide the American people into blacks and whites, males and females and, thereby, to weaken America.

A weakening of American prestige was also put up with in favor of individual Americans when President Carter did not permit—not even for medical treatment—the shah to enter the United States, although the former ruler of Iran had been a long and faithful ally of the United States and whose generous hospitality Carter and his entourage had enjoyed not too long before. Carter obviously feared that such permission might harm the hostages. His attitude probably was approved by most Americans, who thought of their compatriots rather than of their *patria*. The same applies to Vietnam. Loud voices put the return of American soldiers above their victory. They were not particularly worried over their country's not living up to its obligations as an ally, its losing its first war, thus jeopardizing its credit as an ally and as a strong nation. Perhaps in the land that has made available to its population more earthly goods than any other nation, in which more of these goods have been wasted than anywhere else, the people felt they could afford this kind of behavior, given all the prosperity around them. These examples show that American foreign policy also is dependent upon the differing egoistic desires of individuals and groups, that, in tune with the principle *divide et impera,* it is weakened by them. A primacy of foreign policy does not seem to exist, for such a priority over internal politics presupposes uniform support by a united nation. Such support, however, can hardly be expected in the potpourri of a melting pot.

Neither can it be expected that in America there would have developed anything other than such a potpourri, with its to and fro, up and down, and its many inefficiencies. This is due in part to the fact that the United States is not just a land of the sons and daughters of emigrants and immigrants but is a country still receiving new emigrants and immigrants, one of steady emancipations. It can also be attributed to the primary documents and leaders of America, that have suggested the many possibilities of liberalism and the most liberal interpretations of the American way of life, leaving possibilities for further interpretations open for all the people in their multiplicity and naïveté.

There is the father of the Declaration of Independence, Jefferson. From his statements and activities one can glean and take what one needs for the time being for one's use and misuse. People have spoken of a Jefferson before, during, and after the French Revolution, of one before, during, and after his presidency, and all these categories can be subdivided. A reference made earlier may well turn up again later on. On the whole, we are faced by a veritable cornucopia for politicians of all shades. Jefferson respected the ethical minimum of the laws but was not too particular with ethics and morals beyond that minimum, much as he might preach them to others. He was some kind of a jack-of-all-trades, basically a bon vivant, living as well as he could and as he liked for the moment.

There is his major contribution, the Declaration of Independence. It is considered, on the one hand, a document heralding the sovereignty of the thirteen colonies vis-à-vis the mother country; on the other hand, it stands for the independence of man from any type of government. Some people consider it a law, others do not. Its formulations have been considered powerful annunciations of important truths as well as vague oratory. Its concepts, especially "the pursuit of happiness," have had a great variety of interpretation, depending upon one's mood. Again, an enormous abundance of possibilities.

The latter is obvious also with respect to the Constitution. A bundle of compromises, it is seen by some as continuing the principles of the Declaration of Independence, by others, as a reaction to these principles. In the case *Elkinson v. Deliesseline,* Justice Johnson commented on it in 1823 that "there is a comprehension and precision that is unparalleled; and I can truly say that after spending my life in studying it, I still daily find in it some new excellence." If he can find in it something new daily, he practically admits that there cannot be as much precision in it as he maintains. And if a judge who obviously was interested in a faithful interpretation of the original Constitution always found new possibilities of its meaning, then others, in view of the different interpretations of that document in the course of time, were likely to discover even more new possibilities of interpretation and to make the most of them. The Constitution in old dress was complemented and replaced by one newly constituted through formal amendments and informal changes that in the sense of Marshall and Jellinek kept it alive as a living Constitution. The distinction between the principles of those who toward the end of the eighteenth century made the Constitution and of those who reinterpreted its provisions and sometimes interpreted them away became evident again in our day. On September 17, 1985, Reagan's Attorney General Edwin Meese III, known for his conservative views, in a Constitution Day speech at Dickinson College emphasized the necessity of respecting the wishes of the Founding Fathers. In the month following, Justice William J. Brennan of the Supreme Court answered him in a lecture given at Georgetown University, entitled, "The Constitution of the United States: Contemporary Ratification." In tune with the concept of the permanent American Revolution, he indicated that the Constitution always has been ratified into new meanings. In the very beginning, he stated, "we are an aspiring people, a people with faith in progress. Our amended Constitution is the lodestar for our aspirations. Like every text worth reading, it is not crystalline. The phrasing is broad and the limitations of its provisions are not clearly marked. Its majestic generalities and ennobling pronouncements are both luminous and obscure. This ambiguity of course calls forth interpretation, the interaction of reader and text. The encounter with the Constitutional text has been, in many sense, my life's work." As did Justice Johnson 150 years earlier, so Justice Brennan, known for his liberal views, at a time when the Supreme Court was rather conservative, discovered many possibilities of constitutional interpretation. This was natural, for in the meantime the Constitution, on account of having undergone changes as a result of formal amendments, judicial interpretations, and reinterpretations, had become an even greater bundle of compromises, an even more comprehensive potpourri of norms than could have been dreamt of by those who originally made it.

Those who made the first comprehensive comments on the Constitution probably did not dream of the kind of constitutional development that would take place, even though their commentary, due to its split personality, left open a great variety of interpretation and even suggested it. Hamilton, who first conceived of the idea of writing this commentary and who therefore can be considered the father of the *Federalist,* chose Madison for his main collaborator—the father of the Constitution, who played an important role, as the Great Compromiser, in its framing. The contributions of that compromiser thus were complemented by those of Hamilton and Jay. They all gave to the *Federalist* the character of a compromise, written in order to bring about the ratification of the constitutional compromise of Philadelphia by a ratification compromise based on the conciliations and reconciliations of those favoring the compromise of the Constitution in the constitutional conventions of the thirteen states.

There are, finally, along with the ambivalent Jefferson and his Declaration of Independence, along with the compromises of the Constitution and its oldest commentary, often considered classic, the two great men of the nineteenth century, Chief Justice Marshall and President Lincoln. Both did their part in establishing and consolidating constitutional compromise. During his long tenure from 1801 to 1835, Marshall saw to it that the Constitution, made for the sake of creating a more perfect Union, actually fulfilled that desire. While he was in the White House, Lincoln did his best to preserve that Union. Both men were liberal relativists. Marshall—like Jefferson, a Virginian—made plain that judicial interpretations had to adjust the Constitution to new conditions, much as his far-reaching protection of private property made him known for his conservatism. Lincoln, hailing from the conservative heartland of the United States, the Midwest, known for his support of Whig causes, generously interpreted the Constitution, going so far as to ignore constitutional provisions and acting against them—in the name of the people.

They all—Jefferson, Hamilton, Marshall, and Lincoln—demonstrated by their behavior a great number of liberal variants, all contributing to making American liberal democracy a potpourri in a melting pot and to gaining the United States the reputation of a land of unlimited opportunities. And since they all left no doubt that, in the last analysis, the people were running that democracy, they encouraged all to always find new liberal variations, to make use of them, and to broaden them liberally as they saw fit. The same is done by the documents mainly determining American democracy, namely, the Declaration of Independence and the Constitution.

In the United States it often has been emphasized that judges look for already existing law and, so to speak, reach into heaven to grasp it. But I have asked myself whether today Americans, rather than looking for norms limiting the behavior of individuals and groups, including the ruling majority, in order to make measure a treasure, they in a Promethean way in ever greater masses take liberties in challenging the Norns in a continuing drive for more and more freedom, moving on and on toward pure and value-free liberty. Generally speaking, it does not seem to occur to them that they might tempt the gods, as was indicated when they named a spaceship *Challenger*. In England, people challenging the sea had been content with naming a big ocean liner *Titanic*.

Irrespective of disasters and tragedies, Americans basically remain happy and lighthearted, qualities quite often attributable to mere carelessness. A symbol of their optimism, President Reagan, shortly after an attack upon an American embassy that cost lives, attended a pleasant show starring his friend Frank Sinatra, who had supported his campaign with millions of dollars. The show must go on. A musical potpourri belongs to the light muses. It is cheerful and cheers people up. It also is liberating, for its arrangement of various melodies makes it easy to listen to and to leave it, as one desires, in order to turn toward new things. It is comparable to the average programs on American radio and television, with all their interruptions and new beginnings. It symbolizes American democracy very well, with its perpetual vacillations and changes, its liberal variants and variations. I was not at all surprised when, on the occasion of the bicentennial of the signing of the Constitution on September 16, 1987, in front of the Capitol in Washington, the celebration reminded me of a *variété*. Under a huge banner saying "We, the People" were all kinds of entertainments by children, youths, and adults, including Chief

Justice Rehnquist and President Reagan, framed by a great variety of dancing and music.

The presidency of Reagan, a man known for his conservative views, did not change much. Much as people may juxtapose American conservatism to liberalism, it is nothing but an aspect of liberalism and, therefore, its captive. Reagan himself has emphasized that originally he had been a follower of the New Deal, a program understanding liberalism as a quest for governmental regulation of the economy, one not showing the respect for private property characteristic of the nineteenth century. Reagan emphasized that he moved into the conservative camp out of disappointment about what liberals had made out of the New Deal, because conservatives favored free trade and a greater respect for the possessions of individuals.

A closer look at American conservatism reveals that it corresponds to the kind of liberalism current at the time of the Declaration of Independence and the adoption of the Constitution and for a long time prevalent thereafter. Reagan campaigned for the presidency under the slogan "A New Beginning." It reminds one of the words of John F. Kennedy at his inauguration, "But let us begin." And the thought of beginning is a liberal, not a conservative, thought. Conservatism proper is interested in conserving rather than beginning. True, Reagan's attitude toward abortion and school prayer shows conservative traits. Yet above all, he wanted to realize the ideas of Adam Smith. He reads *The Freeman,* the monthly publication of the Foundation for Economic Education, which for more than forty years has advocated free enterprise. His secretary of state, Shultz, as well as his confidant, Attorney General Meese, sport Adam Smith ties, as do other members of the Mont Pelerin Society, a worldwide organization in favor of free market economics. Aside from that, Reagan's use of the word *new* when announcing a new beginning put him in line with the New Freedom, the New Deal, and the New Frontier, much as he may have combated their regulations and social legislation. And when he emphasized that he was for the needy rather than the greedy, he made plain that he was not free from social considerations. Be this as it may, there can be little doubt that Reagan's plan for a new beginning was well suited to the New World, with its constant drive for something new, a drive that is a liberal one toward progression, not a conservative one for the sake of preserving.

Even Russell Kirk, whose *The Conservative Mind* (1953) contributed a great deal to the American conservative movement, stated in the introductory chapter (p. 7): "Conservatism is not a fixed and immutable body of dogma, and conservatives inherit from Burke a talent for re-expressing their convictions to fit the time." In the chapter on frustrated conservatism in America, he demonstrated with the example of the distinguished

Adams family of Boston how the steadfast, nonconformist piety of John Adams was pushed aside by the doubts of John Quincy Adams, the humanitarian considerations of Charles Francis Adams, and the desperation of Henry Adams. According to Kirk, the latter "represents the zenith of American civilization. Unmistakably and almost belligerently American, the end-product of four generations of exceptional rectitude and remarkable intelligence, very likely . . . the best-educated man American society has produced" (p. 311). He felt irresistibly carried away by the progression of things. Moving on, not remaining, characterized the conservatism of New England, the loudest in the United States. Its alterations and changes came to overshadow the conservatism of Burke. I stated above that John Adams was not actually as conservative as Kirk claims. The situation was not different with Burke.

American conservatives like to look upon Burke as their example and spiritual leader. His reputation as a conservative primarily rests on his reflections on the French Revolution, clearly showing the disadvantages of the changes brought about by that event. However, a study of Burke's writings and activities reveals him as a typical liberal. In the 1760s, when the controversy between the thirteen colonies and the mother country began, Burke, with the aid of the ideas of Bolingbroke, gave Lockean liberalism new meaning and direction. In 1791, he published his *Appeal from the New to the Old Whigs,* showing new changes in his attitude. Frank O'Gorman's *Edmund Burke: His Political Philosophy* (1973) brought out at the very beginning the different evaluations of Burke and emphasizes that "Burke was not a philosopher at all. He was essentially a practical politician and a propagandist rather than a thinker with a systematic philosophy to expound. His political objectives had their origin less in his own thought than in his membership of the Rockingham Whig party and his close personal relationship with the Marquis of Rockingham himself." The author accused Burke of partisanship and prejudice (p. 11). C. B. Macpherson, in *Burke* (1980), spoke of "The Burke problem," which due to its many-sidedness and ambiguities turned out to be more complicated than the Adam Smith problem discussed by August Oncken in 1898. In the following chapters, he called Burke "the Irish adventurer," "the English politician," "the Anglo-European wasp," "the bourgeois political economist." We think of Jefferson when Burke is described as a practicing politician and an influential author who was full of ideas and interested in having them transmuted into official measures but who, on the other hand, was too impatient a politician to put down his principles in a comprehensive treatise. Therefore, Macpherson goes on, Burke was interpreted in the most differing ways: as a moderate Whig, as an arch conservative, as a herald of nineteenth-century liberalism, as a reviver of the natural law tradition, as a utilitarian, as a revolutionary and counterrevolutionary. According to Macpherson, Burke actually was all of that and considered all of it quite compatible, for basically, his different positions, activities, and changes were just facets of his opinions on economic policy.

This indeed seems to have been the case. Burke's behavior reflected that of his party, a liberal party. It was that of a typical liberal who pursued his ends the way it appeared opportune to him at the time. It was motivated by the idea of the pursuit of happiness and the well-being of those whose—mainly economic—interests he represented. It was very similar to Jefferson's pursuit of happiness, which leaves open many ways and possibilities and emphasizes a hedonistic way of life, as has been demonstrated to a large extent by the American way of life. In the pursuit of happiness one may make many turns and march on winding ways. Burke, the Irishman who sought and found his luck in England, was not particularly concerned about trying to make the English understand the position of the American colonists during their confrontation with the mother country. Their desire not to pay too high taxes was only too compatible with the beliefs of the English Whig, who as an emigrant and immigrant probably had natural sympathies for the land of emigrants and immigrants on the other side of the Atlantic. Burke also shared with his contemporary Jefferson an idea Locke had emphasized, namely, that laws should be derived from the people. That idea also fit into the liberal concept, for popular government is well in tune with liberal tendencies toward change and adjustment. This was clearly expressed by Madison in essays 49 and 62 of the *Federalist* and has been demonstrated again and again by American history.

When Americans speak of conservatism, they usually have in mind a conservatism *à la américaine,* which, however, is similar to the liberalism shared by Burke and Jefferson. It amounts to what Adam Smith stood for in his classic volume on the wealth of nations. This kind of liberalism proposed to reduce the omnipotence of the government, characterized by absolutist and mercantilist features, in a measured way, without jeopardizing law and order. It favored fair free trade, respecting private contracts and private property. It is this kind of liberalism that American conservatives try to revive, to protect, and to see honored again, often by using arguments not just of an economic nature but also of ethics, morals, and religion. The range of American conservatism is wide. It comprises many variants, many variations. This is not surprising at all in view of the fact that this conservatism is mainly interested in preserving a previously accepted form of liberalism and thus actually is a liberalism.

During the past years, conservative groups have mushroomed in the United States. They compete in their attempts to show that they are more conservative than others, often in order to get more money for their activities. In an opportunistic pursuit of happiness, Leftist liberals have become Rightist liberals. In a liberal fashion, conservative organizations have accepted these turncoats with open arms in hopes of gaining strength. This also demonstrates the influence of Burke and Jefferson and Adam Smith—and the captivity of American conservatives by the liberalism of these men. For there is really not much of a difference between those who take advantage of their opportunities in free economic enterprise and those who in the opportunism of politics change their loyalties, following their desires and moods of the moment, switching their allegiance from socialism to the free market. They all are liberals.

Even during the Reagan administration the flexibility of his conservatism was demonstrated. In the group closest to him there originally were pragmatic and ideological conservatives. Increasingly, the former gained the upper hand over the latter. As David A. Stockman complained in *Triumph of Politics* (1986), even Reagan followed pragmatic considerations, being to a large extent motivated by the present wishes of the American people. Thus he favored first a strong, then a weak, dollar. In the beginning, he opposed sanctions against South Africa; later on, he approved them. In spite of serious difficulties, he had medium-range missiles installed in Europe, only to withdraw them later on. During the summit meeting, I could not help but feel that Reagan was out for "exit applause." Just as it makes an actor feel good when, on leaving the theater, he is applauded, Reagan, having had his prestige damaged by the Iran-contra affair, may well have been interested, toward the end of his presidency, to secure himself a good exit after all, one to be aided further by the summit in Moscow in 1988, an election year. Like his compatriots, Reagan was in some respects more than in others the migrant type.

His liberal-democratic attitude was reflected also in his attitude toward the Supreme Court. An important motive for his running again for the presidency was his expectation to be able to nominate new members of the Court, for like his predecessors, he was well aware of the power of that institution. Now it must not be forgotten that the Supreme Court until 1937 often used its power to protect the very values respected by the Founding Fathers, that is, the very values Reagan and his conservatives hoped to preserve, such as free enterprise and the protection of private property. For a century and a half, the Court acted as a bulwark for these values by exercising judicial review. And it was judicial review that was resented by Reagan! This appears to be paradox. For it is well known that the Court, on account of its declaring New Deal laws null and void because they interfered with free enterprise and regulated private property in a way that hurt property rights, was pressured by Roosevelt to capitulate before the ruling majority favoring such interferences and regulation. Therefore, it could have been expected that Reagan would have been interested in the restoration of a judicial review that would put an end to such interference and regulation. Instead, full of resentment against the Court's voiding laws favoring freedom and private property, as they had been passed in some of the states, including his home state California, Reagan turned against judicial review as such, against the very institution that for the better part of American history had been considered the outstanding means for the protection of the original values of the Constitution from liberal-democratic moods and whims. He thus went further than Franklin Roosevelt. The latter had only attacked the exercise of judicial review vis-à-vis national laws, in agreement with Oliver Wendell Holmes, who in "Law and the Court" had written: "I do not think the United States would come to an end if we lost our power to declare an Act of Congress void. I do think the Union would be imperiled if we could not make that declaration as to the laws of the several States." By contrast, Reagan indicated that for the sake of liberty he in a liberal way opposed the latter type of judicial review. Therefore, he opened up possibilities of a legal dissolution of the United States, the inhabitants of which now could, on both state and national levels, do whatever they pleased. This attitude comes close to that of Holmes when he remarked that a proletarian dictatorship would be permissible if desired by the people. In view of the fact that the Constitution has been considered a law providing for a government of the people, by the people, for the people, Reagan's attitude may well be defensible.

American conservatism as emphasized today thus appears to be one of the many parts of the potpourri of the melting pot. Like the rest in the land of migrants, opportunities, and possibilities, it is mainly determined by liberalism, the insatiable desire for more and more freedom. And that desire basically is motivated by the individuals' egoistic pursuits of happiness, the self-interest of individuals hoping that democracy will make their dreams come true and, with them, the American Dream. Kant's words on the nature of the species in his *Anthropologie in pragmatischer Hinsicht abgefaßt* (1798) come to mind: "The individual's own will always is ready to turn against his fellow-man. It always strives toward asserting his claim of unqualified freedom to determine his own behavior as well as that of others who by nature are his equals." These words can also be applied to that variant of liberalism known to Americans as conservatism.

Final Remarks: American Dreams and Worries

To most Americans, the American Dream means that they may devote life and liberty to the pursuit of their happiness here and now, doing justice to the Declaration of Independence, according to which the inalienable rights of man are especially those of life, liberty, and the pursuit of happiness. Since that pursuit is something dynamic, continually resulting in discontent and the desire for more, it amounts to ever new desires for ever new liberties to live ever better, to become happier and happier with an ever higher standard of living, mostly measured by the possession of material goods and their enjoyment. Most Americans see in popular government a means for the realization of the American Dream: the realization of the American Dream constitutes the essence of American democracy, its rationale.

The best-known observers of the United States have generally emphasized that democracy put its stamp on America. They made less plain that the American people in liberal driving and striving imposed their will upon democracy. Tocqueville was concerned with democracy in America rather than with a typically American democracy, much as he emphasized that democracy in America had proceeded further than in other countries. Certainly the title *De la démocratie en Amérique* indicates that he wanted to describe democracy in America rather than a specifically American democracy. Otherwise, he probably would have spoken of *démocratie américaine*. The word *démocratie* dominates the title and the whole title page. It is set in heavy letters and is twice as large as *en Amérique* underneath, words set in thin, tender, and fragile-looking letters and appearing rather insignificant. The contents of the work, in which I could not find the term *démocratie américaine*, correspond to the impression one gets from looking at the title page. In his introduction Tocqueville wrote that he sought in America "the image of democracy itself, with its inclinations, its character, its prejudices, and its passions." Obviously, the United States to him mainly was the scenery for democracy, a place where that form of government could be observed especially well. He obviously was more interested in democracy per se than in a specifically American democracy. The second volume of his work demonstrates this fact even more clearly than does the first one. The author wanted to show how democracy functioned in a particular nation. This interest can be explained from a desire to draw lessons for political developments in other countries, notably in France, where during the rule of the citizen-king Louis-Philippe the thought of democracy was in the air, which to a large extent made Tocqueville desire to study America. At that time, a typically American democracy can hardly be said to have existed, because both nationhood and democracy were still in a developing stage. It thus could not well be described.

After the Civil War, the United States certainly was more of a nation as well as more of a democracy. On the other hand, many of its citizens were still excluded from the political process. Perhaps this prompted the best-known British observer of the nineteenth century, James Bryce, to choose *The American Commonwealth,* published in 1888, as a title for his work—and not *The American Democracy,* in spite of the fact that, given the many electoral reforms in England, the idea of democracy was quite current there. Still, Bryce went further than Tocqueville. His title is more indicative of an American nation. Although he was more concerned with democracy in a particular country than a specifically national democracy, the combination of the American with the democratic is more visible in his book than in that of the Frenchman. As previously in the text, there is mentioned in the last chapter the term "the American democracy," as if the author could not help emphasizing that concept at the end of his work. Perhaps he realized that sooner or later a book with that title would be published.

In 1948, the time was ripe for it. In Harold J. Laski's *The American Democracy,* America appears to be even more combined with democracy than in the work of his compatriot. This is not surprising. The longer people live under a certain form of government, the more they become united, the more they become identical with it. Time can have an integrating effect. Without much doubt the United States was more of a nation after World War II than two generations earlier. National and democratic elements were better integrated. In spite of the success of Margaret Mitchell's bestseller *Gone with the Wind,* the resentment of the South toward the Yankees had subsided. The various local and ethnic groups had fought side by side in the war. The democratic basis of American life had been broadened. There was less discrimination against minorities. The United States was considered the leading democracy. According to Laski, the United States is essentially democratic; the concepts *America* and *democracy* are melted and make up one particular civilization.

Max Lerner's *America as a Civilization* (1957) shares this opinion. When reading this longest of all the books on America mentioned, one again and again becomes aware of the high degree to which the American is tied up with the democratic and that this far-reaching integration constitutes the essential part of American civilization. According to Lerner's foreword, everything "has converged on the grand theme of the nature and meaning of the American experience." With the many phenomena mentioned by Lerner, that experience has been one of a self-governing nation and the individuals composing it, moving in freedom toward ever more freedom for the pursuit of happiness. Basically, Lerner described the American way of life, which he considered the American civilization.

In view of the fact that I attempt in this book to describe that way of life, the reader will perhaps ask why I chose the title *American Democracy* rather than one such as *American Civilization* or *The American Way of Life*. I did so because my title is more indicative of what I think is essential to American civilization and the American way of life. I consider it more concrete as well as more comprehensive. True, a civilization, a way of life as some kind of an order, may very well correspond to a form of government, but it need not do so. By contrast, a democracy can without doubt be understood as a civilization, a way of life. Furthermore, my title emphasizes the concept of popular government and, with it, that of power and its dangers and temptations. It is also indicative of criticism, for civilization usually is considered something good just by definition. And my study is supposed to be a critical one, to show what may be considered negative and positive. It is meant to be a critique of practical liberalism, which manifests itself in American democracy in greater purity than elsewhere.

Looking at the works of Tocqueville, Bryce, Laski, and Lerner, one is struck by the fact that they became more and more voluminous. This is not surprising. With the growth of the United States and whatever occurred in it, the descriptions of this growth was bound to become more and more extensive. The detailed accounts by the authors mentioned have contributed a great deal to an understanding of America and facilitated my attempt to further elucidate our knowledge of the United States. Detailed as are the descriptions of the authors mentioned, one can still draw conclusions about what appears to be important in them, especially in view of the fact that they emphasize certain features, much as the latter may be overshadowed by the accumulation of facts that came about with the pluralism of the liberal-democratic American society and that, obviously, invited comment. With their length, works on America lost their strength, in the sense of *Strenge*—concentrating on the essential. Tocqueville clearly emphasized what he considered the essential feature of democracy in America, namely, the march of equality. He had a good sense for what is decisive and important. It was different for Bryce. In his review, Woodrow Wilson wrote that his work was not up to that of the Frenchman because it was an exposition of facts rather than good judgment. The same is true of Laski's book. In its preface, we read that in America "there is so much of beauty and ugliness, of good and evil" that he "cannot put it into words." He added that "this book is written out of deep love for America," but it is not well proportioned. He amassed so many facts that it is difficult to find out what is essential. The same applies to Lerner's work. Twelve chapters with nearly a hundred subtitles making up a text of over a thousand large-size pages printed in small type, his book deals with its topic probably more exhaustively than any other work. But the essential thing about American civilization, of which one becomes aware by reading and rereading, namely, the liberal-democratic one, is not clearly focused upon. It is obvious only between the lines. Perhaps the remark in the foreword, "No American can achieve detachment in studying America, and I doubt whether even a European or Asian can," may be expanded by saying that the improbability of an objective evaluation of America makes it difficult especially for Americans to see and make stand out what is essential, for their never-ceasing migrations in an ever changing society, complemented by ever new liberal variations facing and strongly trying to influence them, may, given the enormous variety of new impressions, well make them lose their orientation, prevent them from seeing what is decisive, or let them lose interest in discovering what is important. In *Wohin treibt die Bundesrepublik?*, the existentialist Karl Jaspers voiced similar thoughts when he doubted that a German could judge Germany and the Germans. But then, Germany is so much smaller and much more devoid of movement and liberal variations than the United States.

In 1981, the National Gallery in Washington, D.C.—the capital of the country characterized by Big Business, Big Government, Big Labor, and so on—a gallery that has demonstrated the American quest for the new and the colossal by putting on many special exhibits (usually three or four at the same time), mounted the biggest exhibition of Rodin's works under the title Rodin Rediscovered. It stressed how the sculptor invented his own, new ways of creating, of trying to show the essential. Perhaps today, two hundred years after its formative period, an attempt is in order to show the essence of American democracy, after good books have provided valuable detailed accounts. It goes without saying that a scholarly analysis cannot take the liberties artists can afford, much as the search for scholarly findings, their substantiation, and their dissemination may be an art in itself. A deductive method is to be applied with caution, especially with respect to the evaluation of a way of life, for the actual constitution of a living, aspiring people is not necessarily tantamount to the written constitution of its government as described in books and commentaries. On the other hand, it is advisable to keep in mind Konrad Adenauer's remarks at the beginning of his memoirs—that one should look for what is basic to things in order to know what is essential. Therefore, I attempted in the present study of American democracy to point out what appears to me its very essence, namely, the continuous drive among all inhabitants for an ever greater freedom, as manifested in ever new aspects and variations of liberalism.

Emphasizing that he strictly adhered to facts, Tocqueville stated at the very beginning of his first volume what appeared to him the most outstanding feature of democracy in America. Among the novel objects that attracted his attention during his stay in the United States, nothing struck him more forcibly than the general equality of condition among the people. He began, "I readily discovered the prodigious influence that this primary fact exercises on the whole course of society; it gives a peculiar direction to public opinion and a peculiar tenor to the laws; it imparts new maxims to the governing authorities and peculiar habits to the governed. I soon perceived that the influence of this fact extends far beyond the political character and the laws of the country, and that it has no less effect on civil society than on the government; it creates opinions, gives birth to new sentiments, founds novel customs, and modifies whatever it does not produce. The more I advanced in the study of American society, the more I perceived that this equality of condition is the fundamental fact from which all others seem to be derived and the central point at which all my observations constantly terminated." In the following paragraph, the idea of equality is connected with that of democracy. We read further that it is evident to all alike that there is a great democratic revolution going on and that, throughout history, democratic and egalitarian ideas spread. Tocqueville obviously considered equality to be characteristic of democracy and democracy suited to equality.

Tocqueville's emphasis upon equality and democracy in a large measure probably was due to the fact that he observed America at the time of the egalitarian President Jackson, after the abolition of property qualifications for the right to vote, in the wake of Jacksonian democracy. People are inclined to see new things that are close up more than the old, and to emphasize them accordingly. Visitors from foreign lands especially perceive what impresses them most directly. Tocqueville was mainly impressed by the new that was in the foreground, namely, equality and democracy. His sojourn was short. For that reason he probably can be blamed less for his emphasis on these two features than enthusiastic followers of Jackson, to whom he was exposed. It also must be taken into account that the nobleman from Normandy, whose family had suffered under the French Revolution, was influenced by the liberal orientation of his class, an orientation in favor of liberty; his fear was that egalitarian and democratic trends might threaten the rights of individuals. It thus may well be assumed that his skepticism of democracy and equality made him observe these two important factors with a special interest and let him be apprehensive of their powerful combination in the New World, which indicated to him what might be in store for other nations. After all, he prophesied the conquest of large parts of the globe by egalitarian democracy. Perhaps the slogan of the French Revolution, "Liberty, Equality, Fraternity," indicated to him that emphasis on equality would follow that on liberty, just as the Jacobins had followed the Girondists and as Jacksonian egalitarian democracy had followed a predominantly freedom-oriented republic under Presidents Madison, Monroe, and John Quincy Adams. An observer of the development in the United States can indeed come away with the impression that equality has moved so much to the foreground that it looks as if it was pushing liberty aside. Such a replacement, making equality from a means for freedom to an end in itself, in my opinion cannot be precluded. Perhaps the day will come when people will get tired of competing for freedom and be satisfied with an equal distribution of goods. This could be seen as a natural consequence of the equality of conditions that impressed Tocqueville. The land of the free then would become one of the equals, and liberty would have to make room for equality.

Emphases on features that strike the eye when visiting a foreign country, let alone a foreign continent, do not necessarily produce correct descriptions. It cannot even be said that the person describing those features is convinced that they constitute the complete picture. However, Tocqueville seems to have been somewhat familiar with American history. He knew the *Federalist* and had informed himself in many other ways, even though he shied away from giving the sources of his informations. His book shows that all his emphasis upon equality and democracy did not prevent him from indicating that both could be useful or detrimental to the freedom of the individual. The motto of the French Revolution has been considered a liberal confession and program. A liberal like Tocqueville may well have thought that it does not necessarily show the sequence in which one of its values will be succeeded by the other. Rather, he may have thought that all three of them belong together, that equality and fraternity are even dominated by liberty, which, after all, is mentioned first. Tocqueville's contemporary Heinrich Heine in his "Nachtgedanken" spoke of America as the "great freedom-stable, inhabited by equality-scoundrels," indicating the belongingness of freedom with equality, perhaps even that freedom precedes equality, that equality is nothing but a means for more freedom, conducive to freedom, and its servant.

In view of the fact that Tocqueville never lost sight of liberty, perhaps his emphasis upon equality and democracy can be interpreted to mean that he, the liberal, thought that in the last analysis liberalism with its often-mentioned aspects such as liberty, equality, and democracy was the great moving force behind everything. But this is only a speculation. Obviously, Tocqueville stressed equality and democracy as main features of the United States, not liberty. As was foreseen by him, equality and popular government have grown in America. The march of both has been so successful that they no longer are just considered programs, as they were at the time of Tocqueville. They have become established facts but without thereby losing their programmatic character, which is evident in the constant, continuing drive for more equality and democracy.

This does not preclude that liberty would not have advanced also, that liberalism in all its multiplicity, ambiguity, and duplicity could not constitute the essence of Americanism due to the fact that equality and democracy are nothing but means serving liberalism. This indeed is my opinion. Tocqueville may have surmised it, but he never said so. He probably was the captive of the particular type of liberalism prevalent in his circles. As did other noblemen, he saw in the egalitarian democratic movement a challenge to the status and the liberty of the upper strata, something incompatible with his own concept of freedom. Although he did not doubt that equality and democracy would march on, he did not part from his noble environment, in which liberty was conceived to be the opposite of equality and fraternity. In other words, the liberalism of Tocqueville and his class differed from that of the French revolutionaries. It was a liberalism expressing, and bound by, definite values, not the unlimited, pure, and value-free one under which individuals, in order to broaden their liberties, could use any means, including those of far-reaching egalitarianism and democratism. It also should not be overlooked that Tocqueville observed the United States prior to the big waves of immigration. In his time, there existed relatively few liberalisms. They, furthermore, recognized a certain measure, corresponding, for instance, to the liberalism of Adam Smith rather than that of the Manchester school. With increasing immigration, the range of liberalisms grew. The immigrants brought to the land, which attracted them as one of unlimited opportunities, all kinds of liberalisms, much as the latter may have been considered impossible by many people. Those arriving and their offspring frequently welcomed extreme equalizations and democratizations that perhaps even Tocqueville had not thought of. And they all were compatible with pure liberalism—were even demanded by it.

For from the point of view of pure liberalisms, libertarian, egalitarian, and democratic excesses cannot really exist. There can be only liberal ramifications, all of which are in tune with it and, consequently, cannot appear as impossible aberrations in the sense of something evil, ugly, and so on. When Countess Marion Dönhoff in *Amerikanische Wechselbäder* expressed her disappointment over all the many changes constantly taking place in the United States, she spoke as a liberal for whom, as for most Europeans, liberalism still is credited with certain ethical, moral, and other values. Seen from America, a land full of liberal variants and variations, there can hardly exist disappointment over unsteady behaviors, tos and fros, in American politics. One can only be disappointed about something that is different from, and usually worse than, what is expected. But in American democracy, which approaches pure liberalism more than any other popular government and seems to approach it more and more, constant policies can be expected less and less. Under the pressure of the wishes and the curses of individuals and groups due to present moods and whims, such policies will increasingly disappear. It is not surprising that in 1987 there were published books with opposite titles, such as Dieter Kronzucker's *Unser Amerika* (Our America) and Peter von Zahn's *Verläßt uns Amerika?* (Is America Deserting Us?).

As was said, already by the midtwenties, when the communists in the Soviet Union were busy consolidating their regime, which had not been recognized by the United States because communist leaders, following Lenin, did not feel responsible for Russia's debts made under tsarist rule, Holmes, known for his liberalism, stated that America could become communist if its people so desired. In 1920 Carl L. Becker had published *The United States: An Experiment in Democracy,* where we read at the end that, whereas today the absolutism of the majority was still at the disposal of the capitalist class, tomorrow it could well serve the proletariat. This corresponds to American liberal thinking, which comprises more than just the span from capitalism to communism, from the principle *beati possidentes* to that of *damnati possidentes*. Even more does it correspond to pure liberalism, which increasingly has put its stamp on America. In *America Set Free* (1929), Hermann Count Keyserling pointed to the similarity between the United States and the USSR. He considered the American "the most fanatic believer in liberty the world has ever seen," writing that "in present America youth gives the tone to a degree unparalled in history," and considered the "flaming youth of America . . . almost equally irresponsible" as the "Russian revolutionists, nihilists," revolting against the moral order (pp. 130, 141, 159).

If in the United States nearly everything is compatible with drives for rights of one kind or another, even one for communist dictatorship; if Americans are proud of the melting pot of their New World, of their potpourri of the most different variations; if they believe in America's mission to extend freedom throughout the world: then only those in the land of the free can be justified in resenting anti-American movements, those who believe in specifically anticommunist and antisocialist liberalisms, if these movements are communist or socialist. In that case, they would represent the variation of liberalism that was predominant from the American Revolution to the New Deal. That variation is still strong today, for in spite of all regulations of the economy and all social laws, Americans basically have stuck to free enterprise and the protection of private property. Under President Reagan this liberal variant, also known as American conservatism, was strengthened. However, much as its followers might stress their concept of liberty and free government, they should be careful not to maintain that it is the only correct one. Those who arrogantly assert that they favor liberty as such are lying, whether they are in the capitalist or communist or any other camp. As long as people disagree on the nature of freedom, nobody can assert that his concept of freedom is the only correct one. Even those who in the sense of pure liberalism believe in pure liberty—according to which they can do as they please—should be aware that their concept of liberty is a subjective one.

In view of this, there can be no doubt that the scope of liberty and of liberalism is enormously wide. This has been demonstrated in the land of the free more than in any other nation. Therefore, neither in America nor in any other country should anyone claim that his concept of liberty is more truthful than another. He should show that such a claim is correct. And that will be difficult as long as people cannot agree on the nature of freedom, as they probably cannot for a long time to come. Now since we know that liberty is an ability to do good and evil, beautiful and ugly things, people will strive toward proving that the liberties they desire have it over those of others. This again boils down to ethical, aesthetic, and other limitations of freedom and of liberalism. Whether such a proof is possible in view of the general trend to pure freedom, to pure liberalism, is another question. It will be difficult to answer throughout the world, including the land of unlimited opportunities, although events in the United States and their development according to pure liberalism may facilitate the answer.

In view of their many liberal variations, these events show, among other things, that American representatives of specific facets of liberalism from the standpoint of pure liberalism cannot advance theoretical arguments against other liberalisms, anti-American as they may be. If America is seen as the land of liberalism and if the equation *Americanism = liberalism* is accepted, liberal un- or anti-American liberalisms simply are not possible. This is true also of "un-American activities" and the congressional Committee for Un-American Activities, formed after World War II. Therefore, since the United States will not be able to advance convincing arguments against anti-American movements heralded in the name of liberty, such as those against "American imperialism," America's enemies will triumphantly shout: "America is not dependable, get away from her!" They could add that it was especially the far-reaching realization of pure liberalism in the United States that whetted their appetite for the liberties desired by them, even if these liberties opposed the interests of the United States and its liberals. He who hails liberty as such must respect all those who are looking for liberty and must permit everybody to have his own concept of freedom as an ability to do good and evil, as well as to define what is good and what is evil, and so on. If those whom Americans today consider terrorists look upon themselves as people striving for freedom, for pure freedom, similar to the *purs* during Jacobin terror, Americans of all people cannot very well object to them—certainly not from the point of view of liberalism. On the other hand, the terrorists will find it as difficult as American liberals of all orientations to prove that their concept of liberty is the correct one.

Ten years before his death Jefferson wrote John Adams on August 1, 1816, that he hoped that the United States would be a rallying point for the reason and freedom of the globe. He added: "I like the dreams of the future better than the history of the past,—so good night! I will dream on." The author of the Declaration of Independence, the man who stands at the beginning of American liberalism and American democracy, also stands at the beginning of the American Dream. This dream means that ever more people with ever greater equality will become ever more free and that, by means of their government of the people, for the people, by the people, and in their pursuit of happiness, they will enjoy an ever greater standard of living. It is an attractive, tempting dream in view of the fact that the sage of Monticello did not burden his compatriots with the kind of categorical imperatives the sage of Königsberg had in mind. An attractive, tempting dream stirred up by a politician who tried his hand at many things and who, in contrast to the Prussian professor, in his irregular mode of living did not worry too much over morality. And just as Kant's criticism opened new ways for philosophy, Jefferson's optimism opened up to the new nation in the New World the American Dream for all Americans whose migrant mentality liberated them from self-critical inhibitions and thus facilitated the realization of that dream. In accordance with that dream, their liberal-democratic opinions could show the world seemingly unlimited opportunities in the sense of life enjoyment rather than the fulfillment of duty.

On the title page of a lecture F. A. Hayek delivered at the University of Salzburg in 1970 on Mozart's birthday, dealing with the errors of constructivism and the bases of a legitimate criticism of forms of society, there is a print of an etching by Goya from about 1793, "El sueño de la razon produce monstruos." The picture is gruesome. A man is sitting there, clad in the fashion of his day. As if exhausted, he buries his head in his arms, resting on his desk, asleep. According to the title, he is dreaming, obviously having a bad dream. Behind him, there is an abundance of all kinds of monsters. In a cruel, wild, beastly, malicious way they seem to be torturing him, grinning scornfully, sitting on the ground, on the desk, coming from above, being everywhere. And there seem to arrive more and more of them, endlessly. It is clear that he cannot be saved from them. Hayek, known as a liberal, wrote that the inscription usually is translated "the dream of reason gives birth to monsters." But he felt it should be translated differently, the opposite way, namely, "if reason sleeps, monsters come." All this can be read into Goya's words, and many other things come to mind. Hayek, seeing these monsters, thought of constructions that, reflecting irrationalities of the age of reason, were designed by men and were incompatible with his kind of liberalism, which to a large extent was based upon traditional respect for contracts and private property.

Looking at the picture by the Spanish critic, which reminds me of Goethe's sorcerer's apprentice, I think of the American Dream. I ask myself whether American democracy with its many liberal variations perhaps has brought forth monstrosities that have made worries out of the American Dream. American dreaming is a product of the Enlightenment. Jefferson was right when he saw his country as a rallying point for reason and freedom. The American Dream came into existence after Voltaire, under the word *loi,* had written in the *Dictionnaire Philosophique:* "If you desire good laws, burn the ones you have and make new ones." Similar to Rousseau, next to whom he occupies a place of honor in the Paris Pantheon, this French figure of the Enlightenment believed in the unlimited legislative authority of the people. However, if these words are read out of context, they can be considered an invitation to each individual to disregard the laws and to be his own legislator. With increasing equalization and democratization and the growing impact of slogans connected with them, such behavior actually could be expected. Plain, simple people like what is plain and simple. And if, presumably following Voltaire, they could replace existing laws with new ones, it could be assumed that a fortiori they would do the same with respect to ethical and moral imperatives. This, I believe, has to a large extent occurred in the United States.

Naturally, the probability of such a development was greater there than in other countries. Here was a New World, a tabula rasa, extending over many geographic and climatic zones, waiting for all the new things emigrants and immigrants looking for freedom would bring in. They, their children, and their further descendants in a most varied way influenced America and its society, more or less imposing upon them their good and bad characteristics. Their new homeland was to them the land of unlimited opportunities, in which they used, took advantage of, and abused their freedom for good and evil and all kinds of other things. Migrating, roving around, demonstrating, and agitating, they pursued their happiness on this earth mostly in hedonistic and egoistic ways in the generally accepted belief that their business in America was business. Accordingly, they at any particular time favored that version of free government that was the most conducive to their interests. Citizens mainly interested in practical results, they may here and there have cared more or less about ethical, moral, and legal principles, depending upon their temporary tastes. Their main interest was the extension of freedom, the freedom of the individual the way he saw fit. In these drives for freedom, there often was no holding back. There came about, in the potpourri of the American melting pot, innumerable liberal variants and variations. This situation still exists today. Liberalism continues to be at work, demonstrating itself in ever new and enthusiastic quests for liberty. In liberal fashion, one went from elitist to egalitarian, from representative to direct, from limited to unlimited democracy, until in the end, under the impact of new, liberalistic movements, anarchistic trends became obvious. Due to concessions by the ruling majority during the 1960s, demonstrators and agitators were increasingly encouraged. So constant was the rioting that the original formula "Rights through Riots" seemed to be replaced by "Riots through Rights." It often appeared to me that people were on the way from free government to government-free, to the freedom from any kind of rule, to anarchy. The idea of freedom, according to the introduction of Hegel's philosophy of history the absolute final purpose, with "liveliness, movement and activity," was subjectively seen in a manner he probably would have objected to as much as to his interpretation by Marx. I have asked myself whether Tocqueville's law, according to which too many concessions by a liberal government to the liberal demands of citizens will lead to revolution, will not be proven in the United States. This question is imperative especially in view of the fact that the French observer of democracy in America was right in prophesying the march of equality and democracy, although he did not go so far as to emphasize that march as a means for achieving greater freedom for the individual or to mention pure liberalism, which has increasingly influenced American ways.

I have here attempted to focus on pure liberalism, of which, it seems to me, Americans have become increasingly conscious and which has determined their activities more and more. I have tried to lift it out of the unconscious so that it may consciously be seen in its totality—its disadvantages, its blessings, and its propriety—in its "activisme de désespoir" (Sartre) as well as in its activism of hope. When Americans proceeded from elitist to egalitarian, from representative to direct, from limited to unlimited democracy, they demonstrated their striving for pure popular government, for an ever purer democracy. There are indications that as life becomes more complicated there comes about a longing for the plain and simple, for the pure with its presumed simplifications and, in addition, a desire to see democracy not in the sense of Locke or Rousseau but in that of Bakunin. It is open to doubt whether the emphasis on conservatism will change anything in the long run, especially in view of the fact that American conservatism is, like all liberalisms, nothing but a facet of pure liberalism—as the source of all liberalisms. Reagan has been criticized for his attack on Libya. Against his assertion that terrorist attacks against Americans were incompatible with the American way of life it has been argued that it would have been more in conformity with that way of life to arrest the terrorists and subject them to an ordinary court procedure. From the point of view of pure liberalism, according to which one can do whatever one likes at any particular moment, both positions, as well as others, are justified. But the march toward pure liberalism in the realization of the American Dream makes that dream a worrisome one because one cannot tell what will happen next, how freedom will be used and abused for good or evil—or in any other way. This fear does not even imply that the word *democracy* should be written *democrazy,* that popular government ought to be seen as the erring and confusion of the people. The latter also are absolutely compatible with pure liberalism.

Pure liberalism was perhaps seen by the Irish poet William Butler Yeats, writing after John Stuart Mill, who had defined pure freedom in his *Essay on Liberty*. Poets often are wiser than scholars. To maintain this, we need not think of Nietzsche's "Fröhliche Wissenschaft." In Yeats's "The Second Coming" we read:

> Things fall apart; the center cannot hold;
> Mere anarchy is loosed upon the world.

Perhaps, or, rather, probably, the development in the New World, characterized by steady drives for change, sped up this process. For the Americanization of the world, in a century Americans liked to consider their own, ought not to be overlooked, much as the dream of a Pax Americana may be over.

Today, liberalism in many parts of the world shows itself as anarchism to such a degree as to prompt the question whether anarchy is natural to liberalism. For a long time, this question has been answered in the negative, because generally accepted liberalisms were considered something under which law and morals determined individual behavior; because one did not see, or did not want to see, pure liberalism with its enormous potential in all directions. Even in limited liberalisms there usually did not exist a real center, because to each type of liberalism the idea of movement, of getting on, is inherent. One need think only of the basically recognized liberal principle of freedom of contract. Provisions such as that stipulating that a contract incompatible with morality is null and void are mere exceptions, which with the increasing decline of morals became less and less relevant. However, even if there were certain firm centers in limited liberalisms, they would be threatened by pure liberalism. In pure liberalism, there is no firm center to begin with. There is only a dissemination of all kinds of liberalism for the assertion of all kinds of liberties. It is telling that Charles Ives, who according to Lucas Foss in a lecture in the National Gallery in Washington, D.C., is the man in whose compositions anything surprising can happen any time, is American—and one who, according to Leonard Bernstein, made American music independent.

In the democracy of Freud's land, where the enjoyment of liberty brought about veritable exhilaration among large parts of the population, pure liberalism is more evident than in other countries. Still, many Americans do not yet seem to have become fully aware of it and its total value-freeness. Not all people, presumptuous as they might be, have been aware of the steady growth of freedom. I have attempted here to bring about a certain consciousness of these facts. Since American democracy is carried along by each single individual in the nation, one may ask, in the manner of Parsifal, "Who is American popular government?" I answer: in the last analysis, American democracy is all particular individuals in their individuality, all those who act and work and somehow participate in it, to whom democracy shows their human condition, their *Geworfensein* (Heidegger) into good or evil, as well as other liberal variations of human being and human nature. Whether American democracy, like the *Gral,* will bring redemption, is, in view of its orientation toward this world, open to question—although it probably is not impossible.

In a proposed address to Congress, Washington in 1789 questioned the future of the American Constitution: "If the blessings of Heaven showered thick around us should be spilled on the ground or converted to curses, through the fault of those for whom they were intended, it would not be the first instance of folly or perverseness in short-sighted mortals." In the preceding pages I commented on the present constitution of America, its people, and its democracy. I refrain from remarks on the future, which perhaps will show how Americans, engaged in the pursuit of happiness in the here and now, have made their great nation small.

It is improbable that such a development will detract from the importance of Americanism. The latter is tied up too much with liberalism, which will be with us for a long time, to the advantage and disadvantage of humanity, since it is basically beyond good and evil—because in its purity it does not care about ethical and similar values. Exactly for that reason the world in its quest for more freedom will eventually belong to it.

At the time of Sturm und Drang, of storm and stress, when the United States was founded, the nationalist Alexander Hamilton, perhaps thinking of Shakespeare's words, "O brave new world, That has such people in't!" (*Tempest,* 5, 1, 183), in essay 11 of the *Federalist* hoped that Americans would be able to dictate the terms of the connection between the old and the new world. This expectation brings to mind the remark of Machiavelli, who in many respects influenced Hamilton: "Nothing is more difficult to undertake, more dangerous to carry out or uncertain with respect to its success than to take over leadership in the introduction of a new order" (*The Prince,* chap. 6). This should be even more true if, due to its liberality, the new order turns out to be a disorder, because liberalism with its atomistic, egoistic teachings falls into its own trap and strengthens the individualism of Americans obsessed with freedom. He who takes over leadership easily overestimates his ability. John C. Calhoun, the states' righter and opponent of Hamilton, stated in 1817: "We are greatly and rapidly—I was about to say fearfully—growing."

In 1904 Henry Adams, in the chapter "A Law of Acceleration" from his autobiography, saw the coming of the "new American," a child of the uncalculable might of coal, chemistry, and electricity, of far-reaching energy as well as of new, still unknown forces. He believed this new man, as compared to other known creatures of nature, would be some kind of a god. On this kind of a god Lerner wrote half a century later in his work on America as a civilization that "unlike men of previous ages, it is not salvation he is after, nor virtue, nor saintliness, nor beauty, nor status. He is an amoral man of energy, mastery, and power. Above all else, he is a man for whom the walls have been broken down. He is the double figure in Marlowe, of Tamerlane and Dr. Faustus, the one sweeping like a footloose barbarian across the plains to overleap the barriers of earlier civilizations, the other breaking the taboos against knowledge and experience, even at the cost of his soul. . . . Thus the great themes of the Renaissance and Reformation are fulfilled in the American as the archetypal modern man—the discovery of new areas, the charting of the skies, the lure of power, the realization of self in works, the magic of science, the consciousness of the individual" (pp. 63 f.).

Prognoses and descriptions like that bring to mind Pascal, who thought that men are neither angels nor animals ("ni ange ni bête"), a view shared by the authors of the *Federalist*. One also thinks of Baudelaire's lines on Abel and Cain. We read in the first strophe, Abel's race should sleep, drink, and eat, and God will gracefully smile upon it. In the last one it is urged that the race of Cain should ascend to heaven and throw God down to earth. Under the benign, often spiteful and derisive prognosticating smile of pure liberalism, the liberty-loving inhabitants of Freud's land eat, drink, and sleep and, in the opinion of many people in God's own country, do other things to his pleasure and displeasure. In a Promethean manner they ascend to the sky in order to, in the pursuit of happiness, bring about a paradiselike Golden Age for themselves here on earth, perhaps overestimating their abilities. Baudelaire gave the last word to the race of Cain. In his interpretation of Schelling's remark that freedom is an ability to do good and evil, Heidegger emphasized the importance of the latter. This is in close agreement with the statement Fichte made in 1794 at the end of his criticism of Rousseau, namely that most men are evil. All this is not likely to be popular in optimistic America. But it deserves to be reflected upon, even if one refuses to share the sinister pessimism of Donoso Cortes, with its hopeless, Manichaean view of man, and considers exceptional the highly publicized descent of Americans into the underworld of crime. In 1931, Georges Duhamel spoke of America as a menace. This is not my intention at all. Liberalism can be a blessing as well as a threat, and every people can produce supermen and their opposite: *Übermenschen* as well as *Untermenschen*. However, in accordance with Thomas Mann's warning about Dostoevski, it probably is advisable, as it is with respect to all things human, to say, in spite of all the good many Russian contemporaries of Nietzsche attributed to men: "Americanism—with measure."

Perhaps Tocqueville entertained such thoughts when in the introduction to his work on democracy in America he considered the equality of conditions as *fait providentiel* and wrote that a new science of politics was needed. This suggests that, after democratizations, equalizations, and liberalizations demonstrating the march of liberalism toward its purity, a science of politics limiting, and triumphing over, politics might be even more necessary than it was during the life of the Frenchman and his era's outlooks, which new times and tides easily relegated to the past.

Hegel, who according to his wish was buried next to Fichte in Berlin, in the introduction to his *Philosophy of History*, after emphasizing that freedom was the absolute purpose of world history, considered America "the land of the future that is to reveal in times ahead of us the importance of world history: it is a land of longing for all those who are bored by the historic arsenals of old Europe." He reminded people of the words of Napoleon, the child and executor of the French Revolution, that this old Europe bored him: "Cette vieille Europe m'ennuie." Certainly the importance of liberalism has been demonstrated by American democracy. Whether or not it was the right thing, or whether people in the land of the free possess the armaments to do the right things, are important questions.

One perhaps thinks of Ives's *The Unanswered Question* of 1906, when the American Century supposedly was about to begin. The composer, in his private life rather conservative and inconspicuously following the rules and regulations of daily life, was credited by Leonard Bernstein with having given American music its independence. However, in the composition mentioned—a very short piece—he in an extremely liberal, irregular, and disturbing way made a musical force out of discords, which, in contrast to those of Wagner, cannot be explained. Instruments placed in different parts of the concert hall play in so radically different tempi that they no longer can be controlled by one conductor. Disappearing low tones in the background, which for Ives reflected the quiet times past, are drowned out and nearly annihilated by loud discords. One gets an uneasy feeling from all the new things brought about at the time of the revolt of the masses—and into the new century in Freud's house in the New World. And it is open to doubt whether or not this sentiment is mitigated by the words of Iphigenie in Goethe's measured drama:

> —denn es erzeugt nicht gleich
> Ein Haus den Halgbott, noch das Ungeheuer;
> Erst eine Reihe Böser oder Guter
> Bringt endlich das Entsetzen, bringt die Freude
> Der Welt hervor.

> —for there is not created right away
> By a house the demigod, nor the monster;
> Only a string of evil and good ones
> Will finally bring forth the horror, the joy
> Of the world.

My evaluation of American democracy deals with the nature of practical liberalism. It is the nature of something existing that its existence, its being, is being in time. It is conditioned by time, part of time. It is not timeless. However eternally world history may show, step by step, the evolution of the principle, the content of which is the awareness of freedom; however eternal the drive for freedom and the toil connected with it may appear: liberalisms have not succeeded in separating themselves from the times in which they came about. They lingered on and decayed. Kant, who never left his native Prussia, remarked in *Das Ende aller Dinge* (1794): "Poor mortals, nothing is consistent with you but inconsistency."

Especially in the New World, liberalism has produced a great many liberal variants and variations, which succeeded one another and disappeared with time. Under some of them the United States advanced from a young nation to the most powerful on earth, its people from a modest to a high standard of living. What lies in store for America and for Americanism remains to be seen.

Postscript: Liberalism, Modernism, Americanism

Liberalism is the source of modernism and Americanism.

My presentation in this study of American democracy follows the words of the title and discusses America, the American people, and their popular government. Just as Montesquieu, known for his description of the various branches of government, emphasized that their separation was qualified by checks and balances and their intertwinement, I have stressed that concepts such as America, the American people, and their self-government cannot be strictly kept apart. One flows into the other. America in large measure is what its people make of it by virtue of ruling themselves. American democracy is a melting pot not only of ethnic groups, but of concepts. The subtitle points to what American democracy is all about, namely, aspects of practical liberalism.

Aspects of something may be not only different facets of it. They also can only constitute partial demonstrations. Therefore, aspects of practical liberalism show partial sides of practical liberalism. And since practical liberalism is only the practical side of liberalism, people will assume that there also is a theoretical side and that both derive from liberalism without any qualification, from liberalism as such, from liberalism proper, as a *Ding an sich*. As my subtitle suggests, I am in the preceding pages mainly concerned with practical liberalism, with liberalism as understood by the typical American, the "doer," to use an expression of Alpheus Mason. I shall be doing so also in this postscript.

The title of my book, including its subtitle, begins with the word *America* and ends with *Liberalism*. Liberalism thus comes last, but by no means least, for the subtitle explains what I consider American democracy to be all about. In my opinion, liberalism constitutes the essence of

American democracy and is the source of Americanism as it developed under that form of government. The enormous and overwhelming impact of liberalism on American democracy and Americanism, for better or worse, I hope has been evident to the reader of this volume, in which I attempt to show that liberalism is the source of Americanism, and not the other way around: much as America may have aided liberalism, it is liberalism that has brought about Americanism.

The veritable primeval force of liberalism, of the human desire to be free and ever more free, becomes even more obvious in view of the fact that in recent times a distinction has been drawn between liberalism and modernism. It is here maintained that modernism and all its aspects and demonstrations are nothing but aspects of liberalism; that it is in the very nature of liberalism, its openness and openendedness, that it always will seek to demonstrate itself in new and modern versions, all of which are, therefore, mere aspects of liberalism, that seemingly inexhaustible spawner of liberalisms. In the New World called America, discovered at the beginning of what has been called the modern age, a world that certainly with respect to the United States has been considered a modern world, modernism with all its modernisms no doubt has had its impact upon the American way of life as reflected in American democracy, but only as a part of liberalism. Liberalism and its child, modernism, created Americanism and kept on creating it in ever new dimensions, according to the wishes and whims of freedom-seeking people. This justifies my reversing the sequence of words used in the title and subtitle of my book, and give to this postscript the title "Liberalism, Modernism, Americanism." It demonstrates that liberalism, mentioned last in the title and subtitle of the book as an explanation of American democracy, now with respect to importance comes first, followed by its modern and modernist versions, which can be called by the common term *modernism*. This concept forms a bridge to Americanism, to the new, modern world of America, in which all kinds of modernisms, good and bad, beautiful and ugly, and so on, have found a cozy—and not so cozy—home. But it always must be kept in mind that both modernism and Americanism would not be possible without liberalism, that freedom-thirsty "brooding omnipresence in the sky," to use the words of Oliver Wendell Holmes, one of the great liberal members of the Supreme Court, in *Southern Pacific Co. v. Jensen* (1917). For modernism is nothing but the captive and fleeting appearance of time, receiving its substantive content from the quest for freedom. So also does Americanism, the captive of mere space, something quite accidental if taken all by itself. Liberalism, on the other hand, is timeless and spaceless, and its everlasting substance is the urge to become more and more free.

Let us first consider the distinction between liberalism and modernisms in greater detail. Dr. Benjamin Rush, a signer of the Declaration of Independence, the founder of Dickinson College, and known as the father of American medicine, in January 1787 urged the American people not to confuse the War of Independence with the American Revolution, because the Revolution was not over. A man of basically conservative inclinations, he thus laid the groundwork for the idea of the permanent American revolution, a concept fraught with an enormous liberal potential, which could produce all kinds of liberal variants and variations and let people indulge in innumerable modernisms, such as the decision of the Supreme Court in *United States v. Alvarez-Machain* (1992) that American government agents may kidnap a Mexican in Mexico so that he may be tried in the United States, a decision considered "monstrous" and "shocking" by the dissenting minority of Justices Blackmun, O'Connor, and Stevens.

Similarly, it has become customary to confuse the historical movement known as liberalism with liberalism itself. The former was evident in the English Revolution, also known as the Whig Revolution, which culminated in the Glorious Revolution of 1688. It found major proponents in men like Lord Coke, John Locke, and later, Montesquieu. It could be seen in the American Revolution, often considered a sequence of the Whig Revolution, and in America's Founding Fathers. Adam Smith and Immanuel Kant were outstanding representatives of that movement, as were Wilhelm von Humboldt, the founder of the University of Berlin, and John Stuart Mill, the latter dedicating his *Essay on Liberty* to the former. It has existed down to our day; we need think only of Wilhelm Röpke, F. A. Hayek, and Milton Friedman. It has become known as "classic" liberalism, the kind of liberalism that was considered proper by the men mentioned, providing for a good balance between individual human rights and public power.

However, this kind of liberalism, important as it has been in the history of liberalism, must not be confused with liberalism itself as its source. In a word, the liberalism considered proper by the men just mentioned is not liberalism proper, liberalism as such, liberalism as a Ding an sich, the source of all kinds of liberal variations, including the historical movement known as liberalism. In my *Liberalism Proper and Proper Liberalism* (1985), I arrived at the conclusion that liberalism proper is pure liberalism, liberalism as such, a quest for nothing but the extension of freedom, unhindered by any ethical, moral, legal, or other limitation. That idea I elaborated in *Reiner Liberalismus* (1985), which I defined as a highly egoistic and egotistic drive of the individual for his own greater freedom to do or not to do whatever he sees fit.

Looking at liberalism that way makes us shudder in view of Schelling's statement in *Über das Wesen der menschlichen Freiheit* (1809) that freedom is "an ability to do good and evil." From that point of view, traces of which also can be found in the writings of America's founders, someone fighting for the freedom to hurt others even to the point of killing them could do so under the banner of liberalism, of pure liberalism, or liberalism proper, because he considers himself acting under what he feels is a proper liberalism. The Hobbesian state of nature, characterized by a bellum omnium contra omnes (a war of all against all), was thus one dominated by liberalism, where every individual believed it was proper to steal from others, to hurt them, to kill them. In a word, the very philosopher who generally is considered the defender of monarchical dictatorship would qualify as a liberal. Indeed he does if one takes liberalism as liberalism proper. And those who deny this simply are inclined to interpret liberalism the opposite way, as the historical movement described, a liberalism they consider proper, one that basically fights for the freedom of the individual from dictatorship.

These people would also deny that Karl Marx, proposing dictatorship by the proletariat, the liquidation of the bourgeoisie and capitalists, was a liberal. They are right if they interpret liberalism from the point of view of the historical liberal movement they claim to belong to, from what became known as classic liberalism. They agree with Marx, who strongly resented their kind of liberalism, who saw its Manchester version and decided to write the *Communist Manifesto,* urging proletarians of all lands to unite and liberate themselves from oppression by their capitalist employers. And communist liberation went on: in not too distant times past the leadership of the Soviet Union supported all kinds of "liberation movements" throughout the world to spread communist dictatorships for the sake of the freedom of the proletariat.

Was Stalin, one of the most cruel and bloodthirsty dictators of our age, an outspoken enemy of liberalism, its aspect of capitalism, and Western democracy, a liberal? Certainly not from the point of view of classic liberalism. But surely he was from that of his own liberal interpretation of communism as a dictatorial means of bringing about greater freedom for the proletariat, from that of liberalism in the sense of liberalism proper, or pure liberalism, from that of a liberalism he, Stalin, considered proper.

Of Hitler, the other cruel and bloodthirsty dictator of the twentieth century, the same can be said. His party slogan, always on the front page of the *Völkischer Beobachter,* the official party newspaper, was "Für Freiheit und Brot" (For Freedom and Bread). Freedom came first! I remember songs like the "Niederländische Dankgebet": "Uns ward das Los gegeben, ein freies Volk zu sein" (We were given the lot to be a free people, free from the Treaty of Versailles, the freemasons, and the Jews!). And "Freiheit ist das Feuer, ist der helle Schein, so lang sie noch lodert, ist die Welt nicht klein!" following the words, "nur der Freiheit gehört unser

Leben!" (Our life only belongs to liberty! Freedom is the fire, is the light shine, as long as it is ablaze, the world is not small!). In 1933, when Hitler came to power, he usually would begin his speeches with the statement that fourteen years of serfdom and disgrace—the fourteen years of the Weimar Republic, a republic known for its classic liberalism—were over: a clear confession to the freedom and honor his regime was heralding in. Obviously, Hitler, as far as the historical movement called liberalism is concerned, agreed with his favorite author, Nietzsche, as expressed in the latter's *Vom Nutzen und Nachteil der Historie für das Leben* (On the Usefulness and Disadvantages of History for Life, 1874), that history had to be disregarded because it was detrimental to the *Volk* and its culture.

As stated above, the dangers resulting from freedom were recognized, for instance, by William Blackstone, a commentator on the laws of England who was considered as much of a classic liberal as Locke. His arguments, as those of Locke, were used in the struggle of the American colonists with Great Britain. He had spoken of "wild and savage liberty" and said that "natural liberty consists properly in a power of acting as one thinks fit, without any restraint or control, unless by the laws of nature." These dangers were seen by Americans, and by another great liberal, Kant, who spoke of "wild freedom," who criticized "brutal freedom," "lawless freedom," "barbaric freedom," "crazy freedom," who complained of the "so confused play of human affairs" in a "ruleless freedom," and who mentioned with "deep contempt" the "attachment of the wild beings to their lawless freedom." The exercise of this kind of freedom appeared to him as a "raw, uncouth and beastly degradation of humanity" (*Idee zu einer allgemeinen Geschichte in weltbürgerlicher Absicht,* 1784; *Zum ewigen Frieden,* 1795, in *Kant's Werke,* vol. 8, pp. 22, 24, 25, 26, 30, 354, 367). Hegel feared that man could see in the right to do whatever he desired a direct invitation to theft, murder, sedition, and so on (*Philosophie des Rechts,* sec. 319).

I think these authors sensed liberalism proper and its dangers but did not really dare to clearly call it in all honesty by its proper name, *pure liberalism.* Concerned as they were with securing freedom from the government, they considered freedom something pure in the sense of ethics, a freedom from a government they felt to be impure because it was bad. Doing so, they could not very well use the word *pure* in its innate sense, implying the absence of ethics and morals. They were reluctant to do something similar to what was done later by Hans Kelsen when he brought forth his pure theory of law, maintaining that all that counted with law was its sanction and not whether it was good. Interestingly enough, Kant, who wrote *Critique of Pure Reason* (1781), never wrote a critique of pure freedom or of pure liberalism, much as his *Critique of Practical Reason* (1788) is full of categorical imperatives meant to guard against exercises of freedom that might be encouraged by the allurements and temptations of pure freedom and pure liberalism. I attempted to fill part of that gap in *Reiner Liberalismus,* which, in turn, prompted me to write the present critique of practical liberalism. For I know no other country—even in the New World, where Columbus arrived five hundred years ago (an event that Francisco López de Gómara at the beginning of his *Historia General de la Indias* in 1552 considered the greatest event since the creation of the world, with the exception of the incarnation and death of its creator)—in which the seemingly limitless potential of liberalism would have been better demonstrated than in the United States, the land of the free and of unlimited opportunities. In the *Spirit of the Laws,* Montesquieu wrote that he, the great man of comparative government, knew of no nation where the freedom of the individual citizen was better protected than in England. It was to its American colonies that English men and women left the old country in order to enjoy even more freedom; it has been in the United States that people made the most of their liberties, gave the best demonstration of all aspects of practical liberalism, and more closely approached pure liberalism—for good or evil and beyond.

Given this enormous potential of liberalism, its potency, its ability to effect all kinds of results, the drive for liberty may well be the primary drive in the human mind and in human nature. This would confirm the opinion of Hegel that history shows a continuing quest for greater freedom; of Nietzsche, whose drive for more freedom let him look down upon history; of Hayek, who in the 1960s was among the few refusing to be misled by the trend toward increasing state controls and regulations and who envisioned a final victory of liberty even in the Soviet Union—then still considered a strong nation. This drive for more liberty also includes the emancipations desired by Freud, another scholar from Vienna, whom Hayek, still the captive of classic liberalism, considered about as dangerous to our civilization as Marx. From *potentia* it is but one step to *potestas.* The potency of the potential of liberalism constitutes a power that could well be overwhelming and must be guarded against by heeding warnings like that of Lord Acton that power tends to corrupt and absolute power corrupts absolutely. The same applies to modernism, as a modern aspect of liberalism.

In view of the fact that modernism is nothing but an aspect of liberalism proper, and modernisms are merely partial demonstrations of pure liberalism, it makes no sense to emphasize the distinction between liberalism and modernism or to maintain that the two are different. This does not mean that those who do so act from bad motives. They simply are the captives of classic liberalism, a liberalism full of liberal variants and variations by itself, one to which I have paid allegiance throughout my life, much as I have resented some of its facets. From the point of view of that kind of liberalism, Stalin, Hitler, and other dictators could not qualify as liberals by any stretch of the imagination. On the other hand, liberalism proper permits a seemingly endless stretching of the imagination, far beyond what people may consider proper liberalism. This has been done by many of those who started what has become known as the liberal movement. This movement made the nineteenth century the "liberal century" and is still well under way, after having brought about, under the guidance of Ludwig Erhard, the economic recovery of Germany, known as the German miracle. This miracle was followed by many other economic miracles and by the spreading of constitutional democracy and the free market in the former communist nations. I have been in basic agreement with classic liberals. As they have done, I have criticized Marx, Lenin and Stalin, Mussolini and Hitler, and dictatorship as such.

This does not imply that I would not criticize classic liberals. Not the way they were criticized by "the socialists of all parties," to whom Hayek addressed his *The Road to Serfdom.* But I would criticize them for not being willing to recognize that liberalism is much larger than classic liberalism, that liberalism proper is the source of any kind of liberalism considered proper by those advocating it, that in its pure form it is out only to increase the freedom of the individual or all those who propose it and is devoid of any ethical, moral, or other connotations, all of which can only be limitations on an unlimited striving for, and use of, freedom. As a classic liberal, I am inclined to favor such connotations and to criticize some far-out approaches to pure liberalism. However, I also feel impelled to recognize pure liberalism, or liberalism proper, as the source of all kinds of liberalisms and encompassing all of them, much as I might want to write a constructive critique of it—something I have attempted in this volume, always aware of the fact that freedom is an ability to do good or evil.

Subsuming what has become known as modernism under the general concept of liberalism and rejecting its juxtaposition to liberalism does not mean that modernism could not fulfill a useful function. Any kind of liberalism can do so. Just as John Stuart Mill asserted in his *Essay on Liberty* that the expression of even faulty opinions can contain part of the truth and be of use, likewise the assertion of any kind of liberalism, subject to criticism as it may be, is not necessarily all wrong and can improve things. And while, remindful of Kant's derogatory remarks on *Geniemänner* (*Anthropologie, in pragmatischer Hinsicht abgefaßt,* 1978, *Werke,* vol. 7, p. 226), his warning not to run with modern fashions (ibid., p. 245 f.) and that we must scrutinize modernism carefully, modernism can, in connection with liberalism and Americanism, play an important role, even though it will function only as an aspect of liberalism.

As an aspect of liberalism, modernism and all kinds of modernisms can demonstrate the enormous potential of liberalism. They can show its breadth, depth, its wide dimensions, its potency, its power. For clearly, if there always come about modern versions of liberalism, keeping pace with modernity and modern fashions, the quest for more freedom inherent in liberalism will become increasingly satisfied. New realizations of liberties will bring about new desires for further adjustments of existing liberties to more modern conditions, conditioning people to ever new aspects of freedom and whetting their appetites to newer and newer liberalisms, to further and further drives for greater freedom. This *perpetuum mobile*—and liberalism, especially in the form of modernism, is steadily on the move—may well not further classic liberalism. As a matter of fact, it may leave it by the wayside as something unmodern to be disregarded, even discarded. Still, it is in tune with liberalism proper, which, grinning with satisfaction over its power, may well welcome the demise of its classic aspects, considered old-fashioned and out-of-date.

Alpheus Thomas Mason may have recognized the enormous potential for better or worse of pure liberalism. Heidegger, commenting on Schelling's statement that freedom is the ability to do good and evil, thought that Hegel's roommate in their student days at Tübingen primarily had in mind freedom's potential to do evil; so too Mason, when describing liberal variations, may have harbored similar fears. I do not know. I never asked him. But the more I think about it, I find it strange that the title of a chapter, "Liberal Variations," which appeared in the first edition of his *Free Government in the Making,* could no longer be found in later editions. Was Mason aware of the possibility, even probability, that modern interpretations of liberalism might bring about a modernism that would replace and even eliminate the classic liberalism he believed in, the kind of liberalism reflected in his and most of America's Founding Fathers' concept of government? Did he sense liberalism proper as distinguished from the liberalism he and the majority of America's founders considered proper? Did he envision pure liberalism with its modernism and their potential to do good and, especially, evil?

Be this as it may, there can be little doubt that modernism has brought into focus the great power of liberalism. It has done so especially in the United States. This is not surprising in view of the fact that this country, the liberalism of which inspired Simón Bolívar and Spanish-American revolutions for independence from Spain, emerged as the most prominent liberal nation in the New World, one the Old World became conscious of at the beginning of the modern age—Circa 1492, as J. Carter Brown's last big exhibition at the National Gallery in Washington was entitled. Thus modernism, aside from demonstrating the great power of liberalism, can be considered a link between liberalism and Americanism—the

American way of life as it has developed in American democracy and its aspects of practical liberalism described in the preceding chapters, which show that liberalism has been the major formative force of Americanism.

One could take issue with this thesis and assert that Americanism spawned liberalism, certainly the kind of liberalism that has come to exist in the United States. Such an assertion could be based upon Locke's famous statement in section 49 of his *Second Treatise of Government:* "in the beginning all the world was America." After all, Locke is probably the political philosopher who influenced Americans the most. Furthermore, he made that statement in his chapter "Of Property," and few people will deny that property has played an important role in the American way of life and its liberalism. On top of it, Locke has been considered the father of classic liberalism. Therefore, it could be argued, if he put America first and considered it the beginning, then liberalism could come only thereafter. The assertion that Americanism brought forth liberalism could, especially with respect to modern versions of liberalism, be based upon the argument that certainly such versions, characteristic as they are primarily of the United States, show the mark of American attitudes and thus were preceded by them. One could push this argument even further and, in the vein of Montesquieu who maintained that concepts appear differently under different conditions, claim that from the very beginning Americans formed their own kind of liberalism. This would take us back to Locke's idea that in the beginning all the world was America. One could add that when Goethe wrote "Amerika, du hast es besser" and showed in that poem that Americans enjoyed more freedom than did people in the old world; that when on another occasion he asked what might have become of him had he gone to America and never heard of Kant: he thought that America brought forth freedom. So did many people leaving their old countries for the United States, the land of unlimited opportunities, the land of the free. The American national anthem itself puts the concept of America before that of freedom when it speaks of the land (America) of the free.

Still, the argument that Americanism preceded liberalism can be refuted. As to Locke's statement, it ought not to be taken out of context. A closer reading of his chapter on property reveals that he thought of America in terms of mere space, wild and uncultivated, without spiritual content. While he wrote that in the beginning all the world was that kind of space, he added that by his time America had changed, thus making a clear reference to its having become more cultivated by the efforts of people working there in freedom. That amounts to saying that liberalism preceded Americanism the way it was known to him. As to Goethe's statements, his poem dedicated to the United States clearly praises that country's liberation from a past he regretted and perhaps resented; America was inhabited by free people, whom he urged to remain free. It was freedom ever growing and ever supposed to grow—liberalism—that made, and was going to make, America what it was and was going to be, and thus preceded Americanism. His question, what would have become of him had he gone to America and never heard of Kant, in view of the latter's categorical imperatives restricting freedom, can only be interpreted as a longing for a country whose people have made it a free country by constantly fighting for more freedom. The emigrants leaving for America came because they felt oppressed at home by their governments and saw America as a land free of oppressive governments, because Americans wanted it to be so. And the national anthem? It praised the land because it was inhabited by the free, who had taken care that it would be and remain free. Clearly, mere American space did not matter. What mattered was the spirit of the people inhabiting and making something out of it. That was the spirit of liberalism, creating and maintaining its kind of Americanism. Result: liberalism has created Americanism.

In view of the enormous power of liberalism as described throughout this book and in this postscript, another result could hardly have been expected. Too primeval, too innate in human nature is the quest for freedom not to succeed in, and put its stamp on, environments, including the American one. It is true that in a country that approaches pure liberalism more than any other nation because it is part of and representative of the New World—not only in a geographic sense, but also in that of behavior—many modernisms may have been possible only in America. From that point of view, one is tempted to argue that Americanism, creating the climate for modernism, indeed preceded modernism and, modernism being a part of liberalism, liberalism. But this argument overlooks the fact that Americanism was created by liberalism long before people began talking of modernism, a concept which may result in good and evil as much as liberalism, of which it is part and probably its most far-out aspect. As such, modernism could well be, in cruel modern times, the most dangerous aspect of liberalism and, among other things, could seriously threaten Americanism, as conceived by those considered classic liberals. For to liberals proper, believing in pure liberalism, there cannot actually be a modernist threat to any kind of Americanism brought about in American democracy by aspects of practical liberalism, all of which derive from the nature of practical liberalism or, as the German subtitle of this book reads, from the *Wesen des praktischen Liberalismus*.

The nature, or *Wesen,* of liberalism implies the coming and going of its aspects or partial realizations of pure liberalism. It shows the perpetual striving for more freedom, however conceived by individual desires, bearing out Hegel's evaluation of history. Therefore, there can be no end of history, much as people may want a given historical situation to last. This is true of all such situations. Hitler, perhaps inspired by the length of the First Reich and Wagner's *Lohengrin,* thought his would be a *Tausendjähriges Reich,* but it lasted only twelve years. The workers' paradise envisioned by communists did not last too long either. Neither did capitalist liberal democracies. Maurice Hauriou, like many a Frenchman, felt that in the Third Republic France had finally arrived at the type of government ideally suited to it. The principles guiding that republic were discarded by those of de Gaulle's Fifth Republic. In the 1930s, it generally was assumed that capitalist liberal democracy in Latin America was safe in Argentina, Chile, Colombia, and Uruguay. It survived nowhere, being succeeded in all these countries by military governments.

The bourgeois feeling of contentment and saturation, against which Thomas Mann revolted toward the fin de siècle, was followed by new ideologies. They were modern versions of liberalism. So were neoliberalisms after Hayek took on John Maynard Keynes, then believed to be the apostle of the new millennium. Wishful thinking about perfect conditions continued. For instance, after Jean François Revel published *Comment les démocraties finissent* in 1983, five hundred years after the birth of Luther (English translation, *How Democracies Perish,* 1984), Francis Fukuyama brought out an article, *The End of History?* in the eventful year 1989, two hundred years after the French Revolution and one hundred years after the birth of Martin Heidegger. Fukuyama indicated that the end of history might be accomplished with a general acceptance of capitalist liberal democracy following the rejection of Leftist and Rightist extremes. He elaborated that thesis in *The End of History and the Last Man* (1992), after Claes G. Ryn had come forth with doubts about an end of history in *The New Jacobinism: Can Democracy Survive?* (1991). Optimistic speculations have thus been matched by question marks. The match is probably not yet over, for even Fukuyama does not seem to be sure whether the Eldorado he envisioned will last, perhaps aware of what Eric Voegelin considered obvious, namely, that human nature does not change, as I indicated in *Liberale Demokratie* (1992).

From my critique of practical liberalism here presented it follows that challenges to liberal democracy actually need not come from outside the big field of liberalism. Those claiming the contrary show themselves to be the captives of a liberalism that rejects dictatorship, be it from the Right, the Left, the church, or what have you. In fact, these challenges, as long as their proponents assert that they fight for more freedom, are as much partial realizations of pure liberalism as classic liberalism is (as I attempted to show in my critique of pure liberalism, *Reiner Liberalismus*). They may be considered proper derivatives of liberalism proper as much as other liberal variations usually thought to be in tune with classic liberalism. Therefore, those asserting that challenges to liberal democracy are illiberal often refuse to recognize liberalism in its purity as the source of all liberalisms, to look liberalism proper in the eye, to face up to it. Ignoring Schelling's opinion that freedom is an ability to do good and evil, they do not realize that liberalism is a quest for more freedom to do just that: to do more good and more evil.

To repeat: as long as the drive for freedom exists—and it is likely to exist in the last man—there cannot very well be a end of history. As Max Weber, the first American artist to be given a retrospective exhibition at the Museum of Modern Art in New York City, put it in one of his Cubist Poems of 1914:

> *No End, no beginning*
>
> As there is no end to any end
> So has beginning no beginning
> But in this time is
> And all in time that lives

It is improbable that capitalist liberal democracy will ever bring about general satisfaction among people, for the human drive for change is too strong. If it does, there may indeed come about stagnation as something more or less desired by tired, satisfied, and saturated men, something remindful of the fin de siècle atmosphere with its bored bourgeoisie. But there can be no stagnation in historical development as long as there is life. Schiller's wife, with an air of disapproval, said of Goethe: "Er hat sein' Sach' auf nichts gestellt," a sentence later emphasized by Max Stirner in *Der Einzige und sein Eigentum,* published in 1844. This means: "He doesn't really care about anything" (in contrast to her husband, who could generate much enthusiasm). This statement shows the author of *Faust* to be a liberal able to make ample use of pure liberalism as the more or less praiseworthy as well as dubious source of all kinds of liberal variations and variants—and being tolerant toward them. He saw the coexistence of the diastolic and the systolic as much as that of the diabolic and the divine. And he appeared as a genuine liberal when he remarked: "Es gilt am Ende doch nur vorwärts" (In the last analysis, we are bound to move on). Thomas Mann, at the end of his fantasy on Goethe (1948), emphasized this statement in connection with the latter's poem on America.

In his classic *On Democracy in America,* the classic liberal Tocqueville wrote that in the twentieth century the United States and Russia would emerge as the two major powers. After World War I, the United States was the biggest creditor nation and Imperial Russia became the Soviet Union. Following the Second World War, both countries were the world's superpowers. By now, the USSR has disintegrated and formally no longer exists as one nation. The communist dream has turned sour; much as it believed itself to be the final workers' paradise, another kind of the end of history has proved to be an illusion. The United States for the time being is the only superpower left. Whether it will remain in that position and what will happen to the American Dream remains to be seen. I pose this question not only here at the end of the present study, but also at that of my *America's Political Dilemma: From Limited to Unlimited Democracy,* published twenty years earlier. At that time, student revolts had weakened the United States, and the Soviet Union appeared strong. Today, after the Reagan administration, under which this country became a big debtor nation, people begin to wonder whether the vertical disintegration that destroyed the Soviet Union will, in the land of unlimited opportunities, be followed by a horizontal one due to liberal variations and their liberal interpretations. Arthur M. Schlesinger, Jr., *The Disuniting of America: Reflections on a Multicultural Society* (1991), and Andrew Hacker, *Two Nations: Black and White, Separate, Hostile, Unequal* (1992), point in that direction, as do recent Hispanic riots in Washington and black ones in Los Angeles. The latter prompted gruesome, disturbing title pages. *The Economist* (May 9–15) showed under the caption "Getting Along" a black and a white looking in opposite directions before an American flag. *Newsweek* (May 18) spoke of "Rethinking Race and Crime in America: Beyond Black and White."

At any rate, the quest for freedom is likely to continue for better or worse as a result of the enormous possibilities by still-prevailing classic liberalisms, as they may be derived from liberalism proper or pure liberalism. The continuation of that quest in the United States is beyond much doubt, because Americans traditionally have striven toward the new for more liberty and for the ideal and material things that come with it. In view of these never-ending contentions, contentedness—even with that well-known version of classic liberalism, capitalist liberal democracy—seems to be improbable. This eliminates thoughts of an end of history under that kind of setup. A fortiori, it must eliminate such thoughts in case of other, nonclassic realizations of liberalism, some of which may even make a mockery of classic liberalism.

What is valid for the order of the United States applies even more so to any world order. In 1952, when many people still believed in the Pax Americana, Carl Schmitt, a skeptic of classic liberalism whom Hayek, an enthusiastic defender of that way of thinking, ranked among the great German minds, published an article on the unity of the world in the journal *Merkur.* It voiced doubts about whether the victor in the struggle between the two superpowers could bring about that unity in view of the fact that the world always will be larger than the United States. The new world order conceived by President Bush is supposed to be capitalist, liberal, and democratic in the sense of classic liberalism. Given its greater diversity, there probably will be more ups and downs in it than in the United States, even if it exists within the classic liberal mold. Its liberal variations are likely to be still greater once it goes beyond that mold under the aegis of pure liberalism. There will be a good chance of its falling prey to leaders who, while promising greater freedom, actually oppress people according to their own egoistic interpretation of liberty as their and their followers' right to force others to be free. The classic liberal Max Weber suggested that probability for Germany back in 1919, in his essay on politics as a profession. Simón Bolívars famous *Jamaica Letter* (1815), in which this classic liberal and liberator of Spanish America expressed doubts about these lands becoming as liberal-democratic as the United States, is applicable today to many other parts of the world, where regimes have come about that in many respects are the very opposite of classic liberal democracy.

Talk about an end of history makes sense to me only if it means that historical development strives toward some particular end, such as, for instance, liberalism. In that respect, Hegel, Nietzsche, and Hayek are not far apart. It cannot mean that history comes to an end under a liberal stalemate, for a stalemated liberalism is a contradiction in terms. Talk about an end of history also indicates hybris. Ardent research so far has not discovered the beginning of history. It is doubtful whether it ever will. Why, then, should we think that we're not bound by that same limitation concerning the end of history? To assume that we can know that end would put speculation above fact, quicksilvered quackery above serious scholarship, which, in tune with Ranke, takes pains to find out what actually took place.

In the German misery of 1945, Heidegger, having his roots in the same soil Hegel, Schelling, and Schiller did, and often considered an existentialist, showed no angst, but was full of hope. He wrote to a colleague: "Alles denkt jetzt den Untergang. Wir Deutschen können deshalb nicht untergehen, weil wir noch gar nicht aufgegangen sind und erst durch die Nacht hindurch müssen" (Everybody thinks of going down. We Germans cannot go down because we have not yet risen, and first must pass through the night). He had witnessed some rebirth of Germany when in 1976 he was laid to rest in his little home town, Messkirch, to the sound of the very church bells he had tolled as a boy. The many Japanese who on the occasion of his hundredth birthday flocked to his grave in 1989 may well have applied his words to the lot of their own people back in 1945. There always is hope. But history has shown that disillusion ought not be discounted. As Nietzsche wrote, history has both advantages and disadvantages for the lives of individuals, nations, and cultures. History will go on. And as long as man is alive, it probably will do so under the striving of liberalism, where, according to Tocqueville's chapter on why the Americans are more addicted to practical than theoretical science, "Everyone is in motion, some in quest of power, others of gain." That striving has been indicated in the leading nation of the New World by programs such as the New Freedom, the New Deal, the New Frontier and, now, Clinton's "New Generation"—one implying not just an age group, but a generation of ever-new things for better or worse.

Following these words, we read: "In the midst of this universal tumult, this incessant conflict of jarring interests, this continual striving of men after fortune, where is that calm to be found which is necessary for the deeper combinations of the intellect? How can the mind dwell upon any single point when everything whirls around it, and man himself is swept and beaten onwards by the heady current that rolls all things in its course?"

As I said in the foreword, the book here presented may, I hope, make a contribution by showing what is questionable in democracy and liberalism, both of which have probably developed furthest in the United States—and are likely to continue to do so according to Americanism and modernism as demonstrations of liberalism. They will continue to evolve from the time of this publication, two hundred and fifty years after Jefferson's birth, until the still-unforeseeable end of all things.

Selected Works Referred to in the Text

Adair, Douglass. "The Authorship of the Disputed Federalist Papers." *William and Mary Quarterly* 1 (1944): 97–122, 235–64.

Adams, Henry. *The Education of Henry Adams: An Autobiography.* Boston: Houghton Mifflin, 1918.

Adams, James T. *The Epic of America.* Boston: Little, Brown, 1933.

———. *The Living Jefferson.* New York: Scribner's, 1936.

Adams, John. *A Defence of the Constitutions of Government of the United States of America.* London: C. Dilly, 1787.

Adams, William H., ed. *Jefferson and the Arts: An Extended View.* Washington, D.C.: National Gallery of Art, 1976.

Arnold, Matthew. *Discourses in America.* London: Macmillan, 1885.

Banfield, Edward C. *The Unheavenly City: The Nature and Future of Our Urban Crisis.* Boston: Little, Brown, 1970.

Becker, Carl L. *The History of Political Parties in the Province of New York, 1760–1776.* Madison: University of Wisconsin Press, 1909.

———. *The United States: An Experiment in Democracy.* New York: Harper, 1920.

———. *The Declaration of Independence: A Study of the History of Political Ideas.* New York: Harcourt, Brace, 1922.

———. *Everyman His Own Historian: Essays on History and Politics.* New York: Croft, 1935.

Benson, C. Randolph. *Thomas Jefferson as Social Scientist.* Rutherford: Fairleigh Dickinson University Press, 1971.

Benson, George C. S. *The New Centralization.* New York: Farrar and Rinehart, 1941.

Berman, Eleanor D. *Thomas Jefferson and the Arts: An Essay on Early American Esthetics.* New York: Philosophical Library, 1947.

Bodin, Jean. *The Six Bookes of a Commonweale.* London: Bishop, 1606.

Borch, Herbert von. *Die unfertige Gesellschaft.* Munich: Piper, 1964.
Boyd, Julian, et al., eds. *The Papers of Thomas Jefferson.* Princeton: Princeton University Press, 1950.
Brown, Stuart G. *Thomas Jefferson.* New York: Washington Square, 1963.
Brownlow, Louis. *The President and the Presidency.* Chicago: Public Administration Service, 1949.
Bryce, James. *The American Commonwealth.* London: Macmillan, 1888.
Burns, Edward M. *James Madison: Philosopher of the Constitution.* New Brunswick: Rutgers University Press, 1938.
Burns, James M. *The Deadlock of Democracy: Four-Party Politics in America.* Englewood Cliffs: Prentice-Hall, 1983.
Calhoun, John C. *A Disquisition on Government, and a Discourse on the Constitution and Government of the United States.* Charleston: Walker and James, 1851.
Chinard, Gilbert. *Thomas Jefferson: Apostle of Americanism.* Boston: Little Brown, 1929.
Cornuelle, Richard C. *Reclaiming the American Dream.* New York: Random House, 1965.
Corwin, Edward S. *The "Higher Law" Background of American Constitutional Law.* Ithaca: Cornell University Press, 1929.
———. *The President: Office and Powers, 1787–1984.* New York: New York University Press, 1984.
Corwin, Edward S., and Louis Koenig. *The Presidency Today.* New York: New York University Press, 1956.
Davenport, Russell W., and editors of *Fortune. U.S.A.: The Permanent Revolution.* New York: Prentice-Hall, 1951.
Davidson, Philip. *Propaganda and the American Revolution, 1773–1783.* Chapel Hill: University of North Carolina Press, 1941.
Desvernine, Raoul E. *Democratic Despotism.* New York; Dodd, Mead, 1936.
Dicey, Albert V. *Introduction to the Law of the Constitution.* London: Macmillan, 1885.
Dietze, Gottfried. *The Federalist: A Classic on Federalism and Free Government.* Baltimore: Johns Hopkins University Press, 1960.
———. "Will the Presidency Incite Assassination?" *Ethics* 76 (1965): 14–32.
———. *America's Political Dilemma: From Limited to Unlimited Democracy.* Baltimore: Johns Hopkins University Press, 1968.
———. *Liberalism Proper and Proper Liberalism.* Baltimore: Johns Hopkins University Press, 1985.
———. *Reiner Liberalismus.* Tübingen: Mohr, 1985.
Dönhoff, Marion Gräfin von. *Amerikanische Wechselbäder.* Stuttgart: Deutsche Verlagsanstalt, 1983.
Duhamel, Georges. *America: The Menace.* Boston: Houghton Mifflin, 1931.
Emerson, Ralph W. *Society and Solitude.* Boston: Houghton Mifflin, 1904.
Engels, Friedrich. *Schriften aus der Frühzeit,* ed. Gustav Mayer. Berlin: Springer, 1920.
Farland, Max. *The Framing of the Constitution of the United States.* New Haven: Yale University Press, 1913.

Fichte, Johann Gottlieb. *Einige Vorlesungen über die Bestimmung des Gelehrten.* Jena: Gabler, 1794.
Freud, Sigmund. *Die Frage der Laienanalyse.* Leipzig: Internationaler Psychoanalytischer Verlag, 1926.
———. Abriß der Psychoanalyse, mit einer Rede von Thomas Mann. Frankfurt: Fischer, 1953.
Fukuyama, Francis. "The End of History?" *National Interest,* no. 16 (1989): 3–18.
———. *The End of History and the Last Man.* New York: Free Press, 1992.
Graebner, Norman A. *The Enduring Lincoln.* Urbana: University of Illinois Press, 1959.
Hacker, Andrew. *Two Nations: Black and White, Separate, Hostile, Unequal.* New York: Scribner's, 1992.
Hamilton, Alexander, John Jay, and James Madison. *The Federalist Papers* (1788–89).
Handlin, Oscar. *The Uprooted: The Epic Story of the Great Migrations that Made the American People.* Boston: Little, Brown, 1951.
Hartz, Louis. *The Liberal Tradition in America: An Interpretation of American Political Thought since the Revolution.* New York: Harcourt, Brace, 1955.
Hayek, Friedrich August von. *The Road to Serfdom.* Chicago: University of Chicago Press, 1944.
———. *The Constitution of Liberty.* Chicago: University of Chicago Press, 1960.
———. *Die Irrtümer des Konstruktivismus.* Munich: Fink, 1970.
———. *Law, Legislation and Liberty.* 3 vols. Chicago: University of Chicago Press, 1973–79.
Healey, Robert M. *Jefferson on Religion in Public Education.* Hamden: Archon, 1970 (Ph.D. diss., Yale University, 1962).
Higham, John. *Send These to Me: Jews and Other Immigrants in Urban America.* New York: Atheneum, 1975.
Himelhoch, Jerome, and Sylvia Fleis Fava. *Sexual Behavior in American Society.* New York: Norton, 1955.
Hite, Shere. *The Hite Report: A Nationwide Study on Female Sexuality.* New York: Macmillan, 1976.
Holmes, Oliver Wendell. *The Common Law.* Boston: Little, Brown, 1881.
———. "Law and the Court." In *Collected Legal Papers.* New York: Harcourt, Brace, and Howe, 1920.
Honeywell, Roy. *The Educational Work of Thomas Jefferson.* New York: Russell and Russell, 1964.
Hunt, Morton M. *Sexual Behavior in the 1970s.* Chicago: Playboy Press, 1974.
Jackson, Richard. *U.S. Bicentennial Music.* New York: Institute for Studies in American Music, Brooklyn College, CUNY, 1977.
James, William. *The Varieties of Religious Experience: A Study in Human Nature, being the Gifford Lectures on Natural Religion, delivered at Edinburgh in 1901–1902.* New York: Longmans, Green, 1902.
Jones, Maldwyn A. *American Immigration.* Chicago: University of Chicago Press, 1960.
Jouvenel, Robert de. *La république des camarades.* Paris: Grasset, 1914.

Kant, Immanuel. *Critik der reinen Vernunft*. Riga: Hartknoch, 1781.
———. *Critik der praktischen Vernunft*. Riga: Hartknoch, 1788.
———. *Zum ewigen Frieden*. Königsberg: Nicolovius, 1795.
———. *Der Streit der Fakultäten*. Königsberg: Nicolovius, 1798.
———. *Anthropologie in pragmatischer Hinsicht*. Königsberg: Nicolovius, 1798.
———. (Articles: "Idee zu einer allgemeinen Geschichte in weltbürgerlicher Absicht (1784); "Beantwortung der Frage: Was ist Aufklärung?" (1784); "Muthmaßlicher Anfang der Menschengeschichte" (1786); "Was heiβt: Sich im Denken orientieren?" (1786); "Das Ende alle Dinge" (1794). All published in *Berlinische Monatsschrift*.
———. *Kant's Werke,* ed. Königliche Preußische Akademie der Wissenschaften. Berlin: 1907–1912.
Katz, Leslie, ed. *The Bitch-Goddess of Success: Variations on an American Theme*. New York: Eakins, 1968.
Kennedy, John F. *A Nation of Immigrants*. London: H. Hamilton, 1964.
Keyserling, Hermann A. *America Set Free*. New York: Harper, 1929.
Kinsey, Alfred C., et al. *Sexual Behavior in the Human Male*. Philadelphia: Saunders, 1948.
———. *Sexual Behavior in the Human Female*. Philadelphia: Saunders, 1953.
Kirk, Russell. *The Conservative Mind: An Account of Conservative Ideas from Burke to Santayana*. Chicago: Regnery, 1953.
Kronzucker, Dieter. *Unser Amerika*. Reinbek: Rowohlt, 1987.
Laski, Harold J. *The American Democracy: A Commentary and an Interpretation*. New York: Viking, 1948.
Lehmann, Karl. *Thomas Jefferson, American Humanist*. New York: Macmillan, 1967.
Lerner, Max. *America as a Civilization*. New York: Simon and Schuster, 1957.
Lippmann, Walter. *Public Opinion*. New York: Harcourt, Brace, 1922.
———. *The Phantom Public*. New York: Harcourt, Brace, 1925.
———. *Essays in the Public Philosophy*. Boston: Little, Brown, 1955.
Locke, John. *Two Treatises of Civil Government*. Anonymously published in 1690. Ed. Peter Laslett. Cambridge: Cambridge University Press, 1960.
MacPherson, C. B. *Burke*. New York: Oxford University Press, 1980.
Mann, Thomas. "Dostojewski—mit Maßen," and "Phantasie über Goethe." In *Neue Studien*. Stockholm: Bermann-Fischer, 1948.
Marcuse, Herbert. *Essays in Honor of Herbert Marcuse: The Critical Spirit*. Ed. Kurt H. Wolff and Barrington Moore, Jr. N.p.: Beacon, 1968.
Martin, Edwin T. *Thomas Jefferson, Scientist*. New York: Schuman, 1952.
Mason, Alpheus T. *Brandeis: A Free Man's Life*. New York: Viking, 1946.
———. *Free Government in the Making*. New York: Oxford University Press, 1949.
———. "The Nature of Our Federal Union Reconsidered." *Political Science Quarterly* 65 (1950): 502–21.
———. "The Federalist: A Split Personality." *American Historical Review* 57 (1952): 625–43.

———, ed. *The States Rights Debate: Antifederalism and the Constitution*. New York: Oxford University Press, 1964.
Masters, William H., and Virginia E. Johnson. *Human Sexual Inadequacy*. London: Churchill, 1970.
———. *Homosexuality in Perspective*. Boston: Little, Brown, 1979.
———. *Human Sexual Response*. Boston: Little, Brown, 1966.
Matthews, Mitford M., ed. *A Dictionary of Americanisms on Historical Principles*. Chicago: University of Chicago Press, 1951.
Mayo, Bernard, ed. *Jefferson Himself: The Personal Narrative of a Many-sided American*. Charlottesville: University Press of Virginia, 1970.
Mill, John Stuart. *An Essay on Liberty*. London: J. W. Parker and Son, 1859.
Mitchell, Donald G. *A Bachelor's Reverie*. Privately printed. Wormsloe: G. Wymberley-Jones, 1850.
Mohl, Robert von. "German Criticism of Mr. Justice Story's Commentaries on the Constitution of the United States." *American Jurist* 15 (1836): 8f.
Montesquieu, Charles-Louis, Baron de. *De l'esprit des loix*. Geneva: Barillot, 1748.
Morgan, Edmund S. *The Birth of the Republic, 1763–89*. Chicago: University of Chicago Press, 1956.
Morse, Jedediah. *The American Geography, or, A View of the Present Situation of the United States of America*. Elizabeth Town: Shepard Kollock, 1789.
Myrdal, Gunnar. *An American Dilemma: The Negro Problem and Modern Democracy*. New York: Harper, 1944.
Neustadt, Richard E. *Presidential Power: The Politics of Leadership*. New York: Wiley, 1960.
Nichols, Frederick D. *Thomas Jefferson, Landscape Architect*. Charlottesville: University Press of Virginia, 1978.
Nietzsche, Friedrich. *Die Geburt der Tragödie aus dem Geiste der Musik*. Leipzig: Fritzsch, 1872.
———. *Vom Nutzen und Nachteil der Historie für das Leben*. In *Unzeitgemäße Betrachtungen*. Leipzig: Naumann, 1874.
Niles, Hezekiah, ed. *Principles and Acts of the Revolution in America*. Baltimore: William Ogden Niles, 1822.
O'Gorman, Frank. *Edmund Burke: His Political Philosophy*. London: Allen and Unwin, 1973.
Packard, Vance O. *The Sexual Wilderness: Contemporary Upheaval in Male-Female Relationships*. New York: McKay, 1968.
Parkinson, Richard. *A Tour of America in 1798, 1799, and 1800: Exhibiting Sketches of Society and Manners, and a Particular Account of the American System of Agriculture, with its Recent Improvements*. London: Harding, 1805.
Patterson, C. Perry. *The Constitutional Principles of Thomas Jefferson*. Gloucester: Smith, 1953.
Peterson, Merrill D. *The Jefferson Image in the American Mind*. New York: Oxford University Press, 1960.
Pierson, George W. *The Moving American*. New York: Knopf, 1971.

Postman, Neil. *Amusing Ourselves to Death: Public Discourse in the Age of Show Business.* New York: Viking, 1984.

Randall, James G. *Lincoln, the Liberal Statesman.* New York: Dodd, Mead, 1947.

Revel, Jean François. *Comment les démocracies finissent.* Paris: Grasset, 1983.

Ribble, Frederick D. G. *State and National Power over Commerce.* New York: Columbia University Press, 1937.

Richardson, Albert D. *Beyond the Mississippi: From the Great River to the Great Ocean.* Newark: Bliss, 1867.

Roosevelt, Theodore. *Autobiography.* New York: Scribner's, 1958.

Rousseau, Jean-Jacques. *Du contrat social; ou, principes du droit politique.* Amsterdam: Rey, 1762.

Rüstow, Alexander. *Ortsbestimmung der Gegenwart.* 3 vols. Erlenbach-Zürich: Rentsch, 1950–57.

Ryn, Claes G. *The New Jacobinism: Can Democracy Survive?* Washington, D.C.: National Humanities Institute, 1991.

Sarmiento, Domingo F. *Viajes en Europa, Africa i America.* 2 vols. Santiago: Belin, 1849–51.

Schelling, Friedrich Wilhelm. *Über das Wesen der menschlichen Freiheit und die damit zusammenhängenden Gegenstände.* Reutlingen: Ensslin, 1834. Written in 1809.

Schlesinger, Arthur M., Jr. *The Imperial Presidency.* Boston: Houghton Mifflin, 1973.

———. *The Disuniting of America: Reflections on a Multicultural Society.* Knoxville: Whittle, 1991.

Schmitt, Carl. "Die Einheit der Welt." *Merkur* 4 (1952): 1–11.

Schönemann, Friedrich. *Die Kunst der Massenbeeinflussung in den Vereinigten Staaten von Amerika.* Stuttgart: Deutsche Verlagsanstalt, 1924.

Schuyler, Robert L. *The Constitution of the United States.* New York: Macmillan, 1923.

Siegfried, André. *Les Etats-Unis d'aujourd'hui.* Paris: Colin, 1927.

Smith, Adam. *An Inquiry into the Nature and Causes of the Wealth of Nations.* London: W. Strahan and T. Cadell, 1776.

Sorokin, Pitirim A. *The American Sex Revolution.* Boston: Sargent, 1956.

Steevens, George W. *The Land of the Dollar.* Edinburgh: Blackwood, 1897.

Stirner, Max. Der Einzige und sein Eigenthum. Leipzig: Wigand, 1844.

Stockman, David A. *The Triumph of Politics: How the Reagan Revolution Failed.* New York: Harper and Row, 1986.

Stokes, Anson P. *Church and State in the United States.* New York: Harper and Row, 1950.

Thoreau, Henry David. *Excursions.* Boston: Ticknor and Fields, 1863.

Tocqueville, Alexis de. *De la démocratie en Amérique.* 2 vols. Paris: Gosselin, 1835, 1840.

Veblen, Thorstein. *The Theory of the Leisure Class: An Economic Study in the Evolution of Institutions.* New York: Macmillan, 1899.

Weber, Max. "Die protestantische Ethik und der 'Geist' des Kapitalismus." *Archiv für Sozialwissenschaft und Sozialpolitik* 20, 21 (1905): 1–54; 1–110.

———. *Politik als Beruf.* Munich: Duncker und Humblot, 1919.

———. *Wissenschaft als Beruf.* Munich: Duncker und Humblot, 1919.

Wise, James W., ed. *Thomas Jefferson Then and Now, 1743–1943.* New York: Bill of Rights Sesqui-centennial Committee, 1943.

Williams, William C. *In the American Grain.* New York: Boni, 1925.

Wright, Benjamin F. *Consensus and Continuity 1776–1787.* Boston: Boston University Press, 1958.

Zahn, Peter von. *Verläßt uns Amerika?* Berlin: Ullstein, 1987.

Additional Selected Works

Aaron, Daniel. *Men of Good Hope*. New York: Oxford University Press, 1951.
Adams, Brooks. *The Theory of Social Revolutions*. New York: Macmillan, 1913.
Adams, James Truslow. *Our Business Civilization*. New York: Boni, 1929.
———. *The Tempo of Modern Life*. New York: Boni, 1931.
Aikman, Duncan. *The Turning Stream*. Garden City: Doubleday, 1948.
Allen, Frederick Lewis. *Only Yesterday: An Informal History of the Nineteen Twenties*. New York: Harper, 1931.
———. *The Big Chance: America Transforms Itself, 1900–1950*. New York: Bantam, 1952.
Arnold, Thurman W. *The Folklore of Capitalism*. New Haven: Yale University Press, 1937.
Baldwin, Leland, D. *The Meaning of America*. Pittsburgh: University of Pittsburgh Press, 1955.
———. *The American Quest for the City of God*. Macon: Mercer, 1981.
Barth, Alan. *The Loyalty of Free Men*. New York: Viking, 1951.
———. *Government by Investigation*. New York: Viking, 1955.
Barzini, Luigi. *Americans Are Alone in the World*. New York: Random House, 1953.
Barzun, Jacques. *God's Country and Mine*. Boston: Little, Brown, 1954.
Bates, Ernest Sutherland. *American Faith*. New York: Norton, 1940.
Beard, Charles A., ed. *A Century of Progress*. New York: Harper, 1933.
Beard, Charles A., and Mary B. Beard. *The Rise of American Civilization*. New York: Macmillan, 1930.
Bell, Daniel. *The New American Right*. New York: Criterion, 1955.
Bellamy, Edward. *Looking Backward, 2000–1887*. New York: Houghton Mifflin, 1889.
Berle, Adolf, Jr. *The Emerging Common Law of Free Enterprise: Antidote to the Omnipotent State*. Philadelphia: Brandeis Society, 1951.

———. *The Twentieth Century Capitalist Revolution*. New York: Harcourt, Brace, 1954.
———. *The American Economic Republic*. New York: Harcourt, Brace, and World, 1963.
Berle, Adolf, Jr., and Gardiner C. Means. *The Modern Corporation and Private Property*. New York: Macmillan, 1932.
Blau, Joseph L., ed. *Social Theories of Jacksonian Democracy*. New York: Hafner, 1947.
Bledstone, Albert T. *An Essay on Liberty and Slavery*. Philadelphia: Lippincott, 1856.
Boorstin, Daniel. *The Genius of American Politics*. Chicago: University of Chicago Press, 1953.
Boudin, Louis B. *Government by Judiciary*. New York: Godwin, 1932.
Bowers, Claude G. *Jefferson and Hamilton: The Struggle for Democracy*. Boston: Houghton Mifflin, 1925.
Brady, Robert A. *Business as a System of Power*. New York: Columbia University Press, 1947.
Brandeis, Louis D. *The Curse of Bigness*. New York: Viking, 1934.
Brown, Harrison. *The Challenge of Man's Future*. New York: Viking, 1954.
Brownson, O. A. *The American Republic: Its Constitution, Tendencies and Destiny*. New York: Shea, 1866.
Burlingame, Roger. *The American Conscience*. New York: Knopf, 1957.
Burns, Edward M. *The American Idea of Mission*. New Brunswick: Rutgers University Press, 1957.
Carnegie, Andrew. *Triumphant Democracy*. London: Sampson Low, Marston, Searle, and Rivington, 1886.
Chamberlain, John. *Farewell to Reform: Being a History of the Rise, Life and Decay of the Progressive Mind in America*. New York: Liveright, 1932.
Commager, Henry Steele. *Majority Rule and Minority Rights*. New York: Oxford University Press, 1943.
———. *The American Mind*. New Haven: Yale University Press, 1950.
———. *Freedom, Loyalty, Dissent*. New York: Oxford University Press, 1954.
Corwin, Edward S. *The Doctrine of Judicial Review*. Princeton: Princeton University Press, 1914.
———. *Constitutional Revolution, Ltd*. Claremont: Claremont College, 1941.
Croly, Herbert. *The Promise of American Life*. New York: Macmillan, 1909.
———. *Progressive Democracy*. New York: Macmillan, 1914.
Curti, Merle. *The Growth of American Thought*. 3d ed. New York: Harper, 1964.
De Grazia, Sebastian. *Of Time, Work and Leisure*. New York: Twentieth Century Fund, 1962.
Dewey, John. *Liberalism and Social Action*. New York: Putnam's, 1935.
Donald, David. *An Excess of Democracy: The American Civil War and the Social Process*. Oxford: Oxford University Press, 1960.
Dorfman, Joseph. *The Economic Mind in American Civilization, 1606–1865*. New York: Viking, 1946.
Dos Passos, John. *U.S.A. The Big Money*. New York: Random House, 1930.

Einaudi, Mario. *The Roosevelt Revolution*. New York: Harcourt, Brace, 1959.
Fay, Charles N. *Business in Politics*. Cambridge: Cosmos, 1926.
Ferguson, Harvey. *People and Power: A Study of Political Behavior in America*. New York: Morrow, 1947.
Fine, Sidney. *Laissez-Faire and the Welfare State: A Study of Conflict in American Thought, 1865–1901*. Ann Arbor: University of Michigan Press, 1956.
Ford, Henry Jones. *Rise and Growth of American Politics*. New York: Macmillan, 1898.
Fraenkel, Ernst, ed. *Amerika im Spiegel des deutschen politischen Denkens*. Köln und Opladen: Westdeutscher Verlag, 1959.
Frankel, Charles. *The Case for Modern Man*. New York: Harper, 1956.
———. *The Democratic Prospect*. New York: Harper, 1962.
Galbraith, John Kenneth. *American Capitalism: Concept of Countervailing Power*. Boston: Houghton Mifflin, 1952.
———. *The Affluent Society*. Boston: Houghton Mifflin, 1958.
Garraty, John A. *Constitutional Quarrels that Have Changed History*. New York: Harper and Row, 1964.
George, Henry. *Progress and Poverty*. New York: Appleton, 1879.
Ghent, William J. *Mass and Class: A Survey of Social Divisions*. New York: Macmillan, 1903.
Goldman, Eric. *Rendezvous with Destiny: A History of Modern American Reform*. New York: Knopf, 1952.
Goodwin, Richard N. *The American Condition*. New York: Doubleday, 1974.
Graubard, Stephen R., ed. *A New America?* New York: Norton, 1978.
Greenway, John. *The Inevitable Americans*. New York: Knopf, 1964.
Griswold, A. Whitney. *Farming and Democracy*. New York: Harcourt, Brace, 1948.
Gunther, John. *Inside U.S.A.* New York: Harper, 1947.
Hacker, Andrew. *The Corporation Take-Over*. New York: Harper and Row, 1964.
———. *The End of the American Era*. New York: Atheneum, 1970.
Hacker, Louis M. *Alexander Hamilton in the American Tradition*. New York: McGraw-Hill, 1957.
Hague, John H., ed. *American Character and Culture in a Changing World*. Westport: Greenwood, 1979.
Hammond, Bray. *Banks and Politics in America*. Princeton: Princeton University Press, 1957.
Hand, Learned. *The Bill of Rights*. Cambridge: Harvard University Press, 1958.
Hofstadter, Richard. *Social Darwinism in American Thought, 1860–1915*. Philadelphia: University of Pennsylvania Press, 1945.
———. *The American Political Tradition and the Men Who Made It*. New York: Knopf, 1948.
———. *The Age of Reform*. New York: Knopf, 1955.
Hoover, Herbert. *American Individualism*. Garden City: Doubleday, 1922.
———. *The Challenge to Liberty*. New York: Scribner's, 1934.
Hurd, John C. *The Theory of Our National Existence, As Shown by the Government of the United States Since 1861*. Boston: Little, Brown, 1881.

Jackson, Robert H. *The Struggle for Judicial Supremacy: A Study of a Crisis in American Power Politics*. New York: Knopf, 1941.
Jenkin, Thomas Paul. *Reactions of Major Groups to Positive Government in the United States, 1930–1940*. Berkeley: University of California Press, 1945.
Jones, Howard Mumford. *The Pursuit of Happiness*. Cambridge: Harvard University Press, 1953.
———. *O Strange New World*. New York: Viking, 1964.
———. *The Age of Energy*. New York: Viking, 1971.
Kallen, Horace M. *Individualism: An American Way of Life*. New York: Liveright, 1933.
Kemler, Edgar. *The Deflation of American Ideals: An Ethical Guide for New Dealers*. Washington, D.C.: American Council for Public Affairs, 1941.
King, James M. *Facing the Twentieth Century*. New York: American Union League Society, 1899.
Konvitz, Milton R. *A Century of Civil Rights*. New York: Columbia University Press, 1961.
Krutch, Joseph Wood, et al. *Is the Common Man Too Common?* Norman: University of Oklahoma Press, 1954.
Lerner, Max. *The Unfinished Country*. New York: Simon and Schuster, 1959.
Lilienthal, David. *Big Business: A New Era*. New York: Harper, 1952.
Lindley, Ernest K. *The Roosevelt Revolution*. New York: Viking, 1933.
Lippmann, Walter. *Drift and Mastery*. New York: Holt, 1914.
———. *The New Imperative*. New York: Macmillan, 1935.
Lipset, Seymour Martin. *The First New Nation*. New York: Basic Books, 1963.
Lloyd, Henry Demarest. *Wealth against Commonwealth*. New York: Harper, 1894.
Lukacs, John. *Outgrowing Democracy*. Garden City: Doubleday, 1984.
McCloskey, Robert G. *American Conservatism in the Age of Enterprise*. Cambridge: Harvard University Press, 1951.
McDonald, Forrest. *We the People: The Economic Origins of the Constitution*. Chicago: University of Chicago Press, 1958.
McIlwain, Charles H. *The American Revolution*. New York: Macmillan, 1923.
McLaughlin, Andrew C. *The Courts, the Constitution, and Parties*. Chicago: University of Chicago Press, 1912.
MacPherson, C., *The Political Theory of Possessive Individualism: Hobbes to Locke*. Oxford: Oxford University Press, 1962.
Maritain, Jacques. *Reflections on America*. New York: Scribner's, 1958.
Mason, Alpheus Thomas. *The Supreme Court: Vehicle of Revealed Truth or Power Group?* Boston: Boston University Press, 1953.
———. *Security through Freedom*. Ithaca: Cornell University Press, 1955.
Mencken, H. L. *Notes on Democracy*. New York: Knopf, 1926.
Meyers, Marvin. *The Jacksonian Persuasion*. Stanford: Stanford University Press, 1957.
Miller, John C. *Alexander Hamilton: Portrait in Paradox*. New York: Harper, 1959.
Mills, Ogden L. *What of Tomorrow?* New York: Macmillan, 1935.
———. *Liberalism Fights On*. New York: Macmillan, 1936.

Mims, Edwin. *The Majority of the People*. New York: Modern Age, 1941.
Mitchell, Broadus. *Depression Decade: From New Era through New Deal, 1929–1941*. New York: Rinehart, 1947.
Morgan, E. S. *The Puritan Dilemma*. Boston: Little, Brown, 1958.
Morris, Lloyd R. *The Rebellious Puritan*. New York: Harcourt, Brace, 1927.
Mosier, Richard D. *The American Temper*. Berkeley and Los Angeles: University of California Press, 1952.
Murphy, Carroll D., and Herbert V. Prochnow. *The Next Century is America's*. New York: Greenberg, 1938.
Myers, Gustavus. *The History of American Idealism*. New York: Boni and Liveright, 1925.
———. *America Strikes Back*. New York: Ives Washburn, 1935.
Niebuhr, Reinhold. *The Children of Light and the Children of Darkness*. New York: Scribner's, 1944.
Nossiter, Bernard D. *The Mythmakers: An Essay on Power and Wealth*. Boston: Houghton Mifflin, 1964.
Parrington, Vernon Louis. *Main Currents in American Thought*. New York: Harcourt, Brace, 1946.
Paterson, Isabel. *The God of the Machine*. New York: Putnam, 1943.
Phillips, Arturo Aldunate. *Estados Unidos: Gran Aventura del Hombre*. Santiago de Chile: Nascimento, 1943.
Potter, David M. *People of Plenty: Economic Abundance and American Character*. Chicago: University of Chicago Press, 1954.
Pound, Ezra. *Impact: Essays on Ignorance and the Decline of American Civilization*. Chicago: Regnery, 1960.
Rauschenbusch, Walter. *Christianity and Social Crisis*. New York: Macmillan, 1907.
Reed, Edward, ed. *Challenge to Democracy*. New York: Praeger, 1963.
Riesman, David. *The Lonely Crowd*. New Haven: Yale University Press, 1950.
———. *Abundance for What?* New York: Doubleday, 1964.
Rischin, Moses, ed. *The American Gospel of Success*. Chicago: Quadrangle, 1965.
Robertson, James Oliver. *American Myth, American Reality*. New York: Hill and Wang, 1980.
Roosevelt, Franklin D. *Looking Forward*. New York: Day, 1933.
Savelle, Max. *Seeds of Liberty*. Seattle: University of Washington Press, 1965.
Schlesinger, Arthur, Jr. *The Politics of Upheaval*. Boston: Houghton Mifflin, 1960.
Schneider, H. W. *The Puritan Mind*. New York: Holt, 1930.
———. *A History of American Philosophy*. New York: Columbia University Press, 1946.
Schrag, Peter. *The Decline of the WASP*. New York: Simon and Schuster, 1970.
Smith, J. Allen. *The Spirit of American Government*. New York: Macmillan, 1907.
Soule, George. *Prosperity Decade: A Chapter from American Economic History 1917–1929*. London: Pilot, 1947.

Stillman, Edmund, and William Pfaff. *The Politics of Hysteria*. New York: Harper and Row, 1964.

Sumner, William Graham. *What Social Classes Owe to Each Other*. New York: Harper, 1883.

Swisher, Carl B. *Roger B. Taney*. New York: Macmillan, 1935.

———. *American Constitutional Development*. Boston: Houghton Mifflin, 1954.

Twiss, Benjamin R. *Lawyers and the Constitution: How Laissez-faire Came to the Supreme Court*. Princeton: Princeton University Press, 1942.

Vann Woodward, C. *The Strange Career of Jim Crow*. New York: Oxford University Press, 1957.

Veblen, Thorstein. *The Theory of Business Enterprise*. New York: Scribner's, 1904.

Wallace, Henry. *New Frontiers*. New York: Harcourt, Brace, and World, 1934.

Wertenbaker, T. J. *The Puritan Oligarchy: The Founding of American Civilization*. New York: Scribner's, 1947.

Weyl, Walter. *The New Democracy*. New York: Macmillan, 1912.

Wright, Benjamin F. *American Interpretations of Natural Law*. Cambridge: Harvard University Press, 1931.

Index